WEBMASTER
IN A NUTSHELL

A Desktop Quick Reference

WEBMASTER
IN A NUTSHELL

A Desktop Quick Reference

Stephen Spainhour and Valerie Quercia

O'REILLY™

Bonn • *Cambridge* • *Paris* • *Sebastopol* • *Tokyo*

WebMaster in a Nutshell

by Stephen Spainhour and Valerie Quercia

Published by O'Reilly & Associates, Inc., 101 Morris Street, Sebastopol, CA 95472.

Editor: Linda Mui

Production Editor: Jane Ellin

Printing History:

      October 1996:   First Edition

ISBN: 1-56592-229-8

Table of Contents

Preface

This book is for everyone who works on the content end of the World Wide Web. Do you author or maintain Web documents? Do you work with CGI for creating fill-out forms? Are you a programmer developing Web-based client or server applications? Do you write JavaScript applets? Are you the administrator of a Web site, responsible for maintaining and updating the server software?

There are innumerable books and online resources for learning Web-related skills. What this book does is pare them down to a single desktop-sized volume for easy reference. You may be a whiz at CGI programming, but forget how to use Netscape cookies. You may know HTML fairly well, but can never remember the correct syntax for creating tables. You might forget the directive for creating directory aliases on your server, or how to enforce password protection on documents.

By no means is this book a replacement for more detailed books on the Web. But when those books have been digested and placed onto your bookshelves with pride, this one will remain on your desktop.

Contents

This book is separated into five distinct subject areas. In turn, each subject area is split into chapters. Some chapters are 70 pages, others are 3 pages.

Chapter 1: *Introduction*
Introduces you to the book and to the Web in general.

Part I: HTML

The first section of the book covers the Hypertext Markup Language, or HTML.

Chapter 2: *HTML Overview*
Gives a brief background to HTML syntax.

Chapter 3: *HTML Tags*
>   Lists the HTML tags currently in use.

Chapter 4: *Frames*
>   Shows how to use HTML frames.

Chapter 5: *Tables*
>   Shows how to use HTML tables.

Chapter 6: *Color Names and Values*
>   Lists the names accepted by HTML attributes that accept color values.

Chapter 7: *Character Entities*
>   Lists the special characters recognized by HTML.

Chapter 8: *Browser Comparison*
>   Briefly describes differences between the Microsoft Internet Explorer and Netscape Navigator.

Part II: CGI

The second section of the book covers the Common Gateway Interface, or CGI.

Chapter 9: *CGI Overview*
>   Gives a brief background to CGI.

Chapter 10: *HTML Form Tags*
>   Lists the form tags and demonstrates their usage in a brief example.

Chapter 11: *CGI Environment Variables*
>   Lists the environment variables available to CGI programs.

Chapter 12: *Cookies*
>   Shows how to use cookies in CGI programs.

Chapter 13: *Server Side Includes*
>   Describes SSI, listing directives and environment variables and demonstrating their use.

Chapter 14: *Windows CGI*
>   Describes the Windows CGI, the CGI interface for Windows-based programming languages.

Chapter 15: *Perl Quick Reference*
>   Lists Perl syntax and functions.

Chapter 16: *Other CGI Resources*
>   Lists URLs with libraries and modules that can facilitate CGI programming.

Part III: HTTP

The third section of the book covers Hypertext Transfer Protocol, or HTTP.

Chapter 17: *HTTP Overview*
Introduces HTTP and its general format.

Chapter 18: *Server Response Codes*
Lists the three-digit response codes generated on the server end.

Chapter 19: *HTTP Headers*
Lists the general, request, response, and entity headers for HTTP.

Chapter 20: *Media Types and Subtypes*
Lists the media (content) types in common use.

Part IV: JavaScript

The fourth section of the book covers JavaScript, in a single chapter.

Chapter 21: *JavaScript Quick Reference*
Introduces and provides a lengthy reference to JavaScript.

Part V: Server Configuration

The fifth and final section of the book covers server configuration.

Chapter 22: *Server Configuration Overview*
Describes how servers work.

Chapter 23: *Apache and NCSA Server Configuration*
Lists the directives used by the Apache and NCSA family of servers.

Chapter 24: *CERN Server Configuration*
Lists the directives used by the CERN (W3C) server.

Chapter 25: *Netscape Server Configuration*
Lists the directives used by the Netscape family of servers.

Chapter 26: *WebSite Server Configuration*
Describes how to configure the WebSite server.

Why So Many Chapters?

This book started out as five chapters. Now we have 26. What happened?

All we can say is that we looked at it with five chapters, and it didn't work. It was too hard to find distinct topics. It was too hard to cross-reference between things. It was too hard to work with topics that overlapped several areas.

So we ended up with 26 chapters. So we have some three or four page chapters. So shoot us. Meanwhile, we hope that the format works. Please let us know. (See the section entitled "Request for Comments" below.)

Conventions Used in This Book

The following typographical conventions are used in this book:

Constant width
> is used to indicate headers, directives, attributes, code examples, and HTML tags.

Italic
> is used to indicate variables, filenames, directory names, URLs, and comments in examples.

Request for Comments

We invite you to help us improve this book. If you have an idea that could make this a more useful quick reference, or if you find a bug in an example program or an error in the text, let us know by writing:

O'Reilly & Associates, Inc.
101 Morris Street
Sebastopol, CA 95472
1-800-998-9938 (in the U.S. or Canada)
1-707-829-0515 (international/local)
1-707-829-0104 (FAX)

You can also send us messages electronically. To be put on the mailing list or request a catalog, send email to:

nuts@ora.com (via the Internet)
uunet!ora!info (via UUCP)

To ask technical questions or comment on a book, send email to:

bookquestions@ora.com (via the Internet)

Acknowledgments

A lot of the information from this book was researched from other books that we've either published, or that are very near publication. Some of those books are listed at the end of Chapter 1. Meanwhile, we'd like to thank the authors of those books for giving us permission to use their material as the basis for much of this one. They are: David Flanagan (*JavaScript: The Definitive Guide*), Shishir Gundavaram (*CGI Programming on the World Wide Web*), John Leavitt (*UNIX Web Server Administration*), Chuck Musciano and Bill Kennedy (*HTML: The Definitive Guide*), Susan Peck and Stephen Arrants (*Building Your Own WebSite*), Johan Vromans (*Perl 5 Desktop Reference*), and Clinton Wong (*Web Client Programming in Perl*).

In addition, we'd like to thank Linda Mui, the developmental editor of this book; Tim O'Reilly, the editor of the "in a Nutshell" series; and Frank Willison, for keeping the project going while Linda was on maternity leave. We'd also like to extend special thanks to Bob Denny, who wrote the specification for WinCGI that we adapted for Chapter 14; and to Jerry Peek, who documented some missing topics for us.

Thanks to the production staff at O'Reilly who got this book out speedily, while allowing us to tweak it long after we promised we'd stay away. Thanks to Jane Ellin, our production editor, who gave the book its working title, *WebMasters of the Universe*; Curt Degenhart, who provided production assistance; Nancy Priest, the interior book designer; Edie Freedman, who designed the cover (and found a spider with just the right level of yuckiness); Chris Reilley, who tweaked our screen shots and figures; Clairemarie Fisher O'Leary, who looked over the book with her eagle eye; Kismet McDonough-Chan for quality control; Sheryl Avruch, who kept everyone sane; Seth Maslin, for writing the index; and Lenny Muellner, for his tools support.

CHAPTER 1

Introduction

This is a book that needs no introduction. By this time, if you don't know what the World Wide Web is, then you probably haven't heard of Rollerblades, VCRs, or Boris Yeltsin either.

In this chapter, we give the world's quickest introduction to Web technology and the roles of the WebMasters who breathe life into each Web document. If you want to learn more about the history of the Web, or how to make your Web pages "cool," or the social impact of the Internet, or how to make money online, etc., etc., etc., well, we include a bibliography at the end of this chapter, and we can also recommend many of the books sitting next to this one on the bookstore shelf. But we don't get into those issues.

This is a book by impatient writers for impatient readers. We're less interested in the hype of the Web than we are in what makes it actually tick. We'll leave it to the pundits to predict the future of the Web, or to declare today's technology already outdated. Too much analysis makes our heads spin; we just want to get our Web sites online.

The Web in a Nutshell

We've organized this book in a roughly "outside-in" fashion—that is, with the outermost layer (HTML) first, and the innermost layer (the server itself) last. That way, the material most readers are interested in is immediately accessible, while the material of less general interest remains in the back. But since it's a good idea for all readers to know how everything fits together, let's take a minute to breeze through a description of the Web from the inside-out: no history, no analysis, just the technology basics.

Clients and Servers

The tool that most people use on the Web is a *browser*, such as Netscape Navigator, Internet Explorer, or Mosaic. Web browsers work by connecting over the Internet to remote machines, requesting specific documents, and then formatting the documents they receive for viewing on the local machine.

The language, or *protocol*, used for Web transactions is Hypertext Transfer Protocol, or HTTP. (HTTP is covered in Chapters 17 through 20.) The remote machines containing the documents run HTTP *servers* that wait for requests from browsers and then return the specified document. The browsers themselves are technically HTTP *clients*.

There are several different types of Web server software available, both free and commercial. We cover the configuration of several of the most popular servers in Chapters 22 through 25.

Uniform Resource Locators (URLs)

Now, let's take a short detour in this overview. One of the most important things to grasp when working on the Web is the format for URLs. A URL is basically an address on the Web, identifying each document uniquely (for example, *http://www.ora.com/products.html*). Since URLs are so intrinsic to the Web, we'll discuss them here in a little detail. The simple syntax for a URL is:

    http://*host*/*path*

where:

host is the host to connect to, for example *www.ora.com* or *altavista.digital.com*. (While many Web servers run on hosts beginning with *www*, the *www* prefix is just a convention.)

path is the document requested on that server.

Most URLs you encounter follow this simple syntax. A more generalized syntax, however, is:

    scheme://*host*/*path*/*extra-path-info?query-info*

where:

scheme
        is the protocol used to connect to the site. For Web sites, the scheme is http. For FTP or Gopher sites, the scheme is (respectively) ftp or gopher.

extra-path-info
        is optional extra path information (used by CGI programs). See Chapter 9, *CGI Overview*, for more information.

query-info
        is optional query information (used by CGI programs). See Chapter 9 for more information.

HTML documents also often use a "shorthand" for linking to other documents on the same server, called a *relative URL*. An example of a relative URL is *images/webnut.gif.* The browser knows to translate this into complete URL syntax before sending the request. For example, if the document with URL *http://www.ora.com/books/webnut.html* contains a reference to *images/webnut.gif,* the browser reconstructs the relative URL as a full (or *absolute*) URL, *http://www.ora.com/books/images/webnut.gif,* and requests that document independently (if needed).

Often in this book, you'll see us refer to a URI, not a URL. A URI (Universal Resource Identifier) is a superset of URL, in anticipation of different resource naming conventions being developed for the Web. For the time being, however, the only URI syntax in practice is URL—so while purists might complain, you can safely assume that "URI" is synonymous with "URL" and not go wrong (yet).

Web Content: HTML, CGI, Java, and JavaScript

While Web documents can conceivably be in any format, the one that has been adopted as the standard is Hypertext Markup Language (HTML), a language for creating formatted text interspersed with images, sounds, animation, and hypertext links to other documents anywhere on the Web. Chapters 2 through 8 cover the most current version of HTML.

When static documents aren't sufficient for a Web site's needs, it uses tools such as CGI, Java, and JavaScript. CGI is a way for the Web server to call external programs instead of simply returning a static document. Chapters 9 through 16 are for CGI programmers. Java is an object-oriented language for writing all sorts of programs that can be downloaded over the Web, from animations to spreadsheets. This book does not cover the complexities of Java, but it does cover JavaScript, a related language that can be written directly into the HTML document. (For details on Java, we recommend *Java in a Nutshell,* by David Flanagan.)

Who Are the WebMasters?

So if that's the Web in a Nutshell, who are the WebMasters? The title "WebMaster" vaguely means a person who works on the content end of the Web. When you examine what WebMasters actually do, there are many different definitions.

On a typical Web site, the responsibilities can be broken up into four general groups:

- *Content providers* work on the data itself—creating or editing HTML documents, incorporating images and forms, and maintaining the integrity of the links.

- *Designers* create the images and also define the "look" of the site.

- *Programmers* write CGI, Java, and JavaScript programs for incorporation into the Web site.

- *Administrators* make sure that the server is running properly and efficiently at all times. They might also be responsible for establishing new content development areas, new scripts, and maintaining the security of sensitive documents and the site in general.

On a large site, you might have a staff of 50 content providers, a group of five designers, three or four programmers, and two administrators. On a small site, one person might do it all herself.

Each of these people might justifiably call themselves "WebMasters." And while a programmer may not be especially interested in HTML syntax or server configuration, and someone who works only in HTML markup may not need to know anything about HTTP, this book should be useful to all.

Recommended Books

As we've said, this is a reference book for looking up things you already know. But what if you don't already know it?

Much of the material in this book is adapted from other books that are already published by O'Reilly & Associates, or that are very near publication. At the risk of blatant self-promotion, we really do recommend these books:

- Web content providers will find *HTML: The Definitive Guide*, written by Chuck Musciano and Bill Kennedy, to be an essential reference.

- Designers who are getting started on the Web will find the basics of creating graphics and simple Web pages in *Designing for the Web*, by Jennifer Niederst with Edie Freedman.

- Programmers on Web sites should flock to *CGI Programming on the World Wide Web* by Shishir Gundavaram, *Java in a Nutshell* by David Flanagan, and *JavaScript: The Definitive Guide*, also by David Flanagan. For a Perl tutorial, we recommend *Learning Perl* by Randal Schwartz, and for Perl reference and extensive examples, we recommend the classic "Camel" book, *Programming Perl, Second Edition*, by Larry Wall, Tom Christiansen, and Randal L. Schwartz. Programmers interested in working at the HTTP protocol itself might also be interested in *Web Client Programming* by Clinton Wong (due December 1996), which shows how to write simple specialized Web clients.

- Administrators will want to refer to *Managing Internet Information Services* by Cricket Liu, Jerry Peek, Russ Jones, Bryan Buus, and Adrian Nye, and will want to keep an eye out for *UNIX Web Server Administration* by John Leavitt (due February 1997).

PART I

HTML

CHAPTER 2

HTML Overview

HTML (Hypertext Markup Language) is the language used to encode World Wide Web documents. It is a document-layout and hyperlink-specification language that defines the syntax and placement of special, embedded directions that aren't displayed by a Web browser, but tell it how to display the contents of the document, including text, images, and other supported media. The language also tells you how to make a document interactive through special hypertext links, which connect your document with other documents on your local system, the World Wide Web, and other Internet resources such as FTP and Gopher.

The basic syntax and semantics of HTML are defined in the HTML standard. The HTML standard and all other Web-related standards issues are developed under the authority of the World Wide Web Consortium (W3C). Standards specifications and drafts of new proposals can be found at *http://www.w3.org.*

The most recent work by the HTML working group at the W3C is a working draft for HTML 3.2. Still, the most definitive implementations of HTML for a Web author come from the tag sets that the most popular browsers use.

This section of the book summarizes the current state of HTML in seven chapters, as listed below. For more information on HTML, we recommend *HTML: The Definitive Guide* by Chuck Musciano and Bill Kennedy, published by O'Reilly & Associates, Inc.

- This chapter (Chapter 2) introduces you to the background and general syntax of HTML.

- Chapter 3, *HTML Tags*, describes the syntax of HTML tags and documents with descriptions of all the HTML tags in current use.

- For authors who want to use frames in HTML, Chapter 4, *Frames*, covers the frame tags in more detail and shows examples of using them.

- For authors using tables, Chapter 5, *Tables*, covers the table tags in more detail.

- Chapter 6, *Color Names and Values*, contains listings of valid color values (for tags with attributes for specifying color).

- Chapter 7, *Character Entities*, contains a listing of common character entities recognized in HTML documents.

- Chapter 8, *Browser Comparison*, describes the most important differences between the most popular browsers, Netscape Navigator and Microsoft Internet Explorer.

HTML Document Structure

An HTML document consists of text, which comprises the content of the document, and tags, which define the structure and appearance of the document. The structure of an HTML document is simple, consisting of an outer <html> tag enclosing the document header and body:

```
<html>
<head>
<title>Barebones HTML Document</title>
</head>
<body>
This illustrates in a very <i>simple</i> way,
the basic structure of an HTML document.
</body>
</html>
```

Each document has a *head* and a *body*, delimited by the <head> and <body> tags. The head is where you give your HTML document a title and where you indicate other parameters the browser may use when displaying the document. The body is where you put the actual contents of the HTML document. This includes the text for display and document control markers (tags) that advise the browser how to display the text. Tags also reference special-effects files like graphics and sound, and indicate the hot spots (*hyperlinks* or *anchors*) that link your document to other documents.

HTML Tag Syntax

For the most part, HTML document tags are simple to understand and use since they are made up of common words, abbreviations, and notations. Every HTML tag consists of a tag *name*, sometimes followed by an optional list of tag *attributes*, all placed between opening and closing brackets (< and >). The simplest tags are nothing more than the tag name enclosed in brackets, such as <head> and <i>. More complicated tags have attributes, which may have specific values defined by the author to modify the behavior of a tag.

Tag attributes belong after the tag name, each separated by one or more tab, space, or return characters. The order of attributes in a single tag is not important. An attribute's value, if it has one, follows an equal sign after the attribute name. If an attribute's value is a single word or number, you may simply add it after the equal sign. All other values should be enclosed in single or double quotation marks, especially if they contain several words separated by spaces. The length of an attribute's value is limited to 1024 characters. Here are some examples of tags with attributes:

```
<a href="http://www.ora.com/catalog.html">
<ul compact>
<input name=filename size=24 maxlength=80>
<link title="Table of Contents">
```

Tag and attribute names are not case-sensitive, but attribute values can be. For example, it is especially important to use the proper capitalization when referencing the URLs of other documents with the `href` attribute.

Most HTML tags consist of start and end tags that enclose text and other elements of a document. An end tag is the same as a start tag except it has a forward slash (/) before the tag name. End tags never contain attributes. For example, to italicize text, you enclose it within the `<i>` tags:

```
<i>This text in italics.</i>
```

You should take care when nesting tagged elements in a document. You must end nested tags starting with the most recent one and work your way back out. In this example, a phrase in bold (`<b>`) appears in the text of a link (`<a href= . . . >`) contained in some body text:

```
<body>
This is some text in the body, with a
<a href="another_doc.html">link, a portion of which
is <b>set in bold</b></a>
</body>
```

There are a handful of HTML tags that do not have end tags because they are standalone elements. For example, the image tag (`<img>`) inserts a single graphic into a document and does not require an end tag. Other standalone tags include the linebreak (`<br>`), horizontal rule (`<hr>`), and tags that provide information about a document that doesn't affect its displayed content such as the `<meta>` and `<base>` tags.

In some cases, end tags can be omitted in a document. Browsers often assume the end of one element when another begins. The most common example of this is with the paragraph tag (`<p>`). Since it is so often used in a document, a `<p>` tag usually only appears at the beginning of each paragraph. When one paragraph ends, another `<p>` tag signals the browser to end the paragraph and start another. Most authors do not use an end paragraph tag. There are other end tags that browsers function fine without, such as an ending `</html>` tag. However, it is best to include the end tags as much as possible to avoid confusion and mistakes in displaying your document.

CHAPTER 3

HTML Tags

This section lists the known HTML tags and attributes currently available for use in Web documents. There are many different browsers out there, and they do not all support the same set of tags.

If keeping track of all the browsers and all their differences makes your head spin, no fear. Netscape Navigator and Microsoft's Internet Explorer are the two most popular browsers, and are responsible for almost all of the non-standard extensions to HTML. Chapter 8, *Browser Comparison*, discusses the most important differences between the latest versions of these two browsers.

The most recent version of Netscape Navigator is 3.0. Tags and attributes specific to this browser have *N3* at the beginning of their descriptions. Microsoft's Internet Explorer is also currently at version 3.0. It will be indicated by *IE3*. Browser-specific tags for the earlier versions of the browsers (e.g., *IE2* or *N2*) are assumed to be supported in the later versions.

HTML Tag and Attribute Descriptions

`<a> . . . </a>`	`<a>`

Create a hyperlink (`href` attribute) or fragment identifier (`name` attribute) within a document.

Attributes

   `href=`*url*
      Specify the URL of a hyperlink target (required if not a name anchor).

   `methods=`*list*
      Specify a comma-separated list of browser-dependent presentation methods.

$\rightarrow$

\<a\>
←
	name=*string*
	    Specify the name of a fragment identifier (required if not a hypertext reference anchor).
	rel=*relationship*
	    Indicate the relationship from this document to the target.
	rev=*relationship*
	    Indicate the reverse relationship of the target to this document.
	target=*name*
	    Define the name of the frame or window to receive the referenced document.
	title=*string*
	    Provide a title for the target document.
	urn=*urn*
	    Specify the location-independent Uniform Resource Name for this hyperlink.
	
	Example
	To create an anchor named info at some point in a document called *doc.html*, use the \<a\> tag with the name attribute:
	
	    `<a name="info">Information</a>`
	
	To provide a hyperlink to that point in *doc.html*, use the \<a\> tag with the href attribute appending the anchor name to the filename using a hash mark (#):
	
	    `<a href="doc.html#info">Link to information</a>`

\<address\>	`<address> ... </address>` The enclosed text is an address.

\<applet\>	`<applet> ... </applet>`
	Define an executable applet within a text flow.
	
	Attributes
	align=*position*
	    Align the \<applet\> region to either the top, middle, bottom (default), left, right, absmiddle, baseline, or absbottom of the text in the line.
	alt=*string*
	    Specify alternative text to replace the \<applet\> region within browsers that support the \<applet\> tag, but cannot execute the application.

code=*class*
> Specify the class name of the code to be executed (required).

codebase=*url*
> URL from which the code is retrieved.

height=*n*
> Specify the height, in pixels, of the <applet> region.

hspace=*n*
> Specify additional space, in pixels, to the left and right of the <applet> region.

name=*string*
> Specify the name of this particular instance of the <applet>.

vspace=*n*
> Specify additional space, in pixels, above and below the <applet> region.

width=*n*
> Specify the width, in pixels, of the <applet> region.

<div align="right"><b><applet></b></div>

<area>

<div align="right"><b><area></b></div>

Define a mouse-sensitive area in a client-side image map.

Attributes

coords=*list*
> Specify a comma-separated list of shape-dependent coordinates that define the edge of this area.

href=*url*
> Specify the URL of a hyperlink target associated with this area.

nohref
> Indicate that no document is associated with this area; clicking in the area has no effect.

shape=*shape*
> Define the region's shape to be either circ, circle, poly, polygon, rect, or rectangle.

<b> . . . </b>

<div align="right"><b><b></b></div>

Format the enclosed text using a **bold** typeface.

<base>

<div align="right"><b><base></b></div>

Specify the base URL for all relative URLs in this document.

Attributes

href=*url*
> Specify the base URL.

→

`<base>` ←	`target=`*name* Define the default target window of all `<a>` links in the document. Mostly used for redirecting a link to other frames. There are four special values: `_blank`, `_parent`, `_self`, and `_top`. These values are described in Chapter 4, *Frames*.
`<basefont>`	`<basefont>` Specify the font size for subsequent text. ***Attributes*** `size=`*value* Set the basefont size of 1 to 7 (required; default is 3).

`<bgsound>`	`<bgsound>`
	
	IE2 and later. Define background audio for the document.
	
	Attributes
	`loop=`*value*
	    Set the number of times to play the audio; *value* may be an integer or the value `infinite`.
	`src=`*url*
	    Provide the URL of the audio file to be played.

`<big>`	`<big>` ... `</big>` Format the enclosed text using a bigger typeface.
`<blockquote>`	`<blockquote>` ... `</blockquote>` The enclosed text is a block quotation.

`<body>`	`<body>` ... `</body>`
	
	Delimit the beginning and end of the document body.
	
	Attributes
	`alink=`*color*
	    Set the color of active hypertext links in the document.
	`background=`*url*
	    Specify the URL of an image to be tiled in the document background.
	`bgcolor=`*color*
	    Set the background color of the document.
	`bgproperties=`*value*
	    IE2 and later. When set to `fixed`, prevent the background image from scrolling with the document content.

leftmargin=*value*
> *IE2 and later.* Set the size, in pixels, of the document's left margin.

link=*color*
> Set the color of unvisited hypertext links in the document.

text=*color*
> Set the color of regular text in the document.

topmargin=*value*
> *IE2 and later.* Set the size, in pixels, of the document's top margin.

vlink=*color*
> Set the color of visited links in the document.

<body>

Break the current text flow, resuming at the beginning of the next line.

Attributes

clear=*margin*
> Break the flow and move downward until the desired margin, either left, right, or all, is clear.

<caption> . . . </caption>

<caption>

Define a caption for a table.

Attributes

align=*position*
> For Netscape, set the vertical position of the caption to either top or bottom. Default is top, centered. For Internet Explorer, set the horizontal alignment of the caption to either left, center, or right, or even the vertical position to top or bottom. The default is top, centered. You cannot set both the horizontal and vertical position with this attribute alone. See Chapter 8, *Browser Comparison*, for more information.

valign=*position*
> *IE2 and later.* Set the vertical position of the caption to either top or bottom. Default is top. Use this with a horizontal specification to align to set both vertical and horizontal caption position in Internet Explorer.

See Chapter 5, *Tables*, for more information on using tables.

<center> . . . </center>

<center>

Center the enclosed text.

\<cite\>	`<cite> ... </cite>` The enclosed text is a citation.
\<code\>	`<code> ... </code>` The enclosed text is a code sample.

\<col\>	`<col>`
	
	IE2 and later. Set properties for a column (or columns) within a `<colgroup>` of a table.
	
	Attributes
	
	align=*value*
	    Specify alignment of text in the cells of a column. Value can be `center`, `left`, or `right`.
	
	span=*n*
	    Specify the number of columns to be affected by the `<col>` settings.

\<colgroup\>	`<colgroup>`
	
	IE2 and later. Set properties for designated column or columns within a table Also indicates where vertical rules will be drawn when `rules=groups` is set in the `<table>` tag.
	
	Attributes
	
	align=*value*
	    Specify alignment of text in the cells of columns in the `<colgroup>`. Values can be `center`, `left`, or `right`.
	
	span=*n*
	    Specify the number of columns in the `<colgroup>`.

\<comment\>	`<comment> ... </comment>` *IE2 and later.* Place a comment in the document. Comments will be visible in all other browsers. Comments can be placed within `<!--` *comment text* `-->` for all browsers.
\<dd\>	`<dd> ... </dd>` Define the definition portion of an element in a definition list.
\<dfn\>	`<dfn> ... </dfn>` Format the enclosed text as a definition.

`<dir>` . . . `</dir>`

Create a directory list containing `<li>` tags.

Attributes

   `compact`
      Make the list more compact if possible.

`<div>` . . . `</div>`

Create a division within a document.

Attributes

   `align=`*type*
      Align the text within the division to `left`, `center`, or `right`.

`<dl>` . . . `</dl>`

Create a definition list containing `<dt>` and `<dd>` tags.

Attributes

   `compact`
      Make the list more compact if possible.

`<dt>` . . . `</dt>`

Define the definition term portion of an element in a definition list.

`<em>` . . . `</em>`

Format the enclosed text with additional emphasis.

`<embed>` . . . `</embed>`

Embed an object into a document. Additional parameters to those listed here may be included depending on the embedded object.

Attributes

   `src=`*url*
      Specify the URL of the object to be embedded (required).
   `height=`*n*
      Specify the height of the area the embedded object will occupy.
   `name=`*name*
      Specify the name of the embedded object.

→

HTML

<embed> ←	`width=`*n* Specify the width of the area the embedded object will occupy.

<font>	`<font> ... </font>`
	Set the size, color, or typeface of the enclosed text.
	
	Attributes
	    `color=`*color*
	        Set the color of the enclosed text.
	    `face=`*list*
	        Set the typeface of the enclosed text to the first available font in the comma-separated list of font names.
	    `size=`*value*
	        Set the size to an absolute value (1 to 7), or relative to the `<basefont>` size using +n or -n.

<form>	`<form> ... </form>`
	Delimit a form.
	
	Attributes
	    `action=`*url*
	        Specify the URL of the application that will process the form. The default is the current URL.
	    `enctype=`*encoding*
	        Specify how the form element values will be encoded.
	    `method=`*style*
	        Specify the parameter-passing style, either `get` or `post`. The default is *get*.
	    `target=`*name*
	        IE3 only. Specify a target window for results of form submission to be loaded. The special attributes `_bottom`, `_top`, `_parent`, and `_self` may be used. They are described in Chapter 4.
	
	See Chapter 10, *HTML Form Tags*, for more information on using forms.

<frame>	`<frame> ... </frame>`
	Define a frame within a frameset.
	
	Attributes
	    `bordercolor=`*color*
	        N3 only. Set color for frame border if border is turned on with `frameborder=yes`.

<frame>

frameborder=[1|0]
> *IE3 only.* Enable or disable the displaying of a 3-D border for a frame. Default is 1, which inserts the border. The value 0 turns the border off.

frameborder=[yes|no]
> *N3 only.* Enable or disable the displaying of a 3-D border for a frame or a plain border. The default is yes (for 3-D borders).

marginheight=*n*
> Place *n* pixels of space above and below the frame contents.

marginwidth=*n*
> Place *n* pixels of space to the left and right of the frame contents.

name=*string*
> Define the name of the frame.

noresize
> Disable user resizing of the frame.

scrolling=*type*
> Always add scrollbars (yes), never add scrollbars (no), or add scrollbars when needed (auto).

src=*url*
> Define the URL of the source document for this frame.

See Chapter 4 for more information on using frames.

<frameset>

<frameset> ... </frameset>

Define a collection of frames or other framesets.

Attributes

border=*n*
> *N3 only.* Set size in pixels of frame borders within a frameset. Default border width is 5 pixels.

bordercolor=*color*
> *N3 only.* Set color for frame borders in a frameset.

cols=*list*
> Specify the number and width of frames within a frameset.

frameborder=[yes|no]
> *N3 only.* Enable or disable the displaying of 3-D borders or regular borders for frames. The default is yes (3-D borders).

frameborder=[1|0]
> *IE3 only.* Enable or disable the displaying of 3-D borders for frames within a frameset. The default is 1 (borders on).

→

<frameset>
←
	framespacing=*n*
	    IE3 only. Add additional space between adjacent frames in pixels.
	rows=*list*
	    Specify the number and height of frames within a frameset.
	
	See Chapter 4 for more information on using frames.

<h*n*>	<h*n*> . . . </h*n*> The enclosed text is a level *n* header; for level *n* from 1 to 6. **Attributes** align=*type* Specify the heading alignment as either left (default), center, or right.
<head>	<head> . . . </head> Delimit the beginning and end of the document head.

<hr>	<hr>
	Break the current text flow and insert a horizontal rule.
	Attributes
	align=*type*
	    Specify the rule alignment as either left, center (default), or right.
	noshade
	    Do not use 3-D shading to render the rule.
	size=*pixels*
	    Set the thickness of the rule to an integer number of pixels.
	width=*value*
	    Set the width of the rule to either an integer number of pixels or a percentage of the page width.

<html>	<html> . . . </html> Delimit the beginning and end of the entire HTML document. **Attributes** version=*string* Indicate the HTML version used to create this document.

\<i> ... \</i>

Format the enclosed text in an *italic* typeface.

\<iframe> ... \</iframe>

IE3 only. Define a floating frame within a document with similar placement to \<img>. This element requires a closing tag.

Attributes

align=*type*
> Align the floating frame to either the top, middle, bottom (default), left, or right of the text in the line.

frameborder=[1|0]
> Enable or disable the displaying of a 3-D border for a frame. Default is 1, which inserts the border. The value 0 turns the border off.

height=*n*
> Specify the height of the frame in pixels or as a percentage of the window size.

hspace=*n*
> Specify the space, in pixels, to be added to the left and right of the image.

marginheight=*n*
> Place *n* pixels of space above and below the frame contents.

marginwidth=*n*
> Place *n* pixels of space to the left and right of the frame contents.

name=*string*
> Define the name of the frame.

noresize
> Disable user resizing of the frame.

scrolling=*type*
> Always add scrollbars (yes), never add scrollbars (no), or add scrollbars when needed (auto).

src=*url*
> Define the URL of the source document for this frame.

vspace=*n*
> Specify the vertical space, in pixels, added at the top and bottom of the image.

width=*n*
> Specify the width of the frame in pixels or as a percentage of the window size

See Chapter 4 for more information on using frames.

`<img>`

Insert an image into the current text flow.

Attributes

`alt=`*text*
> Provide alternative text for non-image-capable browsers.

`border=`*n*
> Set the pixel thickness of the border around images contained within hyperlinks.

`controls`
> *IE2 and later.* Add playback controls for embedded video clips.

`dynsrc=`*url*
> *IE2 and later.* Specify the URL of a video clip to be displayed.

`height=`*n*
> Specify the height of the image in pixels.

`hspace=`*n*
> Specify the space, in pixels, to be added to the left and right of the image.

`ismap`
> Indicate that the image is mouse-selectable when used within an `<a>` tag.

`loop=`*value*
> *IE2 and later.* Set the number of times to play the video; *value* may be an integer or the value `infinite`.

`lowsrc=`*url*
> *N2 and later.* Specify a low-resolution image to be loaded by the browser first, followed by the image specified by the `<src>` attribute.

`src=`*url*
> Specify the source URL of the image to be displayed (required).

`start=`*start*
> *IE2 and later.* Specify when to play the video clip, either `fileopen` or `mouseover`.

`usemap=`*url*
> Specify the map of coordinates and links that define the hypertext links within this image.

`vspace=`*n*
> Specify the vertical space, in pixels, added at the top and bottom of the image.

`width=`*n*
> Specify the width of the image in pixels.

`<input type=checkbox>`

Create a checkbox input element within a `<form>`.

Attributes

  checked

      Mark the element as initially selected.

  name=*string*

      Specify the name of the parameter to be passed to the form-processing application if the input element is selected (required).

  value=*string*

      Specify the value of the parameter sent to the form-processing application if this form element is selected (required).

See Chapter 10 for more information on using forms.

`<input type=file>`

Create a file-selection element within a `<form>`.

Attributes

  maxlength=*n*

      Specify the maximum number of characters to accept for this element.

  name=*string*

      Specify the name of the parameter that is passed to the form-processing application for this input element (required).

  size=*n*

      Specify the number of characters to display for this element.

See Chapter 10 for more information on using forms.

`<input type=hidden>`

Create a hidden element within a `<form>`.

Attributes

  maxlength=*n*

      Specify the maximum number of characters to accept for this element.

  name=*string*

      Specify the name of the parameter that is passed to the form-processing application for this input element (required).

  size=*n*

      Specify the number of characters to display for this element.

$\rightarrow$

`<input>` ←	value=*string* Specify the value of this element that is passed to the form-processing application. See Chapter 10 for more information on using forms.

`<input>`	**`<input type=image>`**
	Create an image input element within a `<form>`.
	
	Attributes
	  align=*type*
	    Align the image to either the `top`, `middle`, or `bottom` of the form element's text.
	  name=*string*
	    Specify the name of the parameter to be passed to the form-processing application for this input element (required).
	  src=*url*
	    Specify the source URL of the image (required).
	
	See Chapter 10 for more information on using forms.

`<input>`	**`<input type=password>`**
	Create a content-protected text-input element within a `<form>`.
	
	Attributes
	  maxlength=*n*
	    Specify the maximum number of characters to accept for this element.
	  name=*string*
	    Specify the name of the parameter to be passed to the form-processing application for this input element (required).
	  size=*n*
	    Specify the number of characters to display for this element.
	  value=*string*
	    Specify the initial value for this element.
	
	See Chapter 10 for more information on using forms.

`<input>`	**`<input type=radio>`** Create a radio-button input element within a `<form>`.

checked
> Mark the element as initially selected.

name=*string*
> Specify the name of the parameter that is passed to the form-processing application if this input element is selected (required).

value=*string*
> Specify the value of the parameter that is passed to the form-processing application if this element is selected (required).

See Chapter 10 for more information on using forms.

<input type=reset>   <input>

Create a reset button within a <form>.

Attributes

value=*string*
> Specify an alternate label for the reset button.

See Chapter 10 for more information on using forms.

<input type=submit>   <input>

Create a submit button within a <form>.

Attributes

name=*string*
> Specify the name of the parameter that is passed to the form-processing application for this input element (required).

value=*string*
> Specify an alternate label for the submit button, as well as the value passed to the form-processing application for this parameter if this button is clicked.

See Chapter 10 for more information on using forms.

<input type=text>   <input>

Create a text input element within a <form>. (This is the default input type.)

Attributes

maxlength=*n*
> Specify the maximum number of characters to accept for this element.

$\rightarrow$

\<input\>
←
	name=*string*
	    Specify the name of the parameter that is passed to the
	    form-processing application for this input element
	    (required).
	size=*n*
	    Specify the number of characters to display for this ele-
	    ment.
	value=*string*
	    Specify the initial value for this element.
	
	See Chapter 10 for more information on using forms.

\<isindex\>	\<isindex\>
	
	Create a "searchable" HTML document.
	
	Attributes
	action=*url*
	    IE2 and later. Provide the URL of the program that will
	    perform the searching action.
	prompt=*string*
	    Provide an alternate prompt for the input field.

\<kbd\>	\<kbd\> . . . \</kbd\> The enclosed text is keyboard-like input.

\<li\>	\<li\> . . . \</li\>
	
	Delimit a list item in an ordered (\<ol\>) or unordered (\<ul\>)
	list.
	
	Attributes
	type=*format*
	    Set the type of this list element to the desired format.
	    For \<li\> within \<ol\>: A (capital letters), a (lowercase
	    letters), I (capital Roman numerals), i (lowercase
	    Roman numerals), or 1 (Arabic numerals; default). For
	    \<li\> within \<ul\>: circle, disc (default), or
	    square.
	value=*n*
	    Set the number for this list item to *n*.

\<link\>	\<link\> Define a link in the document \<head\> between this docu- ment and another document.

`href=`*url*

> Specify the hypertext reference URL of the target document.

`methods=`*list*

> Specify a browser-dependent list of comma-separated display methods for this link.

`rel=`*relation*

> Indicate the relationship from this document to the target. For Internet Explorer 3.0, `rel=style` indicates the existence of an external style sheet.

`rev=`*relation*

> Indicate the reverse relationship from the target to this document.

`src=`*url*

> *IE3 only.* Specify the URL for the external style sheet to be used in formatting the document.

`title=`*string*

> Provide a title for the target document.

`type=text/css`

> *IE3 only.* Show type of outside link to be an external cascading style sheet.

`urn=`*urn*

> Provide the location-independent Uniform Resource Name for the target document.

`<listing> ... </listing>` <listing>

Same as `<pre width=132> ... </pre>`; deprecated: don't use.

`<map> ... </map>` <map>

Define a map containing hotspots in a client-side image map.

Attributes

`name=`*string*

> Define the name of this map (required).

`<marquee> ... </marquee>` <marquee>

IE2 and later. Create a scrolling-text marquee.

Attributes

`align=`*position*

> Align the marquee to the `top`, `middle`, or `bottom` of the surrounding text.

$\rightarrow$

\<marquee\>
←
	behavior=*style*
	    Define marquee style to be `scroll`, `slide`, or `alternate`.
	
	bgcolor=*color*
	    Set the background color of the marquee.
	
	direction=*dir*
	    Define the direction, `left` or `right`, the text is to scroll.
	
	height=*value*
	    Define the height, in pixels, of the marquee area.
	
	hspace=*value*
	    Define the space, in pixels, to be inserted left and right of the marquee.
	
	loop=*value*
	    Set the number of times to animate the marquee; value is an integer or `infinite`.
	
	scrollamount=*value*
	    Set the number of pixels to move the text for each scroll movement.
	
	scrolldelay=*value*
	    Specify the delay, in milliseconds, between successive movements of the marquee text.
	
	vspace=*value*
	    Define the space, in pixels, to be inserted above and below the marquee.
	
	width=*value*
	    Define the width, in pixels, of the marquee area.

\<menu\>	`<menu> ... </menu>` Define a menu list containing `<li>` tags. ***Attributes*** compact Make the list more compact.

\<meta\>	`<meta>`
	
	Provides additional information about a document.
	
	Attributes
	
	content=*string*
	    Specify the value for the meta-information (required).
	
	    For client pulls, `content="`*n*`;url=`*url*`"` tells the browser to load the specified *url* after *n* seconds. If no URL is specified, the source document will be reloaded. Must be used with `http-equiv="refresh"` within `<meta>`.

http-equiv=*string*
    Specify the HTTP equivalent name for the meta-information and cause the server to include the name and content in the HTTP header for this document when it is transmitted to the client.
 	
    A value of `refresh` creates a "client-pull" within a document.
name=*string*
    Specify the name of the meta-information.
	\<meta\>

HTML

\<multicol\> ... \</multicol\>   **\<multicol\>**

N3 only. Format enclosed HTML and text in multicolumn format. Text and elements will flow across specified number of columns to give them approximately equal length.

Attributes

cols=*n*
    Specify number of columns (required).
gutter=*n*
    Specify amount of space in pixels between columns. Default is 10 pixels.
width=*n*
    Specify width of columns in pixels.

\<nextid\>   **\<nextid\>**

Define the labeling start point for automatic document-generation tools.

Attributes

n=*n*
    Indicate the starting label number (required).

\<nobr\> ... \</nobr\>   **\<nobr\>**

No breaks allowed in the enclosed text.

\<noframes\> ... \</noframes\>   **\<noframes\>**

Define content to be presented by browsers that do not support frames.

See Chapter 4 for more information on using frames.

\<noscript\> ... \</noscript\>   **\<noscript\>**

N3 only. Specify alternative content for browsers that do not support JavaScript. See Chapter 21, *JavaScript Quick Reference*, for more information on JavaScript.

<object>

<object> ... </object>

IE3 only. Insert an object into the document. This tag is used to specify applets, OLE controls, and other media objects.

Attributes

align=*value*
> Specify how the object is aligned with other elements in the document. Values include: baseline, center, left, middle, right, textbottom, textmiddle, and texttop.

border=*n*
> Set the width of the object's border if it is a hyperlink.

classid=*url*
> Identify the class identifier of the object. The URL syntax of the URL depends on the object type.

codebase=*url*
> Identify the URL of the object's codebase. The syntax of the URL depends on the object.

codetype=*codetype*
> Specify the media type of the code.

data=*url*
> Specify the URL of the data used for the object. The syntax of the URL depends on the object.

declare
> Declare an object without instantiating it.

height=*n*
> Specify the height of the object in pixels.

hspace=*n*
> Specify the amount of space in pixels between the sides of the object and the surrounding elements.

name=*url*
> Specify the name of the object.

shapes
> Indicate shaped hyperlinks in object.

standby=*message*
> Specify message to display during object loading.

type=*type*
> Specify the media type for data.

usemap=*url*
> Specify image map to use with object.

vspace=*n*
> Specify the amount of space in pixels above and below object.

width=*n*
> Specify object width.

`<ol> ... </ol>`

Define an ordered list containing numbered (ascending) `<li>` elements.

Attributes

  `compact`
    Present the list in a more compact manner.
  `start=`*n*
    Start numbering the list at *n*, instead of 1.
  `type=`*format*
    Set the numbering format for this list to either `A` (capital letters), `a` (lowercase letters), `I` (capital Roman numerals), `i` (lowercase Roman numerals), or `1` (Arabic numerals; default).

`<option> ... </option>`

Define an option within a `<select>` item in a `<form>`.

Attributes

  `selected`
    Make this item initially selected.
  `value=`*string*
    Return the specified value to the form-processing application instead of the `<option>` contents.

See Chapter 10 for more information on using forms.

`<p> ... </p>`

Start and end a paragraph.

Attributes

  `align=`*type*
    Align the text within the paragraph to `left`, `center`, or `right`.

`<param> ... </param>`

Supply a parameter to the `<applet>` or `<object>` surrounding this tag.

Attributes

  `name=`*string*
    Define the name of the parameter.
  `value=`*string*
    Define the value of the parameter.
  `valuetype=`*type*
    IE3 only. Indicate the type of value. Can be one of three types: `data` indicates that the parameter's value

→

\<param\> ←	is data (default); ref indicates that the parameter's value is a URL; object indicates that the value is a URL of another object in the document. type=*type* *IE3 only.* Specify the media type.
\<plaintext\>	\<plaintext\> Render the remainder of the document as preformatted plain text.
\<pre\>	\<pre\> . . . \</pre\> Render the enclosed text in its original, preformatted style, honoring line breaks and spacing verbatim. ***Attributes*** width=*n* Size the text, if possible, so that *n* characters fit across the display window.
\<s\>	\<s\> . . . \</s\> The enclosed text is struck through with a horizontal line.
\<samp\>	\<samp\> . . . \</samp\> The enclosed text is a sample.

\<script\>	\<script\> . . . \</script\>
	
	Specify enclosed script in a supported scripting language to be used in the document.
	
	Attributes
	language=*lang*
	    Identify language of the script, e.g., JavaScript or VBScript.
	src=*url*
	    N3 only. Specify the URL of an outside file containing the script to be loaded and run with the document.
	
	See Chapter 21 for more information on JavaScript.

\<select\>	\<select\> . . . \</select\> Define a multiple-choice menu or scrolling list within a \<form\>, containing one or more \<option\> tags.

   `multiple`

      Allow user to select more than one \<option\> within the \<select\>.

   name=*string*

      Define the name for the selected \<option\> values that, if selected, are passed to the form-processing application (required).

   size=*n*

      Display items using a pulldown menu for `size=1` (without `multiple` specified) and a scrolling list of *n* items otherwise.

See Chapter 10 for more information on using forms.

\<small\> . . . \</small\>   **\<small\>**

Format the enclosed text using a smaller typeface.

\<spacer\>   **\<spacer\>**

N3 only. Insert a whitespace element in a document.

Attributes

   type=*type*

      Specify what type of spacer to use. `vertical` inserts space between two lines of text. `horizontal` inserts space between words or characters. `block` inserts a rectangular space like an \<img\> object.

   size=*n*

      Specify size in pixels for either width of `horizontal` spacer, or height of `vertical` spacer.

   width=*n*

      Specify width in pixels of `block` spacer.

   height=*n*

      Specify height in pixels of `block` spacer.

   align=*value*

      Specify alignment of `block` spacer with surrounding text. Values are the same as for the \<img\> tag.

\<span\> . . . \</span\>   **\<span\>**

IE3 only. Specify style-sheet formatting to text between tags.

Attributes

   style=*elements*

      Specify cascading style sheet elements for text in the span.

\<strike\>	`<strike> ... </strike>` The enclosed text is struck through with a horizontal line.
\<strong\>	`<strong> ... </strong>` Strongly emphasize the enclosed text.
\<style\>	`<style> ... </style>` *IE3 only.* Surrounds list of style elements to be used in formatting of document. The `<style>` block comes before the `<body>` tag and outside all other elements except `<html>` `... </html>`.
\<sub\>	`<sub> ... </sub>` Format the enclosed text as a subscript.
\<sup\>	`<sup> ... </sup>` Format the enclosed text as a superscript.
\<table\>	`<table> ... </table>` Define a table. ***Attributes*** `align=`*position* Align the table either `left` or `right` with the surrounding text flow. `background=`*url* Specify an image to be tiled in the background of the table. `bgcolor=`*color* *N3, IE2 and later.* Define the background color for the entire table. `border=`*n* Create a border *n* pixels wide. `bordercolor=`*color* *IE2 and later.* Define the border color for the entire table. `bordercolordark=`*color* *IE2 and later.* Define the dark border-highlighting color for the entire table. `bordercolorlight=`*color* *IE2 and later.* Define the light border-highlighting color for the entire table.

<table>

`cellpadding=`*n*
> Place *n* pixels of padding around each cell's contents.

`cellspacing=`*n*
> Place *n* pixels of spacing between cells.

`frame=[void|above|below|hsides|lhs|rhs|vsides|box|border]`
> *IE3 only.* Specify which sides of a table's outer border will be drawn. `void` removes outer borders. `box` and `border` display all. `hsides` draws horizontal sides, `vsides` draws vertical sides. `lhs` draws left side, `rhs` right side.

`hspace=`*n*
> Specify the horizontal space, in pixels, added at the left and right of the table.

`rules=[all|cols|groups|none|rows]`
> *IE3 only.* Turn off (none) or turn on rules between table cells by `cols`, `rows`, `groups`, or `all`.

`vspace=`*n*
> Specify the vertical space, in pixels, added at the top and bottom of the table.

`width=`*n*
> Set the width of the table to *n* pixels or a percentage of the window width.

See Chapter 5 for more information on tables.

`<tbody>`

<tbody>

IE2 and later. Specify the rows in a table to be grouped as the main table body. Requires no ending tag. This element is used to indicate where rules will be drawn when `rules=groups` is used in the `<table>` tag.

`<td> ... </td>`

<td>

Define a table data cell.

Attributes

`align=`*type*
> Align the cell contents to the `left`, `center`, or `right`.

`background=`*url*
> Specify an image to be tiled in the background of the cell.

`bgcolor=`*color*
> *N3, IE2 and later.* Define the background color for the cell.

→

`<td>` ←	`bordercolor=`*color* *IE2 and later.* Define the border color for the cell. `bordercolordark=`*color* *IE2 and later.* Define the dark border highlighting color for the cell. `bordercolorlight=`*color* *IE2 and later.* Define the light border highlighting color for the cell. `colspan=`*n* Have this cell straddle *n* adjacent columns. `nowrap` Do not automatically wrap and fill text in this cell. `rowspan=`*n* Have this cell straddle *n* adjacent rows. `valign=`*type* Vertically align this cell's contents to the `top`, `center`, `bottom`, or `baseline` of the cell. `width=`*n* Set the width of this cell to *n* pixels or a percentage of the table width. See Chapter 5 for more information on tables.

`<textarea>`

`<textarea>` **...** `</textarea>`

Define a multiline text input area within a `<form>`; content of the `<textarea>` tag is the initial, default value.

Attributes

`cols=`*n*
> Display *n* columns of text within the text area.

`name=`*string*
> Define the name for the text-area value that is passed to the form-processing application (required).

`rows=`*n*
> Display *n* rows of text within the text area.

`wrap=`*style*
> *N2 and later.* Set word wrapping within the text area to `off`, `virtual` (display wrap, but do not transmit to server), or `physical` (display and transmit wrap).

See Chapter 10 for more information on forms.

`<tfoot>`

`<tfoot>`

IE2 and later. Specify the rows that will be grouped as the table footer. Requires no ending tag. Used to indicate where rules will be drawn when `rules=groups` is set in the `<table>` tag. See Chapter 5 for more on tables.

<th>

`<th> ... </th>`

Define a table header cell.

Attributes

align=*type*
> Align the cell contents to the left, center, or right.

background=*url*
> Specify an image to be tiled in the background of the cell.

bgcolor=*color*
> *N3, IE2 and later.* Define the background color for the cell.

bordercolor=*color*
> *IE2 and later.* Define the border color for the cell.

bordercolordark=*color*
> *IE2 and later.* Define the dark border-highlighting color for the cell.

bordercolorlight=*color*
> *IE2 only.* Define the light border-highlighting color for the cell.

colspan=*n*
> Have this cell straddle *n* adjacent columns.

nowrap
> Do not automatically wrap and fill text in this cell.

rowspan=*n*
> Have this cell straddle *n* adjacent rows.

valign=*type*
> Vertically align this cell's contents to the top, center, bottom, or baseline of the cell.

width=*n*
> Set the width of this cell to *n* pixels or a percentage of the table width.

See Chapter 5 for more information on tables.

`<thead>`

<thead>

IE2 and later. Specifies the rows that will be grouped as the table header. Requires no ending tag. This element is used to indicate where rules will be drawn when rules=groups is set in the `<table>` tag. See Chapter 5 for more information on tables.

`<title> ... </title>`

<title>

Define the HTML document's title.

`<tr>`	`<tr> ... </tr>`
	Define a row of cells within a table.
	Attributes
	`align=`*type*
	Align the cell contents in this row to the `left`, `center`, or `right`.
	`background=`*url*
	Specify an image to be tiled in the background of the cell.
	`bgcolor=`*color*
	N3, IE2 and later. Define the background color for this row.
	`border=`*n*
	Create a border *n* pixels wide.
	`bordercolor=`*color*
	IE2 and later. Define the border color for this row.
	`bordercolordark=`*color*
	IE2 and later. Define the dark border-highlighting color for this row.
	`bordercolorlight=`*color*
	IE2 and later. Define the light border-highlighting color for this row.
	`valign=`*type*
	Vertically align the cell contents in this row to the `top`, `center`, `bottom`, or `baseline` of the cell.
	See Chapter 5 for more information on tables.
`<tt>`	`<tt> ... </tt>`
	Format the enclosed text in typewriter-style (monospaced) font.
`<ul>`	`<ul> ... </ul>`
	Define an unordered list of bulleted `<li>` elements.
	Attributes
	`compact`
	Display the list in a more compact manner.
	`type=`*bullet*
	N2 and later. Set the bullet style for this list to either `circle`, `disc` (default), or `square`.
`<var>`	`<var> ... </var>`
	The enclosed text is a variable's name.

`<wbr>`

Indicate a potential word break point within a `<nobr>` section.

| | `<wbr>` |

`<xmp>` ... `</xmp>`

Same as `<pre width=80>` ... `</pre>`; deprecated, do not use.

| | `<xmp>` |

CHAPTER 4

Frames

Version 2.0 of Netscape Navigator introduced a new capability for Web documents called *frames*. Frames allow you to divide the main browser window into smaller sub-windows (frames), each of which simultaneously displays a separate document. Frame support has since been incorporated into Microsoft Internet Explorer as well.

Two tags are used to make frame documents: <frameset> and <frame>. <noframes> tags can be used to provide alternative content for non-frames browsers.

A *frameset* is simply a collection of frames that occupy the browser's window. Column and row definition attributes for the <frameset> tag let you define the number and initial sizes for the columns and rows of frames. The <frame> tag defines what document—HTML or otherwise—initially goes into the frame, and is where you may give the frame a name to use for hypertext link targets.

Here is the HTML source for a simple frame document, which is displayed by the browser in Figure 4-1.

```
<html>
<head>
<title>Frames Layout</title>
</head>
<frameset rows="60%,*" cols="65%,20%,*">
  <frame src="frame1.html">
  <frame src="frame2.html">
  <frame src="frame3.html" name="fill_me">
  <frame scrolling=yes src="frame4.html">
  <frame src="frame5.html">
  <frame src="frame6.html">
  <noframes>
    You are using a browser that does not support frames.
    <a href="frame1.html">Take this link</a> to the first
    HTML document in the set.
```

```
    </noframes>
  </frameset>
  </html>
```

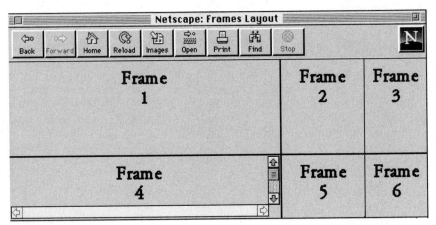

Figure 4-1: A simple six-panel frame layout in Netscape

The first thing to notice in the sample document is that Netscape fills the frames in the frameset in order across each row. Second, frame 4 sports a scrollbar because we told it to, even though the contents may otherwise fit the frame without scrolling. (Scrollbars automatically appear if the contents overflow the frame's dimensions, unless explicitly disabled with `scrolling=no`.)

Another item of interest is the `name` attribute in one of the frame tags. Once named, you can reference a particular frame in which to display a hypertext-linked document. To do that, you add a special `target` attribute to the anchor (`<a>`) tag of the source hypertext link. For instance, to link a document called "new.html" for display in our example window frame 3, which we've named "fill_me", the anchor looks like this:

```
    <a href="new.html" target="fill_me">
```

If the user selects this link, say in frame 1, the *new.html* document will replace the original *frame3.html* contents in frame 3.

Frame Layout

The `<frameset>` tag defines the collection of frames or other framesets in a document. Framesets may be nested, providing a richer set of layout capabilities. The `<frameset>` tag replaces the `<body>` tag in a document. You may not include any other content except valid `<head>` and `<frameset>` content.

The `<frameset>` tag uses two attributes to let you define the size and number of columns (`cols`) and rows (`rows`) of either frames or nested framesets to display in the document window. These attributes divide a frameset up in a grid-like or tabular format. Both attributes accept a quote-enclosed, comma-separated list of values that specify either the absolute or relative width (for columns) or height (for rows) for the frames. The number of attribute values determines how many rows or columns of frames the browser will display in the document window.

Each value in the `rows` and `cols` attributes can be specified in one of three ways: as an absolute number of pixels, as a percentage of the total width or height of the frameset, or as a portion of the space remaining after setting aside room for adjacent elements.

The browser will match the size specifications as closely as possible. However, the browser will not extend the boundaries of the main document window or leave blank space outside of frames. Space is allocated to a particular frame in reference to all other frames across the row or down the column, and the entire document window is filled. Also, the main document window for a frame document does not have scrollbars.

Here is an example of setting row heights in pixels:

```
<frameset rows="150,300,150">
```

This will create three frames, each stretching across the entire document window. The top and bottom rows are set to 150 pixels tall. The middle is set to 300 pixels. Unless the browser window is exactly 600 pixels tall, the browser automatically and proportionally stretches or compresses the top and bottom rows so that each occupies one-quarter of the window space. The middle row occupies the remaining half of the window. This frameset could be expressed with percentages like this:

```
<frameset rows=25%,50%,25%">
```

The percentages should add up to 100%, of course. If they don't, the browser will proportionally resize the rows to make them fit.

To make row and column sizing easier, you can use the asterisk (*) character. The asterisk is used to represent one equal portion of the remaining window space, whatever it is. For example:

```
<frameset cols="50,*">
```

creates one fixed 50-pixel column down the left side of the window, and the remaining space then goes to the right column. The asterisk can also be used for more than one column or row. For example:

```
<frameset rows="*,100,*">
```

creates a 100-pixel tall row across the middle of a frameset and rows above and below it that are equal in height.

If you precede the asterisk with an integer value, the corresponding row or column gets proportionally more of the available space. For example:

```
<frameset cols="10%,3*,*,*">
```

creates four columns: the first column occupies 10% of the overall width of the frameset. The second column then gets three-fifths of the remaining space, and the third and fourth columns each get one-fifth. Using the asterisk makes it easy to divide up remaining space in a frameset.

Be aware that unless you explicitly tell it not to, the browser lets users manually resize the individual columns and rows in a frame document. To prevent this, use the noresize attribute for the <frame> tag.

Nested Framesets

You can achieve more complex layouts by using nested <frameset> tags. Any frame within a frameset can contain another frameset.

For example, Figure 4-2 shows a layout of two columns, the first with two rows and the second with three rows. This is created by nesting two <frameset> tags with row specifications within a top-level <frameset> that specifies the columns:

```
<frameset cols="50%,*">
  <frameset rows="50%,*">
    <frame src="frame1.html">
    <frame src="frame2.html">
  </frameset>
  <frameset rows="33%,33%,*">
    <frame src="frame3.html">
    <frame src="frame4.html">
    <frame src="frame5.html">
  </frameset>
</frameset>
```

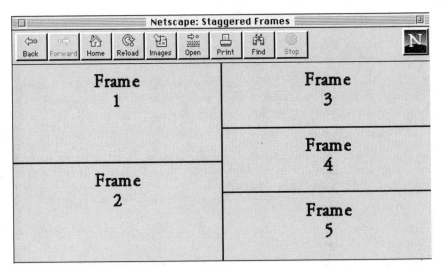

Figure 4-2: Staggered frame layouts using nested <frameset> tags

The <frame> Tag

A frame document contains no displayable content (except for the contents of the <noframes> tag, if applicable). The <frame> tags provide URL references to the individual documents that occupy each frame. <frame> tags are standalone elements, and therefore do not require a closing tag.

Frames are placed into a frameset column by column, from left to right, and then row by row, from top to bottom, so the sequence and number of <frame> tags inside a <frameset> are important.

Netscape displays empty frames for <frame> tags that do not contain a src document attribute and for those trailing ones in a frameset that do not have an associated <frame> tag. Such orphans, however, remain empty; you cannot put content into them later, even if they have a target name attribute for display redirection.

Listed below are the basic attributes that can be used in the <frame> tag.

src=*document_name*
> The value of the src attribute is a URL of the document that is to be displayed in the frame. The document may be any valid HTML document or displayable object, including images and multimedia. The referenced document may itself be another frame document.

name=*frame_name*
> The optional name attribute labels the frame for later reference by a target attribute in a hypertext link anchor <a> tag. If a link that targets a frame's name is selected, the document will be displayed in the named frame. The value of the name attribute is a text string enclosed in quotes.

noresize
> Even though you may explicitly set their dimensions with attributes in the <frameset> tag, users can manually alter the size of a column or row of frames. To suppress this behavior, add the noresize attribute to the frame tags in the row or column whose relative dimensions you want to maintain.

scrolling=[yes,no,auto]
> Normally, the browser displays vertical and horizontal scrollbars for frames whose contents exceed the allotted space. If there is sufficient room for the content, no scrollbars appear. The scrolling attribute gives you explicit control over whether scrollbars appear. A value of yes turns the scrollbars on; no turns them off. The value of auto gives the default scrollbar behavior and is the same as not using the scrolling attribute at all.

marginheight=*height* marginwidth=*width*
> The browser normally places a small amount of space between the edge of a frame and its contents. Those margins can be manually set with the marginheight and marginwidth attributes, whose values are given in pixels. You cannot make a margin less than one pixel, nor so big that there is no room left for the frame's contents.

Frame Targets

The `<frame>` tag includes an attribute that allows you to name the frame. A hypertext link in another frame can load its referenced document into the named frame by using the `target` attribute in the `<a>` tag. For example:

```
<frame src="frame.html" name="display_frame">
```

describes a frame that displays `frame.html` and is named `display_frame`. If another frame or window (or even the same frame) contains this link:

```
<a href="file.html" target="display_frame">
```

and this link is selected, the file `file.html` will replace the file `frame.html` in the frame named `display_frame`. This is the basic use of targeting frames. A useful example is a book with a table of contents. The table of contents is loaded into a frame that occupies a narrow column on the left side of the browser window. The table of contents contains a list of links to each chapter in the book. Each chapter link targets the frame that occupies the rest of the window. You can then view the chapters while keeping the table of contents available for further navigation.

It can be tedious to specify a target for every hyperlink in your documents, especially when most are targeted at the same window or frame. To alleviate this problem, you can use the `target` attribute for the `<base>` tag in the `<head>` of your document. Adding a target to the `<base>` tag sets the default target for every hypertext link in the document that does not contain an explicit `target` attribute.

There are a couple of things to note about the use of targets and named frames:

- If a link without a target is contained within a frame, the referenced document will replace the current contents of the same frame if it is selected.

- If a link contains a target that does not exist, a new window is opened to display the referenced document, and the window is given the target's name. That window can thus be used by other links that target it.

There are four reserved target names for special document redirection actions, listed below. They all begin with the underscore (_) character. You should not use the underscore character as the first letter of any name that you assign a frame as it will be ignored by the browser.

_blank
: A linked document with `target="_blank"` will always be loaded into a newly opened, unnamed window.

_self
: This target value is the default for all `<a>` tags that do not specify a target, causing the referenced document to be loaded in the same frame or window as the source document. The `_self` target is redundant and unnecessary unless used in combination with the `target` attribute of the `<base>` tag to override the default target value for all the links in the source document.

_parent
: The `_parent` target causes the document to be loaded into the parent window or frameset containing the frame containing the hypertext reference. If

the reference is in a window or top-level frame, it is equivalent to the target _self.

_top

This target causes the document to be loaded into the window containing the hypertext link, replacing any frames currently displayed in the window.

Frame Border Attributes

With the version 3.0 release of their browsers, Internet Explorer and Netscape Navigator have added new tags to adjust the style of the borders that surround frames. Although they have the same functions, the attributes are slightly different for each browser.

Netscape uses the frameborder attribute to toggle between 3-D borders and simple rules for borders. The default is to use 3-D borders; a value of no gives simple borders. This attribute can be placed in either the <frameset> tag or in a <frame> tag. A setting in an individual <frame> overrides an outer <frameset> setting.

You can also set the color of the borders in both <frameset> and <frame> with the bordercolor attribute.

In the <frameset> tag, you can set the width of the borders in a whole frameset with the border attribute. The default width is 5 pixels. To achieve borderless frames in Netscape, set border=0 and frameborder=no.

Internet Explorer does all the same things, only with different attributes. It also uses frameborder in the <frameset> and <frame> tags, but the values are 1 for 3-D borders and 0 for simple ones. In the <frameset> tag, you can set the amount of space between frames with the framespacing attribute. By setting framespacing=0 and frameborder=0, you can achieve borderless frames.

Another new feature in Internet Explorer 3.0 is the floating frame. This has all the abilities that a regular frame does, but it is placed within a document like an <img> would be. The tag for a floating frame is <iframe>, and it requires a closing tag. The attributes include all of the regular <frame> attributes, and the sizing, alignment, and placement attributes of <img>.

CHAPTER 5

Tables

HTML tables offer another creative way to lay out the information in your Web documents. Not only can they be used for standard table comparisons, but also as a way to place the elements of your page more precisely. The HTML table standard has never been totally nailed down, but most graphical browsers use a slightly trimmed version of the proposed standard to great effect. There are also many new extensions, which allow you to add to the visual value of your tables.

The main tags that describe tables are: `<table>`, `<caption>`, `<tr>`, `<th>`, and `<td>`. The `<table>` tag surrounds the table and gives default specifications for the entire table such as background color, border size, and spacing between cells. The optional `<caption>` tag is placed within the `<table>` tags and provides a caption for the table. `<tr>` tags denote each row of the table and contain the tags for each cell within a row. `<th>` and `<td>` describe the table cells themselves, `<th>` being a header cell and `<td>` being a regular cell. `<th>` and `<td>` tags surround the information that will be displayed within each table cell.

Table cells are defined across each row of a table. The number of cells in a row is determined by the number of `<th>` or `<td>` tags contained within a `<tr>`. If a table cell spans more than one row (using the `rowspan` attribute), the affected rows below it automatically accomodate the cell, and no additional cell tag is needed to represent it in those rows.

Here is an example of an HTML table. Figure 5-1 shows the table rendered in two different browsers. Note how differently each browser displays the same table. You should keep these differences in mind when designing tables, and test to see how your table will look in different browsers (as with all of your HTML documents).

```
<table border cellspacing=0 cellpadding=5>
  <caption align=bottom> Kumquat versus a poked
  eye, by gender</caption>
  <tr>
    <td colspan=2 rowspan=2></td>
```

```
   <th colspan=2 align=center>Preference</th>
  </tr>
  <tr>
   <th>Eating Kumquats</th>
   <th>Poke In The Eye</th>
  </tr>
  <tr align=center>
   <th rowspan=2>Gender</th>
   <th>Male</th>
   <td>73%</td>
   <td>27%</td>
  </tr>
  <tr align=center>
   <th>Female</th>
   <td>16%</td>
   <td>84%</td>
  </tr>
 </table>
```

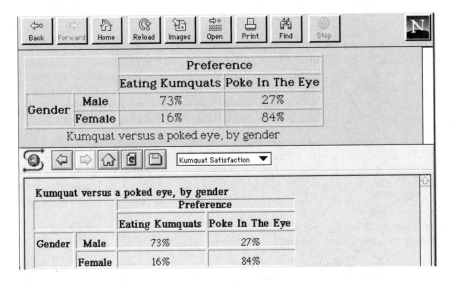

Figure 5-1: HTML table example rendered by Netscape (top) and by Mosaic (bottom)

The contents of table cells may be any data that can can be displayed in an HTML document. This can be plain text, images, tagged text, and other HTML structures. The table cells will be sized according to their contents and in relation to other cells.

The <table> Tag

Tables are normally treated as floating objects within a browser window. They are aligned in the browser window to match the containing text flow, usually left-justified (or centered). Unlike inline images, however, text normally floats above and below a table, but not beside it. Internet Explorer and Netscape allow you to set the alignment of a table and float text around it with the align attribute. align

---

accepts two values, left and right. These values instruct the browser to align the table with either the left or right margin of the text flow around it. Text will then flow along the opposite side of the table, if there is room.

The hspace and vspace attributes are used to add extra space between the table and surrounding content. hspace adds space to the left and right sides of the table; vspace adds space above and below it. The value of each attribute is given in an integer number of pixels.

The width attribute can give you some control over the width of a table. Tables are normally rendered at the width that will fit all of the contents. The width attribute allows you to widen the table beyond the default size to occupy a set number of pixels or a percentage of the window's width. For example:

```
<table width="100%">
```

will always stretch the table to the full width of the browser window. This is a conditional instruction, however. The size of table cells is always determined by the size of the biggest "fixed" content such as an image or a non-breaking line of text. Therefore, a table may need to be wider than you want to allow it. If the table cells contain mostly wrapping text elements such as paragraphs (<p>), the browser will usually accomodate your request.

The border attribute to <table> is used to control the borders within and around the table. Simply using border with no attributes will add default borders to a table, which are not rendered the same in any two browsers. You can set border width by giving the attribute an integer number of pixels as a value. The border=0 and no border attributes turn table borders off completely.

The remaining attributes for the <table> tag get confusing from here on in, because they are supported by different browsers. Netscape only supports the two attributes cellpadding and cellspacing. Each accepts an integer number of pixels as a value. cellpadding sets the space between a cell's contents and its edges, whether borders are on or off. cellspacing sets the space between adjacent table cells. If borders are turned on, cellspacing will add the space outside of the border (half on one side, half on the other). The border width is not included or affected by cellspacing or cellpadding.

Internet Explorer only supports the valign attribute in the <table> tag. valign sets the vertical alignment of the contents of a cell. It accepts values of either top or bottom. The default is to center cell contents. When used in the <table> tag, Internet Explorer sets the vertical alignment for all cells in a table. Both Netscape and Internet Explorer also support valign in the lower-level tags of a table with the same functionality. The lower-level specification overrides the upper-level specification.

The other attributes for the <table> tag are exclusive to Internet Explorer. They can also be used in the <tr>, <th>, and <td> tags. They are discussed in the "Internet Explorer Tables" section at the end of this chapter.

The <caption> Tag

You can add a title or caption to your table by using a <caption> tag within a <table>. The default placement of the caption for Netscape and Internet Explorer is above the table and centered with it. The placement and alignment of the caption is controlled by special alignment attributes that differ between the browsers.

In Netscape and Mosaic, the align attribute accepts two values: top and bottom. These allow you to put the caption above or below the table. The default value is top.

Internet Explorer, on the other hand, uses the align attribute for horizontal placement of the caption. It accepts values of left, right, and center (the default). The vertical positioning of the caption in Internet Explorer is controlled by a special valign attribute, which accepts either top (the default) or bottom. Each browser ignores the attributes and values that it does not accept.

The <tr> Tag

Every row in a table is created with a <tr> tag. Within the <tr> tag are one or more cells containing either headers, each defined with the <th> tag, or data, each defined with the <td> tag.

Every row in a table has the same number of cells as the longest row; the browser automatically creates empty cells to pad rows with fewer defined cells.

Attributes to the <tr> tag are used to control behavior for every cell it contains. There are two commonly used attributes for this tag.

align is used differently in <tr> than it is in <table>. In a table row, align lets you change the default horizontal alignment of the contents of the cells within the row. The attribute accepts values of left, right, or center. For Internet Explorer and Netscape, the default horizontal alignment for header cells (<th>) is centered, and for data cells (<td>) it is left-justified.

The valign attribute allows you to specify the vertical alignment of cell contents within a row. Internet Explorer and Netscape support three values: top, center, and bottom. The default vertical alignment for both browsers is centered.

Netscape also supports a value of baseline for valign. This value specially aligns cell contents to the baseline of the top line of text in other cells in the row.

The remaining attributes for the <tr> tag are specific to Internet Explorer. They are discussed at the end of this chapter.

The <th> and <td> Tags

The <th> (table header) and <td> (table data) tags go inside the <tr> tags of an HTML table to create the cells and contents of each cell within a row. The two tags are identical, except that Netscape and Mosaic render the <th> cells in bold text and centered by default. (Internet Explorer does not use bold text for <th> cells.) <td> cell contents are by default rendered in the regular base font, left justified.

The `align`, `valign`, and Internet Explorer-specific attributes all work the same in the cell tags as they do in the row tag. When specified for `<th>` and `<td>`, these attributes override the same behavior set in the upper-level tags for their specific cell.

The other attributes to the cell tags are very important to the layout of your table. The `width` attribute can be used to set the width of a table cell, and all cells within its column. As with the `<table>` tag, a value may be given in an integer number of pixels or a percentage of the width of the table. A `width` value may be ignored by the browser if contents within the column have a fixed width larger than the value (i.e., an image or non-breaking line of text). You should use only one `width` value in the cells of the same column. If two `width` values are specified in the same column of cells, the browser uses the larger value.

The `nowrap` attribute, when included in a cell tag, disables regular linebreaking of text within a table cell. With `nowrap`, the browser assembles the contents of a cell onto a single line, unless you insert a `<br>` or `<p>` tag, which will force a break.

Cell spanning

It is common to have table cells span several columns or rows. This behavior is set within the `<th>` and `<td>` tags with the `colspan` and `rowspan` attributes. Each value is given in an integer number of columns or rows the cell is to stretch across. For example:

```
<td colspan=3>
```

tells the browser to make the cell occupy the same horizontal space as three cells in rows above or below it. The browser flows the contents of the cell to occupy the entire space.

If there aren't enough empty cells on the right, the browser just extends the cell over as many columns as exist to the right; it doesn't add extra empty cells to each row to accomodate an over-extended `colspan` value.

Similar to the `colspan` attribute, `rowspan` stretches a cell down two or more rows in a table. You include the `rowspan` attribute in the `<th>` or `<td>` tag of the uppermost row of a table where you want the cell to begin and set its value equal to the number of rows you want it to span. The cell then occupies the same space as the current row and an appropriate number of cells below that row. For example:

```
<td rowspan=3>
```

creates a cell that occupies the current row plus two more rows below that. The browser ignores overextended `rowspan` values and will only extend the current cell down rows you've explicitly defined by other `<tr>` tags following the current row.

You may combine `colspan` and `rowspan` attributes to create a cell that spans both rows and columns. In our example table in Figure 5-1, the blank cell in the upper-left corner does this with the tag:

```
<td colspan=2 rowspan=2></td>
```

Internet Explorer Tables

Beginning with version 2.0, Internet Explorer added a number of attributes to its table tags. These attributes let you set colors for the backgrounds and borders of table elements. They can be used to set values for the whole table, individual rows, and individual cells. Values can be set in a nested fashion, so that a specification for a single cell can override the broader setting for its row or the whole table.

Each attribute accepts a value specified as either an RGB color value or a standard color name, both of which are described in Chapter 6, *Color Names and Values*.

The `bgcolor` attribute is used to set the background color of cells within a table. You can set a single background color for the whole table, or specify different colors for individual rows and cells. This functionality is also available in Netscape 3.0.

Similar to setting a background color, both Navigator and Internet Explorer allow you to set a background image for the entire table or individual cells. The image will automatically be tiled behind the appropriate table element. The value of the `background` attribute is the URL of the image file.

Borders in Netscape and Internet Explorer create a 3-D effect by using three differently colored strips. There is a thick center strip with much thinner strips on each side. One of the outer strips is colored darker than the center strip, and one is lighter, producing a shadowed effect. Internet Explorer allows you to set the colors for each of these elements when you have borders turned on with the `border` attribute in the `<table>` tag.

The `bordercolor` attribute sets the color of the main center strip of a border.

The `bordercolorlight` attribute sets the color of the light strip of a border, the top- or left-most strip. `bordercolordark` sets the color of the dark strip, the bottom or right-most strip.

You needn't specify all three border colors. The default for Internet Explorer's table borders sets the lighter and darker strips about 25% brighter and darker than the main border color.

A number of other formatting options are available in Internet Explorer. These include setting header and footer rows, grouping columns, and controlling where rules are drawn in the table. These tags include: `<col>`, `<colgroup>`, `<tbody>`, `<thead>`, `<tfoot>`, and the `rules` and `frame` attributes of the `<table>` tag.

CHAPTER 6

Color Names and Values

Within Netscape Navigator and Internet Explorer, you can change the colors of various elements of your document. The following table lists some of the tags and attributes that give you color choice.

Element	Associated Tag and Attribute
Document background	`<body bgcolor=color>`
All document text	`<body text=color>`
Active hyperlinks	`<body alink=color>`
Visited hyperlinks	`<body vlink=color>`
Regular hyperlinks	`<body link=color>`
Small portion of text	`<font color=color>`
Table cells	`<table bgcolor=color>`
	`<tr bgcolor=color>`
	`<td bgcolor=color>`
	`<th bgcolor=color>`
Table borders (Internet Explorer only)	`<table bordercolor=color>`
	`<table bordercolorlight=color>`
	`<table bordercolordark=color>`
	(same for `<tr>`, `<td>`, and `<th>`)

Color Values

In all cases, you may specify the color value as a six-digit hexadecimal number that represents the red, green, and blue (RGB) components of the color. The first two digits correspond to the red component of the color, the next two to the green component, and the last two are the blue component. A value of 00 corresponds to the component being completely off; a value of FF (255) corresponds to

55

the component being completely on. Thus, bright red is FF0000, bright green is 00FF00, and bright blue is 0000FF. Other primary colors are mixtures of two components, such as yellow (FFFF00), magenta (FF00FF), and cyan (00FFFF). White (FFFFFF) and black (000000) are also easy to figure out.

You use these values in a tag by replacing the color with the RGB triple, preceded by a hash (#) symbol. Thus, to make all visited links display as magenta, use this body tag:

```
<body vlink="#FF00FF">
```

Color Names

Unfortunately, determining the hexadecimal value for more esoteric colors like "papaya whip" or "navajo white" is very difficult. You can go crazy trying to adjust the RGB triple for a color to get the shade just right, especially when each adjustment requires loading a document into your browser to view the result.

The folks at Microsoft and Netscape thought so, too, and gave their browsers the ability to use color names directly in any of the color tags. Simply use the color name for the color-attribute value enclosed in quotes. Single-word color names don't require enclosing quotes, but it's good practice to include them anyway. For example, you can make all visited links in the display magenta with the following attribute and value for the body tag:

```
<body vlink="magenta">
```

The standard color names currently supported by Internet Explorer are:

aqua	gray	navy	silver
black	green	olive	teal
blue	lime	purple	yellow
fuchsia	maroon	red	white

Not to be outdone, Netscape 2.0 and higher supports named colors as well; they just don't document the fact. Even better, Netscape supports the several hundred color names defined for use in the X Window System. Note that color names may contain no spaces; also, the word *gray* may be spelled *grey* in any color name.

Colors marked with an asterisk (*) represent a family of colors numbered one through four. Thus, there are actually four variants of blue, named blue1, blue2,blue3, and blue4, along with plain old blue. Blue1 is the lightest of the four; blue4 the darkest. The unnumbered color name is the same color as the first; thus, blue and blue1 are identical.

Finally, if all that isn't enough, there are one hundred variants of gray (and grey) numbered 1 through 100. Gray1 is the darkest, gray100 is the lightest, and gray is very close to gray75.

The Netscape-supported colors are:

aliceblue	darkturquoise	lightseagreen	palevioletred*
antiquewhite*	darkviolet	lightskyblue*	papayawhip
aquamarine*	deeppink*	lightslateblue	peachpuff*
azure*	deepskyblue*	lightslategray	peru

beige
bisque*
black
blanchedalmond
blue*
blueviolet
brown*
burlywood*
cadetblue*
chartreuse*
chocolate*
coral*
cornflowerblue
cornsilk*
cyan*
darkblue
darkcyan
darkgoldenrod*
darkgray
darkgreen
darkkhaki
darkmagenta
darkolivegreen*
darkorange*
darkorchid*
darkred
darksalmon
darkseagreen*
darkslateblue
darkslategray*

dimgray
dodgerblue*
firebrick*
floralwhite
forestgreen
gainsboro
ghostwhite
gold*
goldenrod*
gray
green*
greenyellow
honeydew*
hotpink*
indianred*
ivory*
khaki*
lavender
lavenderblush*
lawngreen
lemonchiffon*
lightblue*
lightcoral
lightcyan*
lightgoldenrod*
lightgoldenrodyellow
lightgray
lightgreen
lightpink*
lightsalmon*

lightsteelblue*
lightyellow*
limegreen
linen
magenta*
maroon*
mediumaquamarine
mediumblue
mediumorchid*
mediumpurple*
mediumseagreen
mediumslateblue
mediumspringgreen
mediumturquoise
mediumvioletred
midnightblue
mintcream
mistyrose*
moccasin
navajowhite*
navy
navyblue
oldlace
olivedrab*
orange*
orangered*
orchid*
palegoldenrod
palegreen*
paleturquoise*

pink*
plum*
powderblue
purple*
red*
rosybrown*
royalblue*
saddlebrown
salmon*
sandybrown
seagreen*
seashell*
sienna*
skyblue*
slateblue*
slategray*
snow*
springgreen*
steelblue*
tan*
thistle*
tomato*
turquoise*
violet
violetred*
wheat*
white
whitesmoke
yellow*
yellowgreen

CHAPTER 7

Character Entities

The following table collects the defined standard, proposed, and several nonstandard (but generally supported) character entities for HTML.

Entity names, if defined, appear for their respective characters and can be used in the HTML character-entity sequence &name; to define any character for display by the browser. Otherwise, or alternatively for named characters, use the character's three-digit numerical value in the sequence &#nnn; to specifically define an HTML character entity. Actual characters, however, may or may not be displayed by the browser depending on the computer platform and user-selected font for display.

Not all 256 characters in the ISO character set appear in the table. Missing ones are not recognized by the browser as either named or numeric entities.

To be sure that your documents are fully compliant with the HTML 2.0 standard, use only those named character entities whose conformance column is blank. Characters whose conformance columns contain a "P" (Proposed) are generally supported by the current browsers, although are not part of the HTML standard. Defy compliance by using the nonstandard (N) entities.

Numeric Entity	Named Entity	Symbol	Description	Conformance
&#009;			Horizontal tab	
&#010;			Line feed	
&#013;			Carriage return	
&#032;			Space	
&#033;		!	Exclamation point	
&#034;	&quot;	"	Quotation mark	
&#035;		#	Hash mark	
&#036;		$	Dollar sign	
&#037;		%	Percent sign	

Numeric Entity	Named Entity	Symbol	Description	Conformance
&#038;	&amp;	&	Ampersand	
&#039;		'	Apostrophe	
&#040;		(	Left parenthesis	
&#041;		)	Right parenthesis	
&#042;		*	Asterisk	
&#043;		+	Plus sign	
&#044;		,	Comma	
&#045;		-	Hyphen	
&#046;		.	Period	
&#047;		/	Slash	
0 – 9		0 - 9	Digits 0 – 9	
&#058;		:	Colon	
&#059;		;	Semicolon	
&#060;	&lt;	<	Less than	
&#061;		=	Equal sign	
&#062;	&gt;	>	Greater than	
&#063;		?	Question mark	
&#064;		@	Commercial "at" sign	
A – Z		A – Z	Letters A – Z	
&#091;		[	Left square bracket	
&#092;		\	Backslash	
&#093;		]	Right square bracket	
&#094;		^	Caret	
&#095;		_	Underscore	
&#096;		`	Grave accent	
a – z		a – z	Letters a – z	
&#123;		{	Left curly brace	
|				Vertical bar	
&#125;		}	Right curly brace	
&#126;		~	Tilde	
&#130;		‚		N
&#131;		ƒ	Florin	N
&#132;		„	Right double quote	N
&#133;		...	Ellipsis	N
&#134;		†	Dagger	N
&#135;		‡	Double dagger	N
&#136;		^	Circumflex	N

Numeric Entity	Named Entity	Symbol	Description	Conformance
&#137;		‰	Permil	N
&#138;		_		N
&#139;		<	Less than sign	N
&#140;		Œ	Capital OE ligature	N
&#145;		'	Left single quote	N
&#146;		'	Right single quote	N
&#147;		"	Left double quote	N
&#148;		"	Right double quote	N
&#149;		•	Bullet	N
&#150;		—	Em dash	N
&#151;		–	En dash	N
&#152;		~	Tilde	N
&#153;		™	Trademark	N
&#154;		_		N
&#155;		>	Greater than sign	N
&#156;		œ	Small oe ligature	N
&#159;		Ÿ	Capital Y, umlaut	N
			Nonbreaking space	P
&#161;	&iexcl;	¡	Inverted exclamation point	P
&#162;	&cent;	¢	Cent sign	P
&#163;	&pound;	£	Pound sign	P
&#164;	&curren;	¤	General currency sign	P
&#165;	&yen;	¥	Yen sign	P
&#166;	&brvbar;	¦	Broken vertical bar	P
&#167;	&sect;	§	Section sign	P
&#168;	&uml;	¨	Umlaut	P
&#169;	&copy;	©	Copyright	P
&#170;	&ordf;	ª	Feminine ordinal	P
&#171;	&laquo;	«	Left angle quote	P
&#172;	&not;	¬	Not sign	P
&#173;	&shy;	–	Soft hyphen	P
&#174;	&reg;	®	Registered trademark	P
&#175;	&macr;	¯	Macron accent	P
&#176;	&deg;	°	Degree sign	P
&#177;	&plusmn;	±	Plus or minus	P
&#178;	&sup2;	^{2}	Superscript 2	P
&#179;	&sup3;	^{3}	Superscript 3	P
&#180;	&acute;	´	Acute accent	P
&#181;	&micro;	µ	Micro sign (Greek mu)	P

Numeric Entity	Named Entity	Symbol	Description	Conformance
&#182;	&para;	¶	Paragraph sign	P
&#183;	&middot;	·	Middle dot	P
&#184;	&cedil;	¸	Cedilla	P
&#185;	&sup1;	¹	Superscript 1	P
&#186;	&ordm;	º	Masculine ordinal	P
&#187;	&raquo;	»	Right angle quote	P
&#188;	&frac14;	¼	Fraction one-fourth	P
&#189;	&frac12;	½	Fraction one-half	P
&#190;	&frac34;	¾	Fraction three-fourths	P
&#191;	&iquest;	¿	Inverted question mark	P
&#192;	&Agrave;	À	Capital A, grave accent	
&#193;	&Aacute;	Á	Capital A, acute accent	
&#194;	&Acirc;	Â	Capital A, circumflex accent	
&#195;	&Atilde;	Ã	Capital A, tilde	
&#196;	&Auml;	Ä	Capital A, umlaut	
&#197;	&Aring;	Å	Capital A, ring	
&#198;	&AElig;	Æ	Capital AE ligature	
&#199;	&Ccedil;	Ç	Capital C, cedilla	
&#200;	&Egrave;	È	Capital E, grave accent	
&#201;	&Eacute;	É	Capital E, acute accent	
&#202;	&Ecirc;	Ê	Capital E, circumflex accent	
&#203;	&Euml;	Ë	Capital E, umlaut	
&#204;	&Igrave;	Ì	Capital I, grave accent	
&#205;	&Iacute;	Í	Capital I, acute accent	
&#206;	&Icirc;	Î	Capital I, circumflex accent	
&#207;	&Iuml;	Ï	Capital I, umlaut	
&#208;	&ETH;	Ð	Capital eth, Icelandic	
&#209;	&Ntilde;	Ñ	Capital N, tilde	
&#210;	&Ograve;	Ò	Capital O, grave accent	
&#211;	&Oacute;	Ó	Capital O, acute accent	
&#212;	&Ocirc;	Ô	Capital O, circumflex accent	
&#213;	&Otilde;	Õ	Capital O, tilde	
&#214;	&Ouml;	Ö	Capital O, umlaut	
&#215;	&times;	×	Multiply sign	P
&#216;	&Oslash;	Ø	Capital O, slash	
&#217;	&Ugrave;	Ù	Capital U, grave accent	
&#218;	&Uacute;	Ú	Capital U, acute accent	
&#219;	&Ucirc;	Û	Capital U, circumflex accent	
&#220;	&Uuml;	Ü	Capital U, umlaut	
&#221;	&Yacute;	Ý	Capital Y, acute accent	

Numeric Entity	Named Entity	Symbol	Description	Conformance
&#222;	&THORN;	Þ	Capital thorn, Icelandic	
&#223;	&szlig;	ß	Small sz ligature, German	
&#224;	&agrave;	à	Small a, grave accent	
&#225;	&aacute;	á	Small a, acute accent	
&#226;	&acirc;	â	Small a, circumflex accent	
&#227;	&atilde;	ã	Small a, tilde	
&#228;	&auml;	ä	Small a, umlaut	
&#229;	&aring;	å	Small a, ring	
&#230;	&aelig;	æ	Small ae ligature	
&#231;	&ccedil;	ç	Small c, cedilla	
&#232;	&egrave;	è	Small e, grave accent	
&#233;	&eacute;	é	Small e, acute accent	
&#234;	&ecirc;	ê	Small e, circumflex accent	
&#235;	&euml;	ë	Small e, umlaut	
&#236;	&igrave;	ì	Small i, grave accent	
&#237;	&iacute;	í	Small i, acute accent	
&#238;	&acirc;	î	Small i, circumflex accent	
&#239;	&iuml;	ï	Small i, umlaut	
&#240;	&eth;	ð	Small eth, Icelandic	
&#241;	&ntilde;	ñ	Small n, tilde	
&#242;	&ograve;	ò	Small o, grave accent	
&#243;	&oacute;	ó	Small o, acute accent	
&#244;	&ocirc;	ô	Small o, circumflex accent	
&#245;	&otilde;	õ	Small o, tilde	
&#246;	&ouml;	ö	Small o, umlaut	
&#247;	&divide;	÷	Division sign	P
&#248;	&oslash;	ø	Small o, slash	
&#249;	&ugrave;	ù	Small u, grave accent	
&#250;	&uacute;	ú	Small u, acute accent	
&#251;	&ucirc;	û	Small u, circumflex accent	
&#252;	&uuml;	ü	Small u, umlaut	
&#253;	&yacute;	ý	Small y, acute accent	
&#254;	&thorn;	þ	Small thorn, Icelandic	
&#255;	&yuml;	ÿ	Small y, umlaut	

CHAPTER 8

Browser Comparison

This chapter lists the discrepancies in HTML tag support between Netscape Naviga-tor and Internet Explorer. These two browsers, which are in competition with each other, are both striving not only to be the better browser but to improve the quality of Web documents. There are many different features between the two, such as scripting language support and extra media "plug-ins." This chapter will focus on HTML support, because it is the most crucial element in designing and authoring documents for the greatest number of users to see.

For the most part, the browsers support the same set of tags. In cases where an element is not supported by the other browser, workarounds are easily accom-plished. For example, the floating frame tag from Internet Explorer (`<iframe>`) uses an opening and closing tag. Browsers that don't recognize these tags ignore them, but anything between the tags is read as a regular part of the document. Therefore, you can place the same content between the tags (albeit in a different format) and not worry about withholding any information from the reader. This scheme works the same for many elements, such as `<noframes>` and `<multicol>`.

Internet Explorer HTML Exclusives

The following tags are supported only by Internet Explorer:

HTML Tag or Attribute	Description
`<bgsound>`	Inserts background audio file in page
`<body>` `bgproperties=`*value*	Sets "watermark" background, which does not scroll with the document
`<body>` `leftmargin=`*n* `topmargin=`*n*	Sets the margins around the document body

HTML Tag or Attribute	Description
<caption> valign=position	One way of setting vertical position of table caption
<col>	Sets text alignment for table columns
<colgroup>	Groups table columns
<comment>	Place a comment in the HTML source file
<form> target=name	Specifies a target window or frame for the output of a form
<frameset> framespacing=n	Sets amount of space between frames in the <frameset> tag
<iframe>	Creates floating frames

<img>
    dynsrc=url
    controls
    loop=n
    start=action
	Settings for embedded video and audio clips

<isindex> action=url	Provides URL of the program that will perform the search

<link>
    src=url
    rel=relation
    type=text/css
	Various different ways to support Cascading Style Sheets

<marquee>	Places scrolling marquee text in page
<object>	Inserts Java applets, OLE controls, other objects into page
<span>	Specifies style-sheet formatting
<style>	Groups style elements

<table>
    bordercolor=color
    bordercolordark=color
    bordercolorlight=color
	Sets colors for 3-D table borders in the <table>, <td>, <th>, and <tr> tags

<table> frame=value	Controls the display of outer borders of a table in the <table> tag
<table> rules=value	Controls the drawing of table rules in the <table> tag
<tbody>	Indicates table body rows
<tfoot>	Indicates table footer rows
<thead>	Indicates table header rows

Netscape Navigator HTML Exclusives

The following tags are supported only by Netscape Navigator:

HTML Tag or Attribute	Description
`<frame>` `bordercolor=`*color*	Specifies color for frame border. Also works in `<frameset>` tag.
`<frameset>` `border=`*n*	Sets the amount of space between frames
`<img>` `lowsrc=`*url*	Provides low-res source for faster image loading
`<multicol>`	Produces a multicolumn format
`<noscript>`	Provides alternative information to non-JavaScript enabled browsers
`<script>` `src=`*url*	Loads an outside file containing JavaScript code
`<spacer>`	Provides whitespace objects to use in page design
`<textarea>` `wrap=`*style*	Specifies line-wrapping options for textareas in forms
`<ul>` `type=`*bullet*	Specifies bullet style for unordered lists

Tags of Contention

In the continual struggle to be the best or most popular browser, the competitors do not always see it fit to be compatible. Here are two attributes that are used differently in each browser:

`<caption align=`*position*`>`

The table caption has not received fair treatment in regard to its placement by either browser. The default placement in both Navigator and Explorer is centered at the top of the table. In Netscape, `align` can be set to either `top` (the default) or `bottom`. There appears to be no way to get it flush right or flush left.

In Internet Explorer, `align` was originally intended for horizontal placement. In version 2.0, the values could be `left`, `right`, or `center`. The `valign` attribute controlled `top` or `bottom` placement. In version 3.0, however, `align` is designated to do everything, taking the additional values `top` and `bottom`. Documentation for 3.0 does not list the `valign` attribute. You can still use it, though. It is not possible to set both a vertical and horizontal placement for the table caption with `align` only.

`<frameset frameborder=?>`

In both browsers, this attribute controls whether frames will have 3-D borders or simple rules around them. It is also usable in the `<frame>` tag. The trouble is that "on/off" values conflict. For Navigator, you use `yes` for 3-D and `no` for rules. In Internet Explorer, the value 1 means 3-D and 0 means rules. Go figure.

PART II

CGI

CHAPTER 9

CGI Overview

The Common Gateway Interface (CGI) is an essential tool for creating and managing comprehensive Web sites. With CGI, you can write scripts that create interactive, user-driven applications.

CGI is the part of the Web server that can communicate with other programs that are running on the server. With CGI, the Web server can invoke an external program, while passing user-specific data to the program (such as what host the user is connecting from, or input the user has supplied through an HTML form). The program then processes that data and the server passes the program's response back to the Web browser (see Figure 9-1).

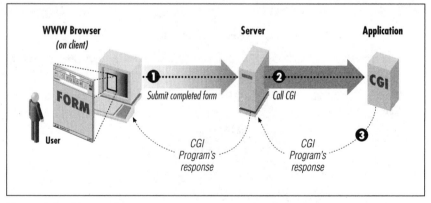

Figure 9-1: CGI overview

Rather than limiting the Web to documents written ahead of time, CGI enables Web pages to be created on the fly, based upon the input of users. You can use CGI scripts to create a wide range of applications, from surveys to search tools, from Internet service gateways to quizzes and games. You can count the number of users who access a document or let them sign an electronic guestbook. You can provide users with all types of information, collect their comments, and respond to them.

Teaching CGI programming from scratch is beyond the scope of this book—for that, we recommend *CGI Programming on the World Wide Web*, by Shishir Gundavaram (O'Reilly & Associates).

Chapters 9 through 16 summarize the essential components of CGI:

- The current chapter (Chapter 9) gives a quick introduction to the mechanism of CGI.

- Chapter 10, *HTML Form Tags*, lists the form tags used as the interface for many CGI applications, and shows an example of using them.

- Chapter 11, *CGI Environment Variables*, lists the environment variables that are commonly defined by servers for CGI programs.

- Chapter 12, *Cookies*, describes how to use Netscape persistent cookies to maintain state across multiple connections.

- Chapter 13, *Server Side Includes*, covers Server Side Includes, which are used with many CGI applications.

- Chapter 14, *Windows CGI*, covers WinCGI, the CGI interface for Windows-based servers.

- Chapter 15, *Perl Quick Reference*, is a quick reference to the Perl programming language, the most common language used for writing CGI programs.

- Chapter 16, *Other CGI Resources*, lists URLs with other resources for CGI, such as libraries and modules that can facilitate CGI programming.

In addition, much of the backbone of CGI resides in the HTTP protocol itself. Effective CGI programming requires some knowledge of HTTP headers and status codes, which are presented in this book as follows:

- Chapter 17, *HTTP Overview*, gives a brief introduction to HTTP.

- Chapter 18, *Server Response Codes*, lists HTTP status codes that can be used by CGI programs that provide their own complete headers.

- Chapter 19, *HTTP Headers*, lists HTTP headers that CGI programs can use in their responses.

- Chapter 20, *Media Types and Subtypes*, lists the media types commonly used in the Content-type headers output by CGI programs.

A Typical CGI Interaction

For an example of a CGI application, suppose you see a fill-in form, such as the one in Figure 9-2.

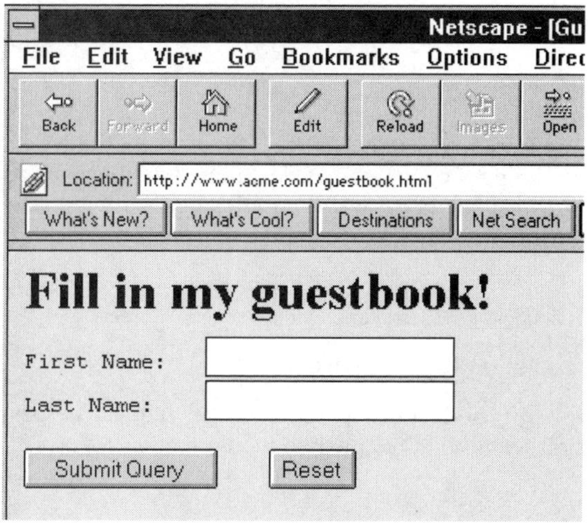

Figure 9-2: A fill-in form

The HTML that produces this form might read as follows:

```
<HTML><HEAD><TITLE>Guestbook</TITLE></HEAD>
<BODY>
<H1>Fill in my guestbook!</H1>
<FORM METHOD="GET" ACTION="/cgi-bin/guestbook.pl">
<PRE>
First Name:    <INPUT TYPE="TEXT" NAME="firstname">
Last Name:     <INPUT TYPE="TEXT" NAME="lastname">

<INPUT TYPE="SUBMIT">    <INPUT TYPE="RESET">
</FORM>
```

The form is written using special "form" tags (discussed in detail in Chapter 10):

- The <form> tag defines the *method* used for the form (either GET or POST) and the *action* to take when the form is submitted—that is, the URL of the CGI program to pass the parameters to.

- The <input> tag can be used in many different ways. In its first two invocations, it creates a text input field and defines the variable name to associate with the field's contents when the form is submitted. The first field is given the variable name "firstname" and the second field is given the name "lastname."

- In its last two invocations, the <input> tag creates a "submit" button and a "reset" button.

- The </form> tag indicates the end of the form.

When the user presses the "submit" button, the data entered into the <input> text fields is passed to the CGI program specified by the action attribute of the <form> tag.

Transferring the Form Data

Parameters to a CGI program are transferred either in the URL or in the body text of the request. The method used to pass parameters is determined by the method attribute to the <form> tag. The GET method says to transfer the data within the URL itself; for example, under the GET method, the browser might initiate the HTTP transaction as follows:

```
GET HTTP/1.0 /cgi-bin/guestbook.pl?firstname=Joe&lastname=Schmoe
```

See Chapter 17 for more information on HTTP transactions.

The POST method says to use the body portion of the HTTP request to pass parameters. The same transaction with the POST method would read as follows:

```
POST HTTP/1.0 /cgi-bin/guestbook.pl
    ... [More headers here]

firstname=Joe&lastname=Schmoe
```

In both these examples, you should recognize the "firstname" and "lastname" variable names that were defined in the HTML form, coupled with the values entered by the user. An ampersand (&) is used to separate the variable=value pairs.

The server now passes the variable=value pairs to the CGI program. It does this either through UNIX environment variables or in standard input (STDIN). If the CGI program is called with the GET method, then parameters are expected to be embedded into the URL of the request, and the server transfers them to the program by assigning them to the QUERY_STRING environment variable. The CGI program can then retrieve the parameters from QUERY_STRING as it would read any environment variable (for example, from the %ENV associative array in Perl). If the CGI program is called with the POST method, parameters are expected to be embedded into the body of the request, and the server passes the body text to the program as standard input (STDIN).

(Other environment variables defined by the server for CGI programs are listed in Chapter 11. These variables store such information as the format and length of the input, the remote host, the user, and various client information. They also store the server name, the communication protocol, and the name of the software running the server.)

The CGI program needs to retrieve the information as appropriate and then process it. The sky's the limit on what the CGI program actually does with the information it retrieves. It might return an anagram of the user's name, or tell them how many times their name uses the letter "t," or it might just compile the name into a list that the programmer regularly sells to telemarketers. Only the programmer knows for sure.

Creating Virtual Documents

The CGI program must then create a new document to be served to the browser, or point to an existing document. On UNIX, programs send their output to standard output (STDOUT) as a data stream that consists of two parts. The first part is either a full or partial HTTP header that (at minimum) describes the format of the returned data (e.g., HTML, ASCII text, GIF, etc.). A blank line signifies the end of the header section. The second part is the body of the output, which contains the data conforming to the format type reflected in the header. For example:

```
Content-type: text/html

<HTML>
<HEAD><TITLE>Thanks!</TITLE></HEAD>
<BODY><H1>Thanks for signing my guest book!</H1>
  ...
</BODY></HTML>
```

In this case, the only header line that is output is the Content-type, which gives the media format of the output as HTML (text/html). This line is essential for every CGI program, since it tells the browser what kind of format to expect. The blank line separates the header from the body text (which, in this case, is in HTML format as advertised). See Chapter 20 for a listing of other media formats that are commonly recognized on the Web.

(Notice that it does not matter to the Web server what language the CGI program is written in. On the UNIX platform, the most popular language for CGI programming is Perl (covered in Chapter 15). Other languages used on UNIX are C, C++, Tcl, and Python. On Macintosh computers, programmers use Applescript and C/C++, and on Microsoft Windows programmers use Visual Basic, Perl, and C/C++. As long as there's a way in a programming language to get data from the server and send data back, you can use it for CGI.)

The server transfers the results of the CGI program back to the browser. The body text is not modified or interpreted by the server in any way, but the server generally supplies additional headers with information such as the date, the name and version of the server, etc. See Chapter 19 for a listing of valid HTTP response headers.

CGI programs can also supply a complete HTTP header itself, in which case the server does not add any additional headers but transfers the response verbatim as returned by the CGI program.

Here is the sample output of a program generating an HTML virtual document, with a complete HTTP header:

```
HTTP/1.0 200 OK
Date:  Thursday, 28-June-96 11:12:21 GMT
Server: NCSA/1.4.2
Content-type: text/html
Content-length: 2041
```

```
<HTML>
<HEAD><TITLE>Thanks!</TITLE></HEAD>
<BODY>
<H1>Thanks for signing my guestbook!</H1>
    . . .
</BODY>
</HTML>
```

The header contains the communication protocol, the date and time of the response, and the server name and version. (The 200 OK is a *status code* generated by the HTTP protocol to communicate the status of a request, in this case successful. See Chapter 18 for a list of valid HTTP status codes.) Most importantly, it also contains the content type and the number of characters (equivalent to the number of bytes) of the enclosed data.

The result is that after the user clicks the "Submit" button, he or she sees a response such as that in Figure 9-3.

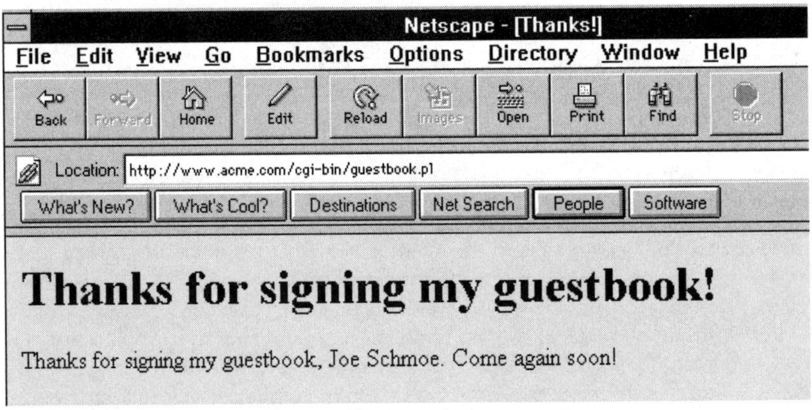

Figure 9-3: Guestbook acknowledgment

URL Encoding

Before data supplied on a form can be sent to a CGI program, each form element's name (specified by the name attribute) is equated with the value entered by the user to create a key-value pair. For example, if the user entered "30" when asked for his or her age, the key-value pair would be "age=30". In the transferred data, key-value pairs are separated by the ampersand (&) character.

Since under the GET method the form information is sent as part of the URL, form information can't include any spaces or other special characters that are not allowed in URLs, or characters that have other meanings in URLs, like slashes (/). (For the sake of consistency, this constraint also exists when the POST method is being used.) Therefore, the Web browser performs some special encoding on user-supplied information.

Encoding involves replacing spaces and other special characters in the query strings with their hexadecimal equivalents. (Thus, URL encoding is also sometimes called *hexadecimal encoding*.) Suppose a user fills out and submits a form containing his or her birthday in the syntax mm/dd/yy (e.g., 11/05/73). The forward slashes in the birthday are among the special characters that can't appear in the client's request for the CGI program. Thus, when the browser issues the request, it encodes the data. The following sample request shows the resulting encoding:

```
POST /cgi-bin/birthday.pl HTTP/1.0
Content-length: 21

birthday=11%2F05%2F73
```

The sequence %2F is actually the hexadecimal equivalent of the slash character.

CGI scripts have to provide some way to "decode" form data the client has encoded. Here's a short CGI program, written in Perl, that can process this form:

```
#!/usr/local/bin/perl

$size_of_form_information = $ENV{'CONTENT_LENGTH'};
read (STDIN, $form_info, $size_of_form_information);

$form_info =~ s/%([\dA-Fa-f][\dA-Fa-f])/pack ("C", hex ($1))/eg;

($field_name, $birthday) = split (/=/, $form_info);

print "Content-type: text/plain", "\n\n";
print "Hey, your birthday is on: $birthday. That's what you
told me, right?", "\n";

exit (0);
```

The line:

```
$form_info =~ s/%([\dA-Fa-f][\dA-Fa-f])/pack ("C", hex ($1))/eg;
```

is a regular expression in Perl that converts the hex "%2F" back to a "/" character. To dissect this program further, see Chapter 15, which provides some quick-reference material on Perl.

As a special case, the space character can be encoded as a plus sign (+) in addition to its hexadecimal notation (%20).

Extra Path Information

In addition to passing query strings, you can pass additional data, known as *extra path information*, as part of the URL. The server gauges where the CGI program name ends; anything following is deemed "extra" and is stored in the environment variable PATH_INFO. The following line calls a script with extra path information:

```
http://some.machine/cgi-bin/display.pl/cgi/cgi_doc.txt
```

Everything after *display.pl* is the extra path. The PATH_TRANSLATED variable is also set, mapping the PATH_INFO to the document root (DOCUMENT_ROOT) directory (e.g., */usr/local/etc/httpd/public/cgi/cgi_doc.txt*).

CHAPTER 10

HTML Form Tags

Many CGI programs use HTML forms to gather user input. This chapter summarizes the tags used to produce forms, and then gives an example of how to use them.

See Chapter 3, *HTML Tags*, for a more complete listing of all available HTML tags.

Summary of Form Tags

Forms are comprised of one or more text-input boxes, clickable radio buttons, multiple-choice checkboxes, and even pull-down menus and clickable images, all placed inside the <form> tag. Within a form, you may also put regular body content, including text and images.

The <form> Tag

You place a form anywhere inside the body of an HTML document with its elements enclosed by the <form> tag and its respective end tag </form>. All of the form elements within a <form> tag comprise a single form. The browser sends all of the values of these elements—blank, default, or user-modified—when the user submits the form to the server.

The required action attribute for the <form> tag gives the URL of the application that is to receive and process the form's data. A typical <form> tag with the action attribute looks like this:

```
<form action="http://www.ora.com/cgi-bin/update">
...
</form>
```

The example URL tells the browser to contact the server named *www.ora.com* and pass along the user's form values to the application named *update* located in the *cgi-bin* directory.

The browser specially encodes the form's data before it passes that data to the server so it does not become scrambled or corrupted during the transmission. It is up to the server to either decode the parameters or to pass them, still encoded, to the application.

The standard encoding format is the media type named application/x-www-form-urlencoded. You can change that encoding with the optional enctype attribute in the <form> tag. If you do elect to use an alternative encoding, the only other supported format is multipart/form-data.

The standard encoding—application/x-www-form-urlencoded—converts any spaces in the form values to a plus sign (+), nonalphanumeric characters into a percent sign (%) followed by two hexadecimal digits that are the ASCII code of the character, and the line breaks in multiline form data into %0D%0A. (See Chapter 9, *CGI Overview*, for more information on URL encoding.)

The multipart/form-data encoding encapsulates the fields in the form as several parts of a single MIME-compatible compound document.

The other required attribute for the <form> tag sets the method by which the browser sends the form's data to the server for processing. There are two ways: the POST method and the GET method. See Chapter 9 for more information on GET and POST.

The <input> Tag

Use the <input> tag to define any one of a number of common form elements, including text fields, multiple-choice lists, clickable images, and submission buttons. Although there are many attributes for this tag, only the type and name attributes are required for each element (only type for a submission button). Each type of input element uses only a subset of the allowed attributes. Additional <input> attributes may be required based upon which type of form element you specify.

You select the type of element to include in the form with the <input> tag's required type attribute, and you name the field (used during the form-submission process to the server) with the name attribute.

The most useful (as well as the most common) form-input element is the text-entry field. A text-entry field appears in the browser window as an empty box on one line and accepts a single line of user input that becomes the value of the element when the user submits the form to the server. To create a text entry field inside a form in your HTML document, set the type of the <input> form element to text. You must include a name attribute as well.

The size and maxlength attributes allow you to dictate the width, in characters, of the text-input display box, and how many total characters to accept from the user, respectively. The default value for size is dependent upon the browser; the default value for maxlength is unlimited.

A text-entry field is usually blank until the user types something into it. You may, however, specify an initial default value for the field with the value attribute.

Password fields

Password fields behave just like a regular text field in a form, except that the user-typed characters don't appear onscreen. Rather, the browser obscures the characters in a masked text to keep such things as passwords and other sensitive codes from prying eyes.

To create a password field, set the value of the `type` attribute to `password`. All other attributes and semantics of the conventional text field apply to the masked field. Note that a masked text field is not all that secure, since the browser transmits it unencrypted when the form is submitted to the server.

File-selection fields

The file-selection form field (introduced by Netscape Navigator) lets users select a file stored on their computer and send it to the server when they submit the form. Browsers present the file-selection form field to the user like other text fields, but it's accompanied by a button labeled "Browse." Users either type the pathname directly as text into the field or, with the Browse option, select the name of a locally stored file from a system-specific dialog box.

Create a file-selection field in a form by setting the value of the `type` attribute to `file`. Like other text fields, the `size` and `maxlength` of a file-selection field should be set to appropriate values.

Checkboxes

The checkbox element gives users a way to quickly and easily select or deselect an item in your form. Checkboxes may also be grouped to create a set of choices, any of which may be selected or deselected by the user.

Create individual checkboxes by setting the `type` attribute for each `<input>` tag to `checkbox`. Include the required `name` and `value` attributes. If the item is selected, it will contribute a value when the form is submitted. If it is not selected, that element will not contribute a value. The optional `checked` attribute (no value) tells the browser to display a checked checkbox and include the value when submitting the form to the server unless the user specifically clicks the mouse to deselect (uncheck) the box.

The browsers includes the value of selected (checked) checkboxes with other form parameters when they are submitted to the server. The value of the checked checkbox is the text string you specify in the required `value` attribute.

By giving several checkboxes the same `name` attribute value, you create a group of checkbox elements. The browser automatically collects the values of a checkbox group and submits their selected values as a comma-separated string to the server, significantly easing server-side form processing.

Radio buttons

Radio buttons are similar in behavior to checkboxes, except only one in the group may be selected by the user. Create a radio button by setting the `type` attribute of the `<input>` element to `radio`. Like checkbox elements, radio buttons each require a `name` and `value` attribute; buttons with the same name value are members of a group. One of them may be initially checked by including the `checked` attribute with that element. If no element in the group is checked, the browser automatically checks the first element in the group.

You should give each radio button element a different value, so the server can sort them out after submission of the form.

Submission buttons

The submit button (`<input type=submit>`) does what its name implies, setting in motion the form's submission to the server from the browser. You may have more than one submit button in a form. You may also include `name` and `value` attributes with a submit button.

With the simplest submit button (that is, without a `name` or `value` attribute), the browser displays a small rectangle or oval with the default label "Submit." Otherwise, the browser will label the button with the text you include with the tag's `value` attribute. If you provide a `name` attribute, the `value` attribute for the submit button will be added to the parameter list the browser sends along to the server.

Reset buttons

The reset type of form `<input>` button is nearly self-explanatory: it lets the user reset—erase or set to some default value—all elements in the form. By default, the browser displays a reset button with the label "Reset" or "Clear." You can change that by specifying a `value` attribute with your own button label.

Custom buttons

With the image type of `<input>` form element, you create a custom button, one that is a "clickable" image. It's a special button made out of your specified image that, when clicked by the user, tells the browser to submit the form to the server, and includes the x,y coordinates of the mouse pointer in the form's parameter list. Image buttons require a `src` attribute with the URL of the image file, and you can include a `name` attribute. You may also include the `align` attribute to control image alignment within the current line of text, much like the `align` attribute for the `<img>` tag.

Hidden fields

The last type of form `<input>` element we describe in this chapter is a way to embed information into your forms that cannot be ignored or altered by the browser or user. Rather, the `<input type=hidden>` tag's required `name` and `value` attributes automatically get included in the submitted form's parameter list. These serve to "label" the form and can be invaluable when sorting out different forms or form versions from a collection of submitted and saved forms.

The <textarea> Tag

The `<textarea>` tag creates a multiline text-entry area in the user's browser display. In it, the user may type a nearly unlimited number of lines of text. When the form is submitted, the browser sends the text along with the name specified by the required `name` attribute.

You may include plain text between the `<textarea>` tag and its end tag `</textarea>`. The browser uses that text as the default value for the text area.

You can control the dimensions of a multiline text area by defining the cols and rows attributes for the visible rectangular area set aside by the browser for multi-line input.

Normally, text typed in the text area by the user is transmitted to the server exactly as typed, with lines broken only where the user pressed the Enter key. With the wrap attribute set to virtual, the text is wrapped within the text area for presentation to the user, but the text is transmitted to the server as if no wrapping had occurred, except where the user pressed the Enter key. With the wrap attribute set to physical, the text is wrapped within the text area and is transmitted to the server as if the user had actually typed it that way. To obtain the default action, set the wrap attribute to off.

The <select> Tag

Checkboxes and radio buttons give you powerful means for creating multiple-choice questions and answers, but they can lead to long forms that are tedious to write and put a fair amount of clutter onscreen. The <select> tag gives you two compact alternatives: pulldown menus and scrolling lists.

By placing a list of <option> tagged items inside the <select> tag of a form, you create a pull-down menu of choices.

As with other form tags, the name attribute is required and used by the browser when submitting the <select> choices to the server. Unlike radio buttons, however, no item is preselected, so if the user doesn't select any, no values are sent to the server when the form is submitted. Otherwise, the browser submits the selected item or collects multiple selections, each separated with commas, into a single parameter list and includes the name attribute when submitting <select> form data to the server.

To allow more than one option selection at a time, add the multiple attribute to the <select> tag. This causes the <select> to behave like an <input type=checkbox> element. If multiple is not specified, exactly one option can be selected at a time, just like a group of radio buttons.

The size attribute determines how many options are visible to the user at one time. The value of size should be a positive integer. If size is set to 1 and multiple is not specified, the <select> list is typically implemented as a pop-up menu, while values greater than 1 or specifying the multiple attribute cause the <select> to be displayed as a scrolling list.

Use the <option> tag to define each item within a <select> form element. The browser displays the <option> tag's contents as an element within the <select> tag's menu or scrolling list, so the content must be plain text only, without any other sort of markup.

Use the value attribute to set a value for each option the browser sends to the server if that option is selected by the user. If the value attribute has not been specified, the value of the option is set to the content of the <option> tag.

By default, all options within a multiple-choice `<select>` tag are unselected. Include the `selected` attribute (no value) inside the `<option>` tag to preselect one or more options, which the user may then deselect. Single-choice `<select>` tags will preselect the first option if no option is explicitly preselected.

An Example Form

Figure 10-1 presents an HTML form showing as many form features as we can fit in the example.

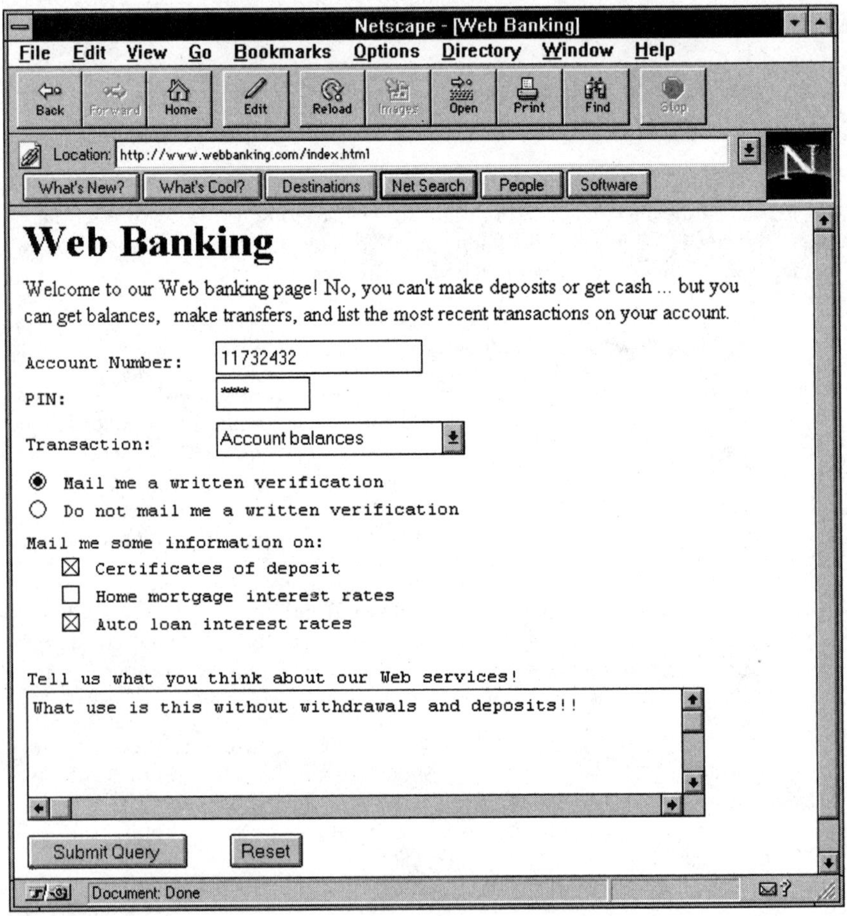

Figure 10-1: The completed form

The HTML used to create this form is shown below:

```
<html><head><title>Web Banking</title></head>
<body>
<h1>Web Banking</h1>
Welcome to our Web banking page!  No, you can't make
```

```
deposits or get cash ... but you can get balances, make
transfers, and list the most recent transactions on your account.
<form method="post" action="/cgi-bin/banking.pl">
<pre>
Account Number:    <input type="text" name="acct">
PIN:               <input type="password" name="pin" size=8>

Transaction:       <select name="transaction">
                   <option selected>Account balances
                   <option>Transfers
                   <option>Show recent transactions
                   <option>Stop payment on a check
                   </select>

<input type="radio" name="verify_by_mail" value="yes" checked> Mail me
a written verification
<input type="radio" name="verify_by_mail" value="no"> Do not mail me a
written verification

Mail me some information on:
    <input type="checkbox"name="info" value="cds"> Certificates of
deposit
    <input type="checkbox" name="info" value="mortgages"> Home mortgage
interest rates
    <input type="checkbox" name="info" value="autoloans"> Auto loan
interest rates


Tell us what you think about our Web services!
<textarea rows=5 cols=60 name="comments">
</textarea>

<input type="submit">    <input type="reset">
</form>
</body></html>
```

First, we use an `<input>` text field to get the user's bank account number. For the user's Personal Identification Number (PIN), we use an `<input>` password field so that the numbers don't appear on screen. (In real life, this wouldn't be considered sufficient for protecting someone's PIN, since the data entered is sent unencrypted across the Internet.)

Next, we use a selection box to have the user choose a transaction. The user can choose to get account balances, transfer money, see a listing of the most recent transactions on that account, or stop payment on a check.

We use a radio box to let the user choose whether to get a written verification of this transaction. The default is to send written verification. In a radio box, the user can choose exactly one of the options. Notice that with radio boxes, each item needs to have the same name but different value attributes.

Next, we use a series of checkboxes to find out what additional information a user might want us to send them.

For any loose ends, we use a `<textarea>` box to allow the user a chance to blow off steam.

Finally, we provide submit and reset buttons.

When the user submits this query, the browser sends a request to the server similar to the following:

```
POST HTTP/1.0 /cgi-bin/banking.pl
Content length: 154
Accept: image/gif
       ... (more headers )

acct=11732432&pin=0545&transaction=Account+balances&verify_by_mail=YES
&info=cds,autoloans&comments=What+use+is+this+without+withdrawals+and+
deposits%21%21
```

CHAPTER 11

CGI Environment Variables

Much of the information needed by CGI programs is made available via UNIX environment variables. Programs can access this information as they would any environment variable (e.g., via the %ENV associative array in Perl). The table below lists the environment variables commonly available through CGI. However, since servers occasionally vary on the names of environment variables they assign, check with your own server documentation for more information.

Environment Variable	Content Returned
AUTH_TYPE	The authentication method used to validate a user. See REMOTE_USER and REMOTE_IDENT.
CONTENT_LENGTH	The length of the query data (in bytes or the number of characters) passed to the CGI program through standard input.
CONTENT_TYPE	The media type of the query data, such as "text/html." See Chapter 20, *Media Types and Subtypes*, for a listing of commonly-used content types.
DOCUMENT_ROOT	The directory from which Web documents are served.
GATEWAY_INTERFACE	The revision of the Common Gateway Interface that the server uses.
HTTP_ACCEPT	A list of the media types that the client can accept.
HTTP_FROM	The email address of the user making the query (many browsers do not support this variable).

Environment Variable	Content Returned
HTTP_REFERER	The URL of the document that the client points to before accessing the CGI program.
HTTP_USER_AGENT	The browser the client is using to issue the request.
PATH_INFO	Extra path information passed to a CGI program. See Chapter 9, *CGI Overview*, for more information on extra path information.
PATH_TRANSLATED	The translated version of the path given by the variable PATH_INFO.
QUERY_STRING	The query information passed to the program. It is appended to the URL following a question mark (?). See Chapter 9 for more information on query strings.
REMOTE_ADDR	The remote IP address from which the user is making the request.
REMOTE_HOST	The remote hostname from which the user is making the request.
REMOTE_IDENT	The user making the request.
REMOTE_USER	The authenticated name of the user making the query.
REQUEST_METHOD	The method with which the information request was issued (e.g., GET, POST, HEAD). See Chapters 9 and 17 for more information on request methods.
SCRIPT_NAME	The virtual path (e.g., */cgi-bin/program.pl*) of the script being executed.
SERVER_NAME	The server's hostname or IP address.
SERVER_PORT	The port number of the host on which the server is running.
SERVER_PROTOCOL	The name and revision of the information protocol the request came in with.
SERVER_SOFTWARE	The name and version of the server software that is answering the client request.

Here's a simple Perl CGI script that uses environment variables to display various information about the server:

```perl
#!/usr/local/bin/perl

print "Content-type: text/html", "\n\n";

print "<HTML>", "\n";
print "<HEAD><TITLE>About this Server</TITLE></HEAD>", "\n";
print "<BODY><H1>About this Server</H1>", "\n";
print "<HR><PRE>";
print "Server Name:        ", $ENV{'SERVER_NAME'}, "<BR>", "\n";
print "Running on Port:    ", $ENV{'SERVER_PORT'}, "<BR>", "\n";
print "Server Software:    ", $ENV{'SERVER_SOFTWARE'}, "<BR>", "\n";
print "Server Protocol:    ", $ENV{'SERVER_PROTOCOL'}, "<BR>", "\n";
print "CGI Revision:       ", $ENV{'GATEWAY_INTERFACE'}, "<BR>", "\n";
print "<HR></PRE>", "\n";
print "</BODY></HTML>", "\n";

exit (0);
```

The preceding program outputs the contents of five environment variables into an HTML document. In Perl, you can access the environment variables using the %ENV associative array. Here's a typical output of the program:

```
<HTML>
<HEAD><TITLE>About this Server</TITLE></HEAD>
<BODY><H1>About this Server</H1>
<HR><PRE>
Server Name:        ora.com
Running on Port:    80
Server Software:    NCSA/1.4.2
Server Protocol:    HTTP/1.0
CGI Revision:       CGI/1.1
<HR></PRE>
</BODY></HTML>
```

CHAPTER 12

Cookies

Persistent state, client side cookies were introduced by Netscape Navigator to enable a server to store client-specific information on the client's machine, and use that information when a server or a particular page is accessed again by the client. The cookie mechanism allows servers to personalize pages for each client, or remember selections the client has made when browsing through various pages of a site—all without having to use a complicated (or more time-consuming) CGI/database system on the server's side.

Cookies work in the following way: When a CGI program identifies a new user, it adds an extra header to its response containing an identifier for that user and other information that the server may glean from the client's input. This header informs the cookie-enabled browser to add this information to the client's *cookies* file. After this, all requests to that URL from the browser will include the cookie information as an extra header in the request. The CGI program uses this information to return a document tailored to that specific client. The cookies are stored on the client user's hard drive, so the information remains even when the browser is closed and reopened.

The Set-Cookie Response Header

A cookie is created when a client visits a site or page for the first time. A CGI program will look for previous cookie information in the client request, and if it is not there, will send a response containing a `Set-Cookie` header. This header contains a name/value pair (the actual cookie) which comprises the special information you want the client to maintain. There are other optional fields you may include in the header.

The `Set-Cookie` header uses the following syntax:

```
Set-Cookie: name=value; expires=date;
path=pathname; domain=domain-name; secure
```

Multiple Set-Cookie headers may be included in the server response. The *name=value* pair is the only required attribute for this header, and it should come first. The remaining attributes can be in any order and are defined as follows:

name=*value*

Both *name* and *value* can be any strings that do not contain either a semi-colon, space, or tab. Encoding such as URL encoding may be used if these entities are required in the *name* or *value*, as long as your script is prepared to handle it.

expires=*date*

This attribute sets the date when a cookie becomes invalid. The date is formatted in a nonstandard way like this:

```
Wednesday, 01-Sep-96 00:00:00 GMT
```

After this date, the cookie will become invalid, and the browser will no longer send it. Only GMT (Greenwich Mean Time) is used. If no expires date is given, the cookie is used only for the current session.

path=*pathname*

The path attribute supplies a URL range for which the cookie is valid. If path is set to /pub, for example, the cookie will be sent for URLs in /pub as well as lower levels such as /pub/docs and /pub/images. A *pathname* of "/" indicates that the cookie will be used for all URLs at the site from which the cookie originated. No path attribute means that the cookie is valid only for the originating URL.

domain=*domain-name*

This attribute specifies a domain name range for which the cookie will be returned. The *domain-name* must contain at least two dots (.), e.g., .ora.com. This value would cover both www.ora.com and software.ora.com, and any other server in the *ora.com* domain.

secure

The secure attribute tells the client to return the cookie only over a secure connection (via SHTTP and SSL). Leaving out this attribute means that the cookie will always be returned regardless of the connection.

The Cookie Request Header

Each time a browser goes to a Web page, it checks its cookies file for any cookies stored for that URL. If there are any, the browser includes a Cookie header in the request containing the cookie's *name=value* pairs.

```
Cookie: name1=value1; name2=value2; . . .
```

Returned cookies may come from multiple entries in the cookies files, depending on path ranges and domain ranges. For instance, if two cookies from the same site are set with the following headers:

```
Set-Cookie: Gemstone=Diamond; path=/
Set-Cookie: Gemstone=Emerald; path=/caves
```

when the browser requests a page at the site in the */caves* path, it will return

```
Cookie: Gemstone=Emerald; Gemstone=Diamond
```

Both items share the same name, but since they are separate cookies, they both apply to the particular URL in */caves*. When returning cookies, the browser will return the most specific path or domain first, followed by less specific matches.

The preliminary cookies specification places some restrictions on the number and size of cookies:

- Clients should be able to support at least 300 total cookies. Servers should not expect a client to store more.

- The limit on the size of each cookie (name and value combined) should not exceed 4 kilobytes.

- A maximum of 20 cookies per server or domain is allowed. This limit applies to each specified server or domain, so *www.ora.com* is allowed 20, and *software.ora.com* is allowed 20, if they are each specified by their full names.

An issue arises with proxy servers in regard to the headers. Both the Set-Cookie and Cookie headers should be propagated through the proxy even if a page is cached or has not been modified (according to the If-Modified-Since condition). The Set-Cookie header should also never be cached by the proxy.

CGI

CHAPTER 13

Server Side Includes

Server Side Includes (SSI) are directives you can place into an HTML document to execute other programs or to output data, such as file statistics or the contents of environment variables. SSI directives can save you the trouble of writing complete CGI programs to output documents containing a small amount of dynamic information. While Server Side Includes technically are not CGI, they can become an important tool for incorporating CGI-like information as well as output from CGI programs.

Keep in mind, however, that not all servers support these directives; in particular, the CERN server cannot handle SSI without some modification to the server's configuration, although the Apache, NCSA, Netscape, and WebSite servers can.

When a client requests a document from an SSI-enabled server, and the document is coded appropriately, the server parses the specified document looking for SSI directives. We've already considered the advantages to this system; there are also a couple of liabilities. First, parsing documents before sending them to the client represents additional server overhead. And second, enabling SSI creates a security risk. For example, an unwise user might embed directives to execute system commands that output confidential information. So, SSI can be very handy, but it must be used efficiently and cautiously.

The current chapter summarizes the Server Side Includes. There aren't many, but they perform some of the most basic CGI-like operations, and can spare you quite a bit of coding.

Configuring the Apache and NCSA Servers for SSI

In order to tell the NCSA and Apache servers which files to parse, you must modify two server configuration files, *srm.conf* and *access.conf*, as follows:

1. In the server configuration file, *srm.conf*, specify the extension(s) of the files the server should parse. For example, the following line specifies that the server will parse all files that end in the suffix *.shtml*:

```
AddType text/x-server-parsed-html .shtml
```

Alternatively, specifying the suffix *.html* would make the server parse all HTML documents; however, keep in mind that parsing every HTML file could present a noticeable server drain.

2. In the access configuration file, *access.conf*, specify the type of SSI directives you can place in your documents.

- To embed SSI directives that display environment variables and file statistics, enable the `Includes` feature.

- To use SSI directives that execute external programs (both CGI and system applications), enable the `Exec` feature.

- To enable both features, add the following line to your *access.conf* file:

```
Options Includes ExecGCI
```

See Chapter 23, *Apache and NCSA Server Configuration*, for more information on configuring the Apache and NCSA servers.

Faking SSI for the CERN Server

For servers that don't offer SSI support, use the *fakessi.pl* Perl program to emulate SSI behavior. (The program is at *http://sw.cse.bris.ac.uk/WebTools/fakessi.html*.)

To use *fakessi.pl* with the CERN server, specify that the server executes the program whenever a client requests a file ending in *.shtml*:

1. Install *fakessi.pl* into the *cgi-bin* directory.

2. Add the following directive to *httpd.conf*:

```
Exec /*.shtml /usr/local/etc/httpd/cgi-bin/fakessi.pl
```

(assuming that *usr/local/etc/httpd/cgi-bin* is the proper directory).

Basic SSI Directives

All SSI directives have the format:

```
<!--#command parameter(s)="argument"-->
```

Each of the symbols is important; be careful not to forget the pound sign (#).

Following is a list of the primary Server Side Includes, the parameters they take, and what they do.

echo	`echo var="`*environment_variable*`"`
	Inserts value of special SSI variables, as well as other environment variables. For example:

```
<H1>Welcome to my server at
<!--#echo var="SERVER_NAME"-->...</H1>
```

See also Chapter 11, *CGI Environment Variables*, and "SSI Environment Variables" later in the current chapter.

`include file|virtual="`*path*`"`

Inserts text of document into current file.

Arguments

`file`
> Pathname relative to a document on the server.

`virtual`
> Virtual path to a document on the server.

For example:

```
<!--#include file="stuff.html"-->
<!--#include virtual="/personal/stuff.html"-->
```

`fsize file="`*path*`"`

Inserts the size of a specified file.

```
The size of the file is
<!--#fsize file="/mybook.ps"--> bytes.
```

`flastmod file="`*path*`"`

Inserts the last modification date and time for a specified file.

```
The file was last modified on
<!--#flastmod file="/mybook.ps"-->bytes.
```

You can specify the format of the date and time returned using the `config` directive with the `timefmt` argument; `timefmt` takes a wide range of values described in the section "Configurable Time Formats For SSI Output" later in this chapter.

`exec cmd|cgi="`*string*`"`

Executes external programs and inserts output in the current document.

Arguments

`cmd`
> Any application on the host.

$\rightarrow$

exec
←
	cgi
	    CGI program.
	
	For example:
	
	`<!--#exec cmd="/bin/finger $REMOTE_USER@$REMOTE_HOST"-->`
	
	`This page has been accessed`
	`<!--#exec cgi="/cgi-bin/counter.pl"-->`
	`times.`

config	`config errmsg|sizefmt|timefmt="`*string*`"`
	Modifies various aspects of SSI.
	
	Arguments
	  `errmsg`
	    Default error message.
	
	    `<!--#config errmsg="Error: File not found"-->`
	
	  `sizefmt`
	    Format for the size of the file (returned by the `fsize` directive). Acceptable values for `sizefmt` are `bytes`, or `abbrev`, which rounds the file size to the nearest kilobyte. For example:
	
	    `<!--#config sizefmt="abbrev"-->`
	
	  `timefmt`
	    Format for times and dates. SSI offers a wide range of formats. See the section "Configurable Time Formats For SSI Output" later in this chapter.

SSI Environment Variables

You can use SSI directives to output the values of environment variables in an otherwise static HTML document. These might be standard CGI variables (listed in Chapter 11); or they might be:

DOCUMENT_NAME
    The current file

```
You are reading a document called:
<!--#echo var="DOCUMENT_NAME"-->
```

DOCUMENT_URL
    Virtual path to the file

```
You can access this document again by pointing to the URL:
<!--#echo var="DOCUMENT_URL"-->
```

QUERY_STRING_UNESCAPED

Undecoded query string with all shell metacharacters escaped with a backslash
(\ )

DATE_LOCAL

Current date and time in the local time zone

```
The time is now <!--#echo var="DATE_LOCAL"-->
```

DATE_GMT

Current date and time in Greenwich Mean Time

```
The Greenwich Mean Time is <!--#echo var="DATE_GMT"-->
```

LAST_MODIFIED

Last modification date and time for current file

```
The current document was last modified on:
<!--#echo var="LAST_MODIFIED"-->
```

Configurable Time Formats for SSI Output

Among its functions, the config SSI command allows you to specify the way the
time and date are displayed with the timefmt argument, and it takes a number of
special values that are summarized in the table below.

The config command in the following example makes use of two of those special time values:

```
<!--#config timefmt="%D %r"-->
The file address.html was last modified on:
      <!--#flastmod file="address.html"-->.
```

where %D specifies that the date appear in "mm/dd/yy" format, and %r specifies
that the time appear as "hh/mm/ss AM|PM."

Thus the previous example would produce output such as:

```
The file address.html was last modified on: 12/23/95 07:17:39 PM
```

SSI Time Formats

Status Code	Meaning	Example
%a	Day of the week abbreviation	Sun
%A	Day of the week	Sunday
%b	Month name abbreviation (also %h)	Jan
%B	Month name	January
%d	Date	01
%D	Date as "%m/%d/%y"	06/23/95
%e	Date	1 (*not* 01)

Status Code	Meaning	Example
%H	24-hour clock hour	13
%I	12-hour clock hour	01
%j	Decimal day of the year	360
%m	Month number	11
%M	Minutes	08
%p	AM | PM	AM
%r	Time as "%I:%M:%S %p"	09:21:13 PM
%S	Seconds	09
%T	24-hour time as "%H:%M:%S"	12:22:40
%U	Week of the year (also %W)	37
%w	Day of the week number (starting with Sunday=0)	2
%y	Year of the century	96
%Y	Year	1996
%Z	Time zone	EST

CHAPTER 14

Windows CGI

Many Windows-based Web servers use a modified CGI interface that allows users to write CGI programs in native Windows programming environments, such as Visual Basic, Delphi, or Visual C++. While many of the CGI basics still apply, WinCGI has its own implementation, covered in this chapter. See Chapter 9, *CGI Overview*, for basic CGI information.

Since the UNIX concepts of standard input and environment variables are foreign to Microsoft Windows, WinCGI-compliant servers transfer data to the program using external temporary files. CGI programs can then retrieve CGI information directly from these files, or they can use a framework such as the CGI.BAS module supplied for Visual Basic programmers using the WebSite server.

This chapter covers the generic WinCGI interface as well as the variables and functions defined on the WebSite server for Visual Basic programming.

The Windows CGI Framework for Visual Basic Programmers

The WebSite server is distributed with CGI.BAS and CGI32.BAS modules, to facilitate CGI programming under (respectively) Visual Basic Version 3 and Visual Basic Version 4. The framework module defines the `Main()` routine of the program, CGI variables for use by the program, and several functions for simplifying CGI programming and error handling.

The Main() Routine

Projects you create for CGI programs that use the framework should be set to start in `Sub Main()` (rather than in a form). When the CGI program starts, it enters at `Main()` in the framework. The framework extracts all of the variables, special request headers, and form content, if any, and stores them in global variables. It also establishes a global exception handler (On Error) so that runtime errors in your CGI program are trapped, preventing the CGI program from exiting without producing a response.

Once the CGI environment has been set up, the framework calls a routine called CGI_Main() that you must write. This is where your code starts. *Always return from CGI_Main(). Never do an abort or exit within a CGI program using the framework.*

If the CGI executable is double-clicked, it will not have the correct information on its command line (no INI file). If this happens, the Main() routine calls a routine Inter_Main(), which you must also write. For most applications, simply display a message box telling the user that this is a CGI program, then exit.

CGI Variables

The CGI32.BAS module defines variables for use within the CGI program.

Information About the Server

Variable Name	Description	Data Type
CGI_ServerSoftware	The name and version of the server software (e.g., WebSite/1.1)	String
CGI_ServerAdmin	The email address of the server's administrator	String
CGI_Version	The CGI version to which this server complies (e.g., CGI/1.2)	String
CGI_GMTOffset	The number of seconds from GMT	Variant

Information About the Browser or User

Variable Name	Description	Data Type
CGI_RequestProtocol	The name and revision of the information protocol (e.g., HTTP/1.0)	String
CGI_Referer	The URL that referred to the CGI script	String
CGI_From	The email address of the user (rarely supplied by the browser)	String
CGI_RemoteHost	The hostname of the remote host running the browser	String
CGI_RemoteAddr	The IP address of the remote host running the browser	String
CGI_AcceptTypes	The CGI accept types	Tuple
CGI_NumAcceptTypes	The number of CGI accept types	Integer

Executable, Logical, and Physical Paths

Variable Name	Description	Data Type
CGI_ExecutablePath	The path of the CGI program being executed	String
CGI_LogicalPath	The logical path or extra path information	String
CGI_PhysicalPath	The physical path (i.e., translated version of the logical path)	String

Information About the Request

Variable Name	Description	Data Type
CGI_RequestMethod	The method with which the request was made (GET, POST, or HEAD)	String
CGI_ServerPort	The port number associated with the request	Integer
CGI_ServerName	The server hostname for this request (varies in multi-homed configuration)	String
CGI_QueryString	The encoded portion of the URL after the ?, containing GET data or query string (if any)	String
CGI_ContentFile	The full pathname of the file containing any attached data (i.e., POST data)	String
CGI_ContentType	The MIME content type of requests with attached data (i.e., POST data)	String
CGI_ContentLength	The length of the attached data (content file) in bytes	Long
CGI_FormTuples	The name=value pairs supplied in form data, if any	Tuple
CGI_NumFormTuples	The number of name=value pairs	Integer
CGI_HugeTuples	Large name=value pairs	HugeTuple
CGI_NumHugeTuples	The number of huge tuples	Integer

Security

Variable Name	Description	Data Type
CGI_AuthUser	The name of the authorized user	String
CGI_AuthPass	The password of the authorized user (only if enabled)	String
CGI_AuthType	The authorization method	String
CGI_AuthRealm	The realm of the authorized user	String

Miscellaneous

Variable Name	Description	Data Type
CGI_ExtraHeaders	The "extra" headers supplied by the browser	Tuple
CGI_NumExtraHeaders	The number of extra headers	Integer
CGI_OutputFile	The full pathname of the file in which the server expects the CGI program's response	String
CGI_DebugMode	CGI Tracing flag from server	Integer

Utility Functions

The CGI32.BAS module defines these functions for facilitating CGI programming, which give information about the server:

Routine Names	Descriptions	Returns
ErrorHandler()	Global exception handler	n/a
FieldPresent()	Test for the presence of a named form field	T/F
GetSmallField()	Retrieve the contents of a named form field	String
PlusToSpace()	Remove "+" delimiters from a string, converting to spaces	n/a
Send()	Write a string into the output spool file	n/a
SendNoOp()	Send a complete response causing the browser to do nothing, staying on its current page	n/a
Unescape()	Remove URL-escaping from a string, return modified string	String
WebDate()	Return a Web-compliant date/time string (GMT)	String

The CGI Data File

The CGI.BAS and CGI32.BAS modules take care of much of the dirty work in CGI processing for Visual Basic programmers. If you are using another programming language or a server other than WebSite, however, you may need to access the external CGI data file manually.

Under WinCGI, the server saves CGI data in an external file to be processed by the CGI program. The CGI data file contains the following sections:

```
[CGI]
[Accept]
[System]
[Extra Headers]
[Form Literal]
[Form External]
[Form File]
[Form Huge]
```

The CGI Section

The first section of the CGI data file contains most of the CGI data items (accept types, content, and extra headers are defined in separate sections). Each item is provided as a string value. If the value is an empty string, the keyword is omitted. The keywords are listed below:

`Authenticated Password`
> The password that the client used to attempt authentication.

`Authenticated Username`
> The username (in the indicated realm) that the client used to attempt authentication.

`Authentication Method`
> The protocol-specific authentication method specified in the request.

`Authentication Realm`
> The method-specific authentication realm.

`CGI Version`
> The revision of the CGI specification to which the server complies.

`Content File`
> For requests that have attached data (i.e., in a POST request), the server makes the data available to the CGI program by putting it into this file. The value of this item is the complete pathname of that file.

`Content Length`
> For requests that have attached data, the length of the content in bytes.

`Content Type`
> For requests that have attached data, the MIME content type of that data.

`Document Root`
> The physical path to the logical root "/".

`Executable Path`
> The logical path to the CGI program executable, as needed for self-referencing URLs.

`From`
> The email address of the browser user.

`Logical Path`
> The extra path information supplied in the request.

`Physical Path`
> If the request contained logical path information, the path in physical (translated) form.

`Query String`
> The information that follows the ? in the URL that generated the request is the "query" information.

Referer
> The URL of the document that contained the link pointing to this CGI program.

Remote Host
> The network host name of the client system, if available.

Remote Address
> The network (IP) address of the client system.

Request Method
> The method with which the request was made. For HTTP, this is "GET," "HEAD," "POST," etc.

Request Protocol
> The name and revision of the information protocol this request came in with. Format: protocol/revision; Example: "HTTP/1.0"

Request Range
> Byte-range specification received with request (if any).

Server Admin
> The email address of the server's administrator.

Server Name
> The network host name or alias of the server, as needed for self-referencing URLs.

Server Port
> The network port number on which the server is listening, as needed for self-referencing URLs.

Server Software
> The name and version of the information server software answering the request (and running the CGI program). Format: name/version

User Agent
> A string description of the client (browser) software.

The Accept Section

The Accept section contains the client's acceptable data types found in the request header as:

> Accept: *type/subtype* [*parameters*]

The System Section

This section contains items that are specific to the Windows implementation of CGI. The following keys are used:

`Content File`
> The full pathname of the file that contains the content (if any) that came with the request.

`Debug Mode`
> This is No unless the server's script tracing mode is enabled, in which case it is Yes. Useful for providing conditional tracing within the CGI program.

`GMT Offset`
> The number of seconds to be added to GMT to reach local time. For Pacific Standard time, this number is -28,800. Useful for computing GMT.

`Output File`
> The full pathname of the file in which the server expects to receive the CGI program's results.

CGI

The Extra Headers Section

This section contains the "extra" headers that were included with the request, in *key=value* form. The server must URL-decode both the key and the value prior to writing them to the CGI data file.

The Form Literal Section

If the request is a POST request from an HTTP form (with content type of `appli-cation/x-www-form-urlencoded` or `multipart/form-data`), the server decodes the form data and puts it into the `Form Literal` section.

If the form contains any SELECT MULTIPLE elements, there will be multiple occurrences of the same key. In this case, the server generates a normal *key=value* pair for the first occurrence, and it appends a sequence number to subsequent occurrences.

The Form External Section

If the decoded value string is more than 254 characters long, or if the decoded value string contains any control characters or double-quotes, the server puts the decoded value into an external file and lists the field into the Form External section as:

key=pathname length

where *pathname* is the path and name of the tempfile containing the decoded value string, and *length* is the length in bytes of the decoded value string.

The Form Huge Section

If the raw value string is more than 65,535 bytes long, the server does no decoding, but it does get the keyword and mark the location and size of the value in the content file. The server lists the huge field in the Form Huge section as:

key=offset length

where *offset* is the offset from the beginning of the content file at which the raw value string for this key is located, and *length* is the length in bytes of the string. You can use the offset to perform a "Seek" to the start of the raw value string, and use the length to know when you have read the entire raw string into your decoder.

The Form File Section

If the request is in the `multipart/form-data` format, it may contain one or more file uploads. In this case, each file upload is placed into an external temporary file similar to the form external data. Each such file upload is listed in the Form File section as:

key=[pathname] length type xfer [filename]

where *pathname* is the pathname of the external tempfile containing the uploaded file, *length* is the length in bytes of the uploaded file, *type* is the MIME content type of the uploaded file, *xfer* is the content-transfer encoding of the uploaded file, and *filename* is the original name of the uploaded file. The square brackets must be included; they are used to delimit the file and pathnames, which may contain spaces.

Example of Form Decoding

In the following sample, the form contains a small field, a SELECT MULTIPLE with 2 small selections, a field with 300 characters in it, one with line breaks (a text area), and a 230KB field:

```
[Form Literal]
    smallfield=123 Main St. #122
    multiple=first selection
    multiple_1=second selection

[Form External]
    field300chars=C:\TEMP\HS19AF6C.000 300
    fieldwithlinebreaks=C:\TEMP\HS19AF6C.001 43

[Form Huge]
    field230K=C:\TEMP\HS19AF6C.002 276920
```

Results Processing

The CGI program returns its results to the server as a data stream representing (directly or indirectly) the goal of the request. The data stream consists of two parts: the *header* and the *body*. The header consists of one or more lines of text, and is separated from the body by a blank line. The body contains MIME-conforming data whose content type must be reflected in the header.

The server recognizes the following header lines in the results data stream:

`Content-Type:`
> Indicates that the body contains data of the specified MIME content type. The value must be a MIME content type/subtype.

`URI: ` *<value>* (value enclosed in angle brackets)
> The value is either a full URL or a local file reference, either of which points to an object to be returned to the client in lieu of the body. If the value is a local file, the server sends it as the results of the request, as though the client issued a GET for that object. If the value is a full URL, the server returns a "401 redirect" to the client to retrieve the specified object directly.

`Location:`
> Same as URI, but this form is now deprecated. The value must *not* be enclosed in angle brackets with this form.

Any other headers in the result stream are passed unmodified by the server to the client. It is the responsibility of the CGI program to avoid including headers that clash with those used by HTTP.

Direct Return

The server provides for the CGI program to return its results directly to the client, bypassing the server's "packaging" of the data stream for its information protocol. In this case, it is the responsibility of the CGI program to generate a complete message packaged for HTTP.

The server looks at the results in the output file, and if the first line starts with "`HTTP/1.0`", it assumes that the results contain a complete HTTP response, and sends the results to the client without packaging.

CHAPTER 15

Perl Quick Reference

Perl is the most common programming language used for CGI throughout the Web. This chapter gives a quick reference to Perl syntax and functions. To learn Perl from scratch, we recommend *Learning Perl* by Randal Schwartz. For Perl reference, we recommend *Programming Perl, Second Edition* by Larry Wall, Tom Christiansen, and Randal Schwartz. Both are published by O'Reilly & Associates.

Items followed by a dagger (†) will default to $_ if omitted.

Command-Line Options

-a Turns on autosplit mode when used with –n or –p. Splits to @F.

-c Checks syntax but does not execute.

-d Runs the script under the debugger. Use –de 0 to start the debugger without a script.

-D *number*
   Sets debugging flags.

-e *commandline*
   May be used to enter a single line of script. Multiple –e commands may be given to build up a multiline script.

-F *regexp*
   Specifies a regular expression to split on if –a is in effect.

-i*ext*
   Files processed by the < > construct are to be edited in place.

-I*dir*
   With –P, tells the C preprocessor where to look for include files. The directory is prepended to @INC.

-l [*octnum*]
   Enables automatic line-end processing, e.g., –l013.

-n Assumes an input loop around your script. Lines are not printed.

-p Assumes an input loop around your script. Lines are printed.

-P Runs the C preprocessor on the script before compilation by Perl.

-s Interprets –xxx on the command line as a switch and sets the corresponding variable $xxx in the script.

-S Uses the PATH environment variable to search for the script.

-T Forces taint checking.

-u Dumps core after compiling the script. To be used with the *undump*(1) program (where available).

-U
    Allows Perl to perform unsafe operations.

-v Prints the version and patchlevel of your Perl executable.

-w
    Prints warnings about possible spelling errors and other error-prone constructs in the script.

-x [*dir*]
    Extracts Perl program from input stream. If *dir* is specified, switches to this directory before running the program.

-0*val*
    (That's the number zero.) Designates an initial value for the record separator $/. See also –l.

Literals

Numeric
    123 1_234 123.4 5E–10 0xff (hex) 0377 (octal)

String
    'abc'
    Literal string, no variable interpolation or escape characters, except \' and \\. Also: q/abc/. Almost any pair of delimiters can be used instead of /.../.

    "abc"
    Variables are interpolated and escape sequences are processed. Also: qq/abc/.
    Escape sequences: \t (Tab), \n (Newline), \r (Return),\f (Formfeed), \b (Backspace),\a (Alarm), \e (Escape), \033 (octal), \x1b (hex), \c[(control).
    \l and \u lowercase/uppercase the following character. \L and \U lowercase/uppercase until a \E is encountered. \Q quotes regular expression characters until a \E is encountered.

    `command`
    Evaluates to the output of the *command.* Also: qx/*command*/.

Array
    (1, 2, 3) ( ) is an empty array.
    (1..4) is the same as (1,2,3,4), likewise ('a'..'z').
    qw/foo bar.../ is the same as ('foo','bar',...).

Array reference

    [1,2,3]

Hash (associative array)

    (*key1, val1, key2, val2,...*)

    Also (*key1* => *val1, key2* => *val2,...*)

Hash reference

    {*key1, val1, key2, val2,...*}

Code reference

    sub { *statements* }

Filehandles

    STDIN, STDOUT, STDERR, ARGV, DATA.

    User-specified: *handle*, $*var*.

Globs

    <*pattern*> evaluates to all filenames according to the pattern. Use <${*var*}> or glob $*var* to glob from a variable.

Here–Is

    <<*identifier*

    Shell-style "here document."

Special tokens

    __FILE__: filename; __LINE__: line number;

    __END__: end of program; remaining lines can be read using the filehandle DATA.

Variables

$var

    A simple scalar variable.

$var[28]

    29th element of array @var.

$p = \@var

    Now $p is a reference to array @var.

$$p[28]

    29th element of array referenced by $p.

    Also, $p–>[28].

$var[–1]

    Last element of array @var.

$var[$i][$j]

    $j-th element of $i-th element of array @var.

$var{'Feb'}

    A value from hash (associative array) %var.

$p = \%var

    Now $p is a reference to hash %var.

$$p{'Feb'}

    A value from hash referenced by $p.

    Also, $p–>{'Feb'}.

$#var

    Last index of array @var.

@var
>   The entire array; in a scalar context, the number of elements in the array.

@var[3,4,5]
>   A slice of array @var.

@var{'a','b'}
>   A slice of %var; same as ($var{'a'},$var{'b'}).

%var
>   The entire hash; in a scalar context, `true` if the hash has elements.

$var{'a',1,...}
>   Emulates a multidimensional array.

('a'...'z')[4,7,9]
>   A slice of an array literal.

pkg::var
>   A variable from a package, e.g., $pkg::var, @pkg::ary.

object
>   Reference to an object, e.g., \$var, \%hash.

*name
>   Refers to all objects represented by *name*.
>   *n1 = *n2 makes n1 an alias for n2.
>   *n1 = $n2 makes $n1 an alias for $n2.

You can always use a { *block* } returning the right type of reference instead of the variable identifier, e.g., ${...}, &{...}. $$p is just a shorthand for ${$p}.

Operators

**	Exponentiation
+ - * /	Addition, subtraction, multiplication, division
%	Modulo division
& | ^	Bitwise AND, bitwise OR, bitwise exclusive OR
>> <<	Bitwise shift right, bitwise shift left
|| &&	Logical OR, logical AND
.	Concatenation of two strings
x	Returns a string or array consisting of the left operand (an array or a string) repeated the number of times specified by the right operand.

All of the above operators have an associated assignment operator, e.g., .=

->		Dereference operator
\		Reference (unary)
!	~	Negation (unary), bitwise complement (unary)
++	--	Auto-increment (magical on strings), auto-decrement
==	!=	Numeric equality, inequality
eq	ne	String equality, inequality
<	>	Numeric less than, greater than
lt	gt	String less than, greater than
<=	>=	Numeric less (greater) than or equal to
le	ge	String less (greater) than or equal to
<=>	cmp	Numeric (string) compare. Returns −1, 0, or 1.

=~	!~	Search pattern, substitution, or translation (negated)
..		Range (scalar context) or enumeration (array context)
?:		Alternation (if-then-else) operator
,		Comma operator, also list element separator. You can also use =>
not		Low-precedence negation
and		Low-precedence AND
or	xor	Low-precedence OR, exclusive OR

All Perl functions can be used as list operators, in which case they have either very high or very low precedence, depending on whether you look at the left or the right side of the operator. Only the operators not, and, or, and xor have lower precedence.

A "list" is a list of expressions, variables, or lists. An array variable or an array slice may always be used instead of a list.

Parentheses can be added around the parameter lists to avoid precedence problems.

Statements

Every statement is an expression, optionally followed by a modifier, and terminated with a semicolon. The semicolon may be omitted if the statement is the final one in a *block*.

Execution of expressions can depend on other expressions using one of the modifiers if, unless, while, or until, for example:

```
expr1 if expr2 ;
expr1 until expr2 ;
```

The logical operators | |, &&, or ?: also allow conditional execution:

```
expr1 | | expr2 ;
expr1 ? expr2 : expr3 ;
```

Statements can be combined to form a *block* when enclosed in {}. *block*s may be used to control flow:

```
if (expr) block [ [ elsif (expr) block...] else block ]
unless (expr) block [ else block ]
[ label: ] while (expr) block [ continue block ]
[ label: ] until (expr) block [ continue block ]
[ label: ] for ( [ expr ] ; [ expr ] ; [ expr ] ) block
[ label: ] foreach var† (list) block
[ label: ] block [ continue block ]
```

Program flow can be controlled with:

goto *label*
   Continue execution at the specified label.
last [*label*]
   Immediately exits the loop in question. Skips continue block.
next [*label*]
   Starts the next iteration of the loop.

redo [*label*]

> Restarts the loop block without evaluating the conditional again.

Special forms are:

> do *block* while *expr* ;
> do *block* until *expr* ;

which are guaranteed to perform *block* once before testing *expr*, and

> do *block*

which effectively turns *block* into an expression.

Subroutines, Packages, and Modules

&*subroutine list*

> Executes a *subroutine* declared by a sub declaration, and returns the value of the last expression evaluated in *subroutine*. *subroutine* can be an expression yielding a reference to a code object. The & may be omitted if the subroutine has been declared before being used.

bless *ref* [, *package*]

> Turns the object *ref* into an object in *package*. Returns the reference.

caller [*expr*]

> Returns an array ($package, $file, $line, ...) for a specific subroutine call. caller returns this information for the current subroutine, caller(1) for the caller of this subroutine, etc. Returns false if no caller.

do *subroutine list*

> Deprecated form of &*subroutine* .

goto &*subroutine*

> Substitutes a call to *subroutine* for the current subroutine.

import *module* [[*version*] *list*]

> Imports the named subroutines from *module*.

no *module* [*list*]

> Cancels imported semantics. See use.

package *name*

> Designates the remainder of the current block as a package.

require *expr*†

> If *expr* is numeric, requires Perl to be at least that version. Otherwise *expr* must be the name of a file that is included from the Perl library. Does not include more than once, and yields a fatal error if the file does not evaluate to a true value. If *expr* is a bare word, assumes extension .pm for the name of the file.

return *expr*

> Returns from a subroutine with the value specified.

sub *name* { *expr* ; ... }

> Designates *name* as a subroutine. Parameters are passed by reference as array @_. Returns the value of the last expression evaluated.

[sub] **BEGIN** { *expr* ; ... }

> 1 *expr* ; ... } Defines a setup *block* to be called before execution.

[sub] END { *expr* ; ... }
   Defines a cleanup *block* to be called upon termination.

tie *var, package,* [*list*]
   Ties a variable to a package that will handle it. Can be used to bind a *dbm* or *ndbm* file to a hash.

untie *var*
   Breaks the binding between the variable and the package.

use *module* [[*version*] *list*]
   Imports semantics from the named module into the current package.

Object-Oriented Programming

Perl rules of object-oriented programming:

- An object is simply a reference that happens to know which class it belongs to. Objects are blessed, references are not.

- A class is simply a package that happens to provide methods to deal with object references. If a package fails to provide a method, the base classes as listed in @ISA are searched.

- A method is simply a subroutine that expects an object reference (or a package name, for static methods) as the first argument.

Methods can be applied with:

method objref parameters   or
objref–>method parameters

Arithmetic Functions

abs *expr*†
   Returns the absolute value of its operand.

atan2 *y, x*
   Returns the arctangent of y/x in the range $-\pi$ to π.

cos *expr*†
   Returns the cosine of *expr* (expressed in radians).

exp *expr*†
   Returns e to the power of *expr.*

int *expr*†
   Returns the integer portion of *expr.*

log *expr*†
   Returns natural logarithm (base e) of *expr.*

rand [*expr*]
   Returns a random fractional number between 0 and the value of *expr.* If *expr* is omitted, returns a value between 0 and 1.

sin *expr*†
   Returns the sine of *expr* (expressed in radians).

CGI

sqrt *expr*†
> Returns the square root of *expr*.

srand [*expr*]
> Sets the random number seed for the rand operator.

time
> Returns the number of seconds since January 1, 1970. Suitable for feeding to gmtime and localtime.

Conversion Functions

chr *expr*†
> Returns the character represented by the decimal value *expr*.

gmtime *expr*†
> Converts a time as returned by the time function to a 9-element array (0:$sec, 1:$min, 2:$hour, 3:$mday, 4:$mon, 5:$year, 6:$wday, 7:$yday, 8:$isdst) with the time analyzed for the Greenwich time zone. $mon has the range 0..11 and $wday has the range 0..6.

hex *expr*†
> Returns the decimal value of *expr* interpreted as a hex string.

localtime *expr*†
> Converts a time as returned by the time function to *ctime*(3) string. In array context, returns a 9-element array with the time analyzed for the local time zone.

oct *expr*†
> Returns the decimal value of *expr* interpreted as an octal string. If *expr* starts off with 0x, interprets it as a hex string instead.

ord *expr*†
> Returns the ASCII value of the first character of *expr*.

vec *expr*, *offset*, *bits*
> Treats string *expr* as a vector of unsigned integers, and yields the bit at *offset*. *bits* must be between 1 and 32. May have a value assigned to it.

Structure Conversion

pack *template*, *list*
> Packs the values into a binary structure using *template*.

unpack *template*, *expr*
> Unpacks the structure *expr* into an array, using *template*.

template is a sequence of characters as follows:

a	/	A	ASCII string, null- / space-padded
b	/	B	Bit string in ascending / descending order
c	/	C	Native / unsigned char value
f	/	d	Single / double float in native format
h	/	H	Hex string, low / high nybble first.
i	/	I	Signed / unsigned integer value
l	/	L	Signed / unsigned long value
n	/	N	Short / long in network (big endian) byte order
s	/	S	Signed / unsigned short value

u	/	p	Uuencoded string / pointer to a string
v	/	V	Short / long in VAX (little endian) byte order
x	/	@	Null byte / null fill until position
X			Backup a byte

Each character may be followed by a decimal number that will be used as a repeat count; an asterisk (*) specifies all remaining arguments. If the format is preceded with %*n*, unpack returns an *n*-bit checksum instead. Spaces may be included in the template for readability purposes.

String Functions

chomp *list*†

Removes line endings from all elements of the list; returns the (total) number of characters removed.

chop *list*†

Chops off the last character on all elements of the list; returns the last chopped character.

crypt *plaintext, salt*

Encrypts a string.

eval *expr*†

expr is parsed and executed as if it were a Perl program. The value returned is the value of the last expression evaluated. If there is a syntax error or runtime error, an undefined string is returned by eval, and $@ is set to the error message. See also eval in the section "Miscellaneous."

index *str, substr* [, *offset*]

Returns the position of *substr* in *str* at or after *offset*. If the substring is not found, returns –1 (but see $[in the section "Special Variables").

length *expr*†

Returns the length in characters of the value of *expr*.

lc *expr*

Returns a lowercase version of *expr*.

lcfirst *expr*

Returns *expr* with the first character lowercase.

quotemeta *expr*

Returns *expr* with all regular expression metacharacters quoted.

rindex *str, substr* [, *offset*]

Returns the position of the last *substr* in *str* at or before *offset*.

substr *expr, offset* [, *len*]

Extracts a substring of length *len* out of *expr* and returns it. If *offset* is negative, counts from end of the string. May have a value assigned to it.

uc *expr*

Returns an uppercased version of *expr*.

ucfirst *expr*

Returns *expr* with the first character uppercased.

Array and List Functions

delete $*hash*{*key*}
> Deletes the specified value from the specified hash. Returns the deleted value (unless *hash* is tied to a package that does not support this).

each %*hash*
> Returns a 2-element array consisting of the key and value for the next value of the hash. Entries are returned in an apparently random order. After all values of the hash have been returned, a null array is returned. The next call to each after that will start iterating again.

exists *expr*†
> Checks if the specified hash key exists in its hash array.

grep *expr, list*

grep *block list*
> Evaluates *expr* or *block* for each element of the *list*, locally setting $_ to refer to the element. Modifying $_ will modify the corresponding element from *list*. Returns the array of elements from *list* for which *expr* returned true.

join *expr, list*
> Joins the separate strings of *list* into a single string with fields separated by the value of *expr*, and returns the string.

keys %*hash*
> Returns an array of all the keys of the named hash.

map *expr, list*

map *block list*
> Evaluates *expr* or *block* for each element of the *list*, locally setting $_ to refer to the element. Modifying $_ will modify the corresponding element from *list*. Returns the list of results.

pop @*array*
> Pops off and returns the last value of the array.

push @*array, list*
> Pushes the values of *list* onto the end of the array.

reverse *list*
> In array context, returns the *list* in reverse order. In scalar context, returns the first element of *list* with bytes reversed.

scalar @*array*
> Returns the number of elements in the array.

scalar %*hash*
> Returns a true value if the hash has elements defined.

shift [@*array*]
> Shifts the first value of the array off and returns it, shortening the array by 1 and moving everything down. If @*array* is omitted, shifts @ARGV in main and @_ in subroutines.

sort [*subroutine*] *list*
> Sorts the *list* and returns the sorted array value. *subroutine*, if specified, must return less than zero, zero, or greater than zero, depending on how the elements of the array (available to the routine as $a and $b) are to be ordered. *subroutine* may be the name of a user-defined routine, or a *block*.

`splice @`*array, offset* [, *length* [, *list*]]

Removes the elements of @*array* designated by *offset* and *length*, and replaces them with *list* (if specified). Returns the elements removed.

`split` [*pattern* [, *expr†* [, *limit*]]]

Splits a string into an array of strings, and returns it. If *limit* is specified, splits into at most that number of fields. If *pattern* is also omitted, splits at the whitespace. If not in array context, returns number of fields and splits to @_. See also the section called "Search and Replace Functions."

`unshift @`*array, list*

Prepends list to the front of the array, and returns the number of elements in the new array.

`values %`*hash*

Returns a normal array consisting of all the values of the named hash.

Regular Expressions

Each character matches itself, unless it is one of the special characters + ? . * ^ $ ( ) [ ] { } | \. The special meaning of these characters can be escaped using a \.

.   Matches an arbitrary character, but not a newline unless it is a single-line match (see m/ /s).

(. . .)

Groups a series of pattern elements to a single element.

^   Matches the beginning of the target. In multiline mode (see m//m) also matches after every newline character.

$ Matches the end of the line. In multiline mode also matches before every newline character.

[. . .]

Denotes a class of characters to match. [^] negates the class.

(. . . | . . . | . . .)

Matches one of the alternatives.

(?# *text*)

Comment.

(?: *regexp*)

Like (*regexp*) but does not make back-references.

(?= *regexp*)

Zero width positive look-ahead assertion.

(?! *regexp*)

Zero width negative look-ahead assertion.

(? *modifier*)

Embedded pattern-match modifier. *modifier* can be one or more of i, m, s, or x.

Quantified subpatterns match as many times as possible. When followed with a ? they match the minimum number of times. These are the quantifiers:

+   Matches the preceding pattern element one or more times.

?   Matches zero or one times.

*   Matches zero or more times.

{*n,m*}

Denotes the minimum *n* and maximum *m* match count. {*n*} means exactly *n* times; {*n*,} means at least *n* times.

A \ escapes any special meaning of the following character if non-alphanumeric, but it turns most alphanumeric characters into something special:

\w

Matches alphanumeric, including _, \W matches non-alphanumeric.

\s   Matches whitespace, \S matches non-whitespace.

\d   Matches numeric, \D matches non-numeric.

\A   Matches the beginning of the string, \Z matches the end.

\b   Matches word boundaries, \B matches non-boundaries.

\G

Matches where the previous m//g search left off.

\n, \r, \f, \t, etc.

Have their usual meaning.

\w, \s, and \d

May be used within character classes, \b denotes a backspace in this context.

Back-references:

\1 ... \9

Refer to matched subexpressions, grouped with ( ), inside the match.

\10 and up

Can also be used if the pattern matches that many subexpressions.

See also $1 ... $9, $+, $&, $`, and $' in the section "Special Variables."

With modifier x, whitespace can be used in the patterns for readability purposes.

Search and Replace Functions

[*expr* =˜] [m] */pattern/* [g] [i] [m] [o] [s] [x]

Searches *expr* (default: $_) for a pattern. If you prepend an m you can use almost any pair of delimiters instead of the slashes. If used in array context, an array is returned consisting of the subexpressions matched by the parentheses in the pattern, i.e., ($1, $2, $3, . . .).

Optional modifiers: g matches as many times as possible; i searches in a case-insensitive manner; o interpolates variables only once. m treats the string as multiple lines; s treats the string as a single line; x allows for regular expression extensions.

If *pattern* is empty, the most recent pattern from a previous match or replacement is used.

With g the match can be used as an iterator in scalar context.

?pattern?

This is just like the */pattern/* search, except that it matches only once between calls to the reset operator.

[$var =~] s/*pattern*/*replacement*/ [e] [g] [i] [m] [o] [s] [x]

> Searches a string for a pattern, and if found, replaces that pattern with the replacement text. It returns the number of substitutions made, if any; if no substitutions are made, it returns false.

> Optional modifiers: g replaces all occurrences of the pattern; e evaluates the replacement string as a Perl expression; for the other modifiers, see /*pattern*/ matching. Almost any delimiter may replace the slashes; if single quotes are used, no interpolation is done on the strings between the delimiters, otherwise the strings are interpolated as if inside double quotes.

> If bracketing delimiters are used, *pattern* and *replacement* may have their own delimiters, e.g., s(foo)[bar]. If *pattern* is empty, the most recent pattern from a previous match or replacement is used.

[$var =~] tr/*searchlist*/*replacementlist*/ [c] [d] [s]

> Translates all occurrences of the characters found in the search list with the corresponding character in the replacement list. It returns the number of characters replaced. y may be used instead of tr.

> Optional modifiers: c complements the *searchlist*; d deletes all characters found in *searchlist* that do not have a corresponding character in *replacementlist*; s squeezes all sequences of characters that are translated into the same target character into one occurrence of this character.

pos *scalar*

> Returns the position where the last m//g search left off for *scalar*. May have a value assigned to it.

study [$var†]

> Studies the scalar variable $*var* in anticipation of performing many pattern matches on its contents before the variable is next modified.

File Test Operators

These unary operators take one argument, either a filename or a filehandle, and test the associated file to see if something is true about it. If the argument is omitted, they test $_ (except for –t, which tests STDIN). If the special argument _ (underscore) is passed, they use the information from the preceding test or stat call.

–r –w –x

> File is readable/writable/executable by effective uid/gid.

–R –W –X

> File is readable/writable/executable by real uid/gid.

–o –O

> File is owned by effective/real uid.

–e –z

> File exists/has zero size.

–s File exists and has non-zero size. Returns the size.

–f –d

> File is a plain file/a directory.

–l –S –p

> File is a symbolic link/a socket/a named pipe (FIFO).

−b −c
  File is a block/character special file.
−u −g −k
  File has setuid/setgid/sticky bit set.
−t Tests if filehandle (STDIN by default) is opened to a tty.
−T −B
  File is a text/non-text (binary) file. −T and −B return `true` on a null file, or
  a file at EOF when testing a filehandle.
−M −A −C
  File modification/access/inode-change time. Measured in days. Value
  returned reflects the file age at the time the script started. See also $^T in
  the section "Special Variables."

File Operations

Functions operating on a list of files return the number of files successfully
operated upon.

chmod *list*
  Changes the permissions of a list of files. The first element of the list must
  be the numerical mode.

chown *list*
  Changes the owner and group of a list of files. The first two elements of
  the list must be the numerical uid and gid.

truncate *file, size*
  Truncates *file* to *size. file* may be a filename or a filehandle.

link *oldfile, newfile*
  Creates a new filename linked to the old filename.

lstat *file*
  Like `stat`, but does not traverse a final symbolic link.

mkdir *dir, mode*
  Creates a directory with given permissions. Sets $! on failure.

readlink *expr*†
  Returns the value of a symbolic link.

rename *oldname, newname*
  Changes the name of a file.

rmdir *filename*†
  Deletes the directory if it is empty. Sets $! on failure.

stat *file*
  Returns a 13-element array (0:$dev, 1:$ino, 2:$mode, 3:$nlink, 4:$uid,
  5:$gid, 6:$rdev, 7:$size, 8:$atime, 9:$mtime, 10:$ctime, 11:$blksize,
  12:$blocks). *file* can be a filehandle, an expression evaluating to a
  filename, or _ to refer to the last file test operation or `stat` call. Returns a
  null list if the `stat` fails.

symlink *oldfile, newfile*
  Creates a new filename symbolically linked to the old filename.

unlink *list*
  Deletes a list of files.

utime *list*
> Changes the access and modification times. The first two elements of the list must be the numerical access and modification times.

Input/Output

In input/output operations, *filehandle* may be a filehandle as opened by the open operator, a predefined filehandle (e.g., STDOUT), or a scalar variable that evaluates to the name of a filehandle to be used.

<*filehandle*>
> In scalar context, reads a single line from the file opened on *filehandle*. In array context, reads the whole file.

< > Reads from the input stream formed by the files specified in @ARGV, or standard input if no arguments were supplied.

binmode *filehandle*
> Arranges for the file opened on *filehandle* to be read or written in binary mode as opposed to text mode (null-operation on UNIX).

close *filehandle*
> Closes the file or pipe associated with the filehandle.

dbmclose %*hash*
> Deprecated, use untie instead.

dbmopen %*hash*, *dbmname*, *mode*
> Deprecated, use tie instead.

eof *filehandle*
> Returns true if the next read will return end of file, or if the file is not open.

eof Returns the EOF status for the last file read.

eof( )
> Indicates EOF on the pseudo file formed of the files listed on the command line.

fcntl *filehandle*, *function*, $*var*
> Implements the *fcntl*(2) function. This function has nonstandard return values.

fileno *filehandle*
> Returns the file descriptor for a given (open) file.

flock *filehandle*, *operation*
> Calls *flock*(2) on the file. *operation* formed by adding 1 (shared), 2 (exclusive), 4 (non-blocking), or 8 (unlock).

getc [*filehandle*]
> Yields the next character from the file, or an empty string on end of file. If *filehandle* is omitted, reads from STDIN.

ioctl *filehandle, function, $var*
> Performs *ioctl*(2) on the file. This function has nonstandard return values.

open *filehandle* [, *filename*]
> Opens a file and associates it with *filehandle*. If *filename* is omitted, the scalar variable of the same name as the *filehandle* must contain the filename.
>
> The following filename conventions apply when opening a file:
>
> "*file*"
> Open *file* for input. Also "<*file*".
>
> ">*file*"
> Open *file* for output, creating it if necessary.
>
> ">>*file*"
> Open *file* in append mode.
>
> "+>*file*"
> Open *file* with read/write access.
>
> " | *cmd*"
> Opens a pipe to command *cmd*; forks if *cmd* is –.
>
> "*cmd*" |
> Opens a pipe from command *cmd*; forks if *cmd* is –.

file may be &*filehnd*, in which case the new filehandle is connected to the (previously opened) filehandle *filehnd*. If it is &=*n*, *file* will be connected to the given file descriptor. open returns undef upon failure, true otherwise.

pipe *readhandle, writehandle*
> Returns a pair of connected pipes.

print [*filehandle*] [*list*†]
> Prints the elements of *list*, converting them to strings if needed. If *filehandle* is omitted, prints by default to standard output (or to the last selected output channel, see select).

printf [*filehandle*] [*list*]
> Equivalent to print *filehandle* and sprintf *list*.

read *filehandle, $var, length* [, *offset*]
> Reads *length* binary bytes from the file into the variable at *offset*. Returns number of bytes actually read.

seek *filehandle, position, whence*
> Arbitrarily positions the file. Returns true if successful.

select [*filehandle*]
> Returns the currently selected filehandle. Sets the current default filehandle for output operations if *filehandle* is supplied.

select *rbits, wbits, nbits, timeout*
> Performs a *select*(2) system call with the same parameters.

sprintf *format, list*
> Returns a string formatted by (almost all of) the usual *printf*(3) conventions.

sysread *filehandle, $var, length* [, *offset*]
>   Reads *length* bytes into $*var* at *offset*.

syswrite *filehandle, scalar, length* [, *offset*]
>   Writes *length* bytes from *scalar* at *offset*.

tell [*filehandle*]
>   Returns the current file position for the file. If *filehandle* is omitted, assumes the file last read.

Formats

formline *picture, list*
>   Formats *list* according to *picture* and accumulates the result into $^A.

write [*filehandle*]
>   Writes a formatted record to the specified file, using the format associated with that file.

Formats are defined as follows:

format [*name*] =
formlist
.

formlist pictures the lines, and contains the arguments that will give values to the fields in the lines. *name* defaults to STDOUT if omitted.

Picture fields are:

@<<< ...	Left-adjusted field, repeat the < to denote the desired width
@>>> ...	Right-adjusted field
@| | | ...	Centered field
@#.## ...	Numeric format with implied decimal point
@*	A multiline field

Use ^ instead of @ for multiline block filling.

Use ~ at the beginning of a line to suppress unwanted empty lines.

Use ~~ at the beginning of a line to have this format line repeated until all fields are exhausted.

Set $– to zero to force a page break on the next write.

See also $^, $~, $^A, $^F, $–, and $= in the section "Special Variables."

Directory Reading Routines

closedir *dirhandle*
>   Closes a directory opened by opendir.

opendir *dirhandle, dirname*
>   Opens a directory on the handle specified.

readdir *dirhandle*
>   Returns the next entry (or an array of entries) from the directory.

`rewinddir` *dirhandle*
> Positions the directory to the beginning.

`seekdir` *dirhandle, pos*
> Sets position for `readdir` on the directory.

`telldir` *dirhandle*
> Returns the position in the directory.

System Interaction

`alarm` *expr*
> Schedules a SIGALRM to be delivered after *expr* seconds.

`chdir` [*expr*]
> Changes the working directory. Uses $ENV{"HOME"} or $ENV{"LOG-NAME"} if *expr* is omitted.

`chroot` *filename*†
> Changes the root directory for the process and its children.

`die` [*list*]
> Prints the value of *list* to STDERR and exits with the current value of $! (errno). If $! is 0, exits with the value of ($? >> 8). If ($? >> 8) is 0, exits with 255. *list* defaults to "Died."

`exec` *list*
> Executes the system command in *list*; does not return.

`exit` [*expr*]
> Exits immediately with the value of *expr*, which defaults to 0 (zero). Calls END routines and object destructors before exiting.

`fork`
> Does a *fork*(2) system call. Returns the process ID of the child to the parent process and zero to the child process.

`getlogin`
> Returns the current login name as known by the system.

`getpgrp` [*pid*]
> Returns the process group for process *pid* (0, or omitted, means the current process).

`getppid`
> Returns the process ID of the parent process.

`getpriority` *which, who*
> Returns the current priority for a process, process group, or user.

`glob` *pat*
> Returns a list of filenames that match the shell pattern *pat*.

`kill` *list*
> Sends a signal to a list of processes. The first element of the list must be the signal to send (either numeric, or its name as a string).

`setpgrp` *pid, pgrp*
> Sets the process group for the *pid* (0 means the current process).

`setpriority` *which, who, priority*
> Sets the current priority for a process, process group, or a user.

`sleep` [*expr*]
> Causes the program to sleep for *expr* seconds, or forever if no *expr*. Returns the number of seconds actually slept.

`syscall` *list*
> Calls the system call specified in the first element of the list, passing the rest of the list as arguments to the call.

`system` *list*
> Does exactly the same thing as `exec` *list* except that a fork is performed first, and the parent process waits for the child process to complete.

`times`
> Returns a 4-element array (0:$user, 1:$system, 2:$cuser, 3:$csystem) giving the user and system times, in seconds, for this process and the children of this process.

`umask` [*expr*]
> Sets the umask for the process and returns the old one. If *expr* is omitted, returns current umask value.

`wait`
> Waits for a child process to terminate and returns the process ID of the deceased process (–1 if none). The status is returned in $?.

`waitpid` *pid, flags*
> Performs the same function as the corresponding system call.

`warn` [*list*] ´
> Prints the message on STDERR like `die`, but doesn't exit. *list* defaults to "Warning: something's wrong".

Networking

`accept` *newsocket, genericsocket*
> Accepts a new socket.

`bind` *socket, name*
> Binds the *name* to the *socket*.

`connect` *socket, name*
> Connects the *name* to the *socket*.

`getpeername` *socket*
> Returns the socket address of the other end of the *socket*.

`getsockname` *socket*
> Returns the name of the socket.

getsockopt *socket, level, optname*
> Returns the socket options.

listen *socket, queuesize*
> Starts listening on the specified *socket*.

recv *socket, scalar, length, flags*
> Receives a message on *socket*.

send *socket, msg, flags* [, *to*]
> Sends a message on the *socket*.

setsockopt *socket, level, optname, optval*
> Sets the requested socket option.

shutdown *socket, how*
> Shuts down a *socket*.

socket *socket, domain, type, protocol*
> Creates a *socket* in *domain* with *type* and *protocol*.

socketpair *socket1, socket2, domain, type, protocol*
> Works the same as socket, but creates a pair of bidirectional sockets.

System V IPC

You need to require "sys/ipc.ph" before you can use the symbolic names of the operations.

msgctl *id, cmd, args*
> Calls *msgctl*(2). If *cmd* is &IPC_STAT then *args* must be a variable.

msgget *key, flags*
> Creates a message queue for *key*. Returns the message queue identifier.

msgsnd *id, msg, flags*
> Sends *msg* to queue *id*.

msgrcv *id, $var, size, type, flags*
> Receives a message from queue *id* into *var*.

semctl *id, semnum, cmd, arg*
> Calls *semctl*(2). If *cmd* is &IPC_STAT of &GETALL then *arg* must be a variable.

semget *key, nsems, size, flags*
> Creates a set of semaphores for *key*. Returns the message semaphore identifier.

semop *key*, . . .
> Performs semaphore operations.

shmctl *id, cmd, arg*
> Calls *shmctl*(2). If *cmd* is &IPC_STAT then *arg* must be a variable.

shmget *key, size, flags*
> Creates shared memory. Returns the shared memory segment identifier.

shmread *id*, $*var*, *pos*, *size*
> Reads at most *size* bytes of the contents of shared memory segment *id* starting at offset *pos* into *var*.

shmwrite *id*, *string*, *pos*, *size*
> Writes at most *size* bytes of *string* into the contents of shared memory segment *id* at offset *pos*.

Miscellaneous

defined *expr*
> Tests whether the lvalue *expr* has an actual value.

do *filename*
> Executes *filename* as a Perl script. See also require in the section "Subroutines, Packages, and Modules."

dump [*label*]
> Immediate core dump. When reincarnated, starts at *label*.

eval { *expr;* ... }
> Executes the code between { and }. Traps runtime errors as described with eval(*expr*), in the section "String Functions."

local *variable*

local (*list*)
> Creates a scope for the listed variables local to the enclosing block, subroutine, or eval.

my *variable*

my (*list*)
> Creates a scope for the listed variables lexically local to the enclosing block, subroutine, or eval.

ref *expr*†
> Returns a true value if *expr* is a reference. Returns the package name if *expr* has been blessed into a package.

reset [*expr*]
> Resets ?? searches so that they work again. *expr* is a list of single letters. All variables and arrays beginning with one of those letters are reset to their pristine state. Only affects the current package.

scalar *expr*
> Forces evaluation of *expr* in scalar context.

undef [*lvalue*]
> Undefines the *lvalue*. Always returns the undefined value.

wantarray
> Returns trues+1 if the current context expects an array value.

Information from System Files

passwd
Returns ($name, $passwd, $uid, $gid, $quota, $comment, $gcos, $dir, $shell).

endpwent
> Ends lookup processing.

getpwent
> Gets next user information.

getpwnam *name*
> Gets information by name.

getpwuid *uid*
> Gets information by user ID.

setpwent
> Resets lookup processing.

group
Returns ($name, $passwd, $gid, $members).

endgrent
> Ends lookup processing.

getgrgid *gid*
> Gets information by group ID.

getgrnam *name*
> Gets information by name.

getgrent
> Gets next information.

setgrent
> Resets lookup processing.

hosts
Returns ($name, $aliases, $addrtype, $length, @addrs).

endhostent
> Ends lookup processing.

gethostbyaddr *addr, addrtype*
> Gets information by IP address.

gethostbyname *name*
> Gets information by hostname.

gethostent
> Gets next host information.

sethostent *stayopen*
> Resets lookup processing.

networks
Returns ($name, $aliases, $addrtype, $net).

endnetent
> Ends lookup processing.

getnetbyaddr *addr, type*
> Gets information by address and type.

getnetbyname *name*
> Gets information by network name.

getnetent
> Gets next network information.

setnetent *stayopen*
> Resets lookup processing.

services
Returns ($name, $aliases, $port, $proto).

endservent
> Ends lookup processing.

getservbyname *name, proto*
> Gets information by service name.

getservbyport *port, proto*
> Gets information by service port.

getservent
> Gets next service information.

setservent *stayopen*
> Resets lookup processing.

protocols
Returns ($name, $aliases, $proto).

endprotoent
> Ends lookup processing.

getprotobyname *name*
> Gets information by protocol name.

getprotobynumber *number*
> Gets information by protocol number.

getprotoent
> Gets next protocol information.

setprotoent *stayopen*
> Resets lookup processing.

Special Variables

The following variables are global and should be localized in subroutines:

$_ The default input and pattern-searching space.

$. The current input line number of the last filehandle that was read.

$/ The input record separator, newline by default. May be multicharacter.

$, The output field separator for the print operator.

$" The separator that joins elements of arrays interpolated in strings.

$\ The output record separator for the print operator.

$# The output format for printed numbers. Deprecated.

$* Set to 1 to do multiline matching within strings. Deprecated, see the m and s modifiers in the section "Search and Replace Functions."

$? The status returned by the last ` ` command, pipe close, or system operator.

$] The Perl version number, e.g., 5.001.

$[The index of the first element in an array, and of the first character in a substring. Default is 0. Deprecated.

$; The subscript separator for multidimensional array emulation. Default is "\034".

$! If used in a numeric context, yields the current value of errno. If used in a string context, yields the corresponding error string.

$@ The Perl error message from the last eval or do *expr* command.

$: The set of characters after which a string may be broken to fill continuation fields (starting with ^) in a format.

$0 The name of the file containing the Perl script being executed. May have a value assigned to it.

$$ The process ID of the currently executing Perl program. Altered (in the child process) by fork.

$< The real user ID of this process.

$> The effective user ID of this process.

$(The real group ID of this process.

$) The effective group ID of this process.

$^A The accumulator for formline and write operations.

$^D The debug flags as passed to Perl using –D.

$^F The highest system file descriptor, ordinarily 2.

$^I In-place edit extension as passed to Perl using –i.

$^L Formfeed character used in formats.

$^P Internal debugging flag.

$^T The time (as delivered by time) when the program started. This value is used by the file test operators –M, –A, and –C.

$^W The value of the –w option as passed to Perl.

$^X The name by which the currently executing program was invoked.

The following variables are context dependent and need not be localized:

$%   The current page number of the currently selected output channel.

$=   The page length of the current output channel. Default is 60 lines.

$–   The number of lines remaining on the page.

$˜   The name of the current report format.

$^   The name of the current top-of-page format.

$ | If set to nonzero, forces a flush after every write or print on the currently selected output channel. Default is 0.

$ARGV
> The name of the current file when reading from < >.

The following variables are always local to the current block:

$&   The string matched by the last successful pattern match.

$˜   The string preceding what was matched by the last successful match.

$'   The string following what was matched by the last successful match.

$+   The last bracket matched by the last search pattern.

$1 ... $9 ...
> Contain the subpatterns from the corresponding sets of parentheses in the last pattern successfully matched. $10\h'0.4n'... and up are only available if the match contained that many subpatterns.

Special Arrays

@ARGV Contains the command-line arguments for the script (not including the command name).

@EXPORT
> Names the methods a package exports by default.

@EXPORT_OK
> Names the methods a package can export upon explicit request.

@INC
> Contains the list of places to look for Perl scripts to be evaluated by the do *filename* and require commands.

@ISA
> List of base classes of a package.

@_   Parameter array for subroutines. Also used by split if not in array context.

%ENV   Contains the current environment.

%INC
> List of files that have been included with require or do.

%OVERLOAD
> Can be used to overload operators in a package.

%SIG
> Used to set signal handlers for various signals.

Environment Variables

Perl uses the following environment variables:

HOME
> Used if chdir has no argument.

LOGDIR
> Used if chdir has no argument and HOME is not set.

PATH
> Used in executing subprocesses, and in finding the Perl script if –S is used.

PERL5LIB
> A colon-separated list of directories to look in for Perl library files before looking in the standard library and the current directory.

PERL5DB
> The command to get the debugger code. Defaults to BEGIN { require 'perl5db.pl' }.

PERLLIB
> Used instead of PERL5LIB if the latter is not defined.

The Perl Debugger

The Perl symbolic debugger is invoked with perl –d.

h   Prints out a help message.

T   Prints a stack trace.

s   Single steps.

n   Single steps around subroutine call.

RETURN
> Repeats last s or n.

r   Returns from the current subroutine.

c [*line*]
> Continues (until *line*, or another breakpoint, or exit).

p *expr*
> Prints *expr*.

l [*range*]
> Lists a range of lines. *range* may be a number, start-end, start+amount, or a subroutine name. If *range* is omitted, lists next window.

w   Lists window around current line.

–   Lists previous window.

f *file*
> Switches to *file* and starts listing it.

l *sub*
> Lists the named subroutine.

S   Lists the names of all subroutines.

/*pattern*/
> Searches forward for *pattern*.

?pattern?
>Searches backward for *pattern*.

b [*line* [*condition*]]
>Sets breakpoint at *line*; default is the current line.

b *sub* [*condition*]
>Sets breakpoint at the subroutine.

d [*line*]
>Deletes breakpoint at the given line.

D   Deletes all breakpoints.

L   Lists lines that have breakpoints or actions.

a *line command*
>Sets an action for line.

A   Deletes all line actions.

< *command*
>Sets an action to be executed before every debugger prompt.

> *command*
>Sets an action to be executed before every s, c, or n command.

V [*package* [*vars*]]
>Lists all variables in a package. Default package is main.

X [*vars*]
>Like V, but assumes current package.

! [[−]*number*]
>Re-executes a command. Default is the previous command.

H [−*number*]
>Displays the last −*number* commands of more than one letter.

t   Toggles trace mode.

= [*alias value*]
>Sets alias, or lists current aliases.

q   Quits. You may also use your character.

command
>Executes *command* as a Perl statement.

CHAPTER 16

Other CGI Resources

You can simplify many of the basic tasks of CGI programming (such as creating and decoding forms) by using the freely available CGI modules for Perl 5. Several of these are available from the Comprehensive Perl Archive Network (CPAN), the mirror sites of which follow:

ftp://ftp.funet.fi/pub/languages/perl/CPAN/

ftp://ftp.cis.ufl.edu/pub/perl/CPAN/

ftp://ftp.uiarchive.cso.uiuc.edu/pub/lang/perl/CPAN/

ftp://ftp.delphi.com/pub/mirrors/packages/perl/CPAN/

ftp://ftp.uoknor.edu/mirrors/CPAN/

ftp://ftp.sedl.org/pub/mirrors/CPAN/

ftp://ftp.ibp.fr/pub/perl/CPAN/

ftp://ftp.pasteur.fr/pub/computing/unix/perl/CPAN/

ftp://ftp.leo.org/pub/comp/programming/languages/perl/CPAN/

ftp://ftp.rz.ruhr-uni-bochum.de/pub/programming/languages/perl/CPAN/

ftp://ftp.demon.co.uk/pub/mirrors/perl/CPAN/

ftp://ftp.cs.ruu.nl/pub/PERL/CPAN/

ftp://ftp.sunet.se/pub/lang/perl/CPAN/

ftp://ftp.switch.ch/mirror/CPAN/

ftp://ftp.mame.mu.oz.au/pub/perl/CPAN/

ftp://ftp.tekotago.ac.nz/pub/perl/CPAN/

ftp://ftp.lab.kdd.co.jp/lang/perl/CPAN/

ftp://dongpo.math.ncu.edu.tw/perl/CPAN/

ftp://ftp.is.co.za.programming/perl/CPAN/

CGI Modules for Perl 5

The current section gives an overview of some of the available modules. The set of coordinated, commonly available CGI modules for Perl 5 are known collectively as the CGI::* modules. They are available from:

http://www-genome.wi.mit.edu/WWW/tools/scripting/CGIperl/

The CGI::* modules allow you to create and decode forms as well as maintain state between forms. A short description of each CGI::* module follows:

Base.pm

> The core module that contains common methods (i.e., functions) that some of the other classes depend on. These include methods to read form information (the module does not parse or decode the data), log debug messages, implement socket I/O for maintaining state, and access and manipulate data from environment variables, such as the client's acceptable MIME content types.
>
> *Base.pm* represents the base class (re: object-oriented programming), from which other classes "inherit" methods and data structures; the "child" classes can override the methods from the base class to create modified functions, or implement new ones.

BasePlus.pm

> A module consisting of functions to handle the new multipart forms generated by "file upload"—a feature new to Netscape 2.0. This very powerful feature allows users to send files on their local machines as part of a form; however, decoding the data can be a hassle. So you should use either this module or the *CGI_Lite* module to handle multipart forms.

Request.pm

> Module used to parse and decode form and query data.

Form.pm

> A module to help you create forms without remembering and entering every HTML tag. Also helps decode and parse form and query data easily. The functions responsible for this are inherited from the *Base.pm* and *Request.pm* modules.

MiniSvr.pm

> A module that lets you implement a "mini HTTP daemon" that can be forked from a CGI application to maintain state between multiple form invocations.

Response.pm

> Though not part of the official CGI module distribution at the time of this writing, this module contains functions that make it easier to output HTML headers. For example, if you want a document to be cached, you can call a method that will automatically output the `Pragma` and `Expires` headers for you.

Carp.pm

> An independent module (i.e., it does not inherit any functionality from the base class), but very useful; it allows you to format error messages sent to the server log file or redirect them to the browser or another file.

There are also some independent CGI modules for Perl 5, among them:

CGI_Lite

> An alternative to the CGI::* modules, this Perl 5 version of *cgi-lib.pl* (a version 4 library) decodes both URL-encoded and multipart form data produced by the file upload feature present in Netscape 2.0. *CGI_Lite* is simpler and easier to use than the core CGI modules.

Sprite

> A Perl 5 module that allows you to manipulate text-delimited databases (all data and delimiters are text) using a small but important subset of SQL-92. *Sprite* allows you to create your own databases and access them in CGI scripts, even if you don't have a database product like Sybase or Oracle.

CGI_Lite and *Sprite* can be found at any of the CPAN mirror sites, under */modules/by-authors/Shishir_Gundavaram.*

Additional CGI Software

The following libraries and modules are available for use with Perl 4 and/or other languages/platforms:

cgic (CGI C/C++ Library)
> *http://www.bio.cam.ac.uk/web/form.html*

cgi-lib.pl (Perl 4)
> *http://www.bio.cam.ac.uk/web/form.html*

EIT's CGI Library for C/C++
> *http://wsk.eit.com/wsk/dist/doc/libcgi/libcgi.html*

Grant's CGI Framework for the Macintosh
> *http://arpp1.carleton.ca/grant/mac/grantscgi.html*

libwww
> *modules/by-authors/Gisle_A* in the CPAN archives

Python CGI Library
> *http://www.python.org/~mclay/notes/cgi.html*

uncgi
> *http://www.hyperion.com/~koreth/uncgi.html*

Related Utilities and Applications

CGI Lint
> *modules/by-authors/Shishir_Gundavaram* in the CPAN archives

DBI/DBperl
> *authors/Tim_Bunce/DBI* in the CPAN archives

fakessi.pl
> *http://sw.cse.bris.ac.uk/WebTools/fakessi.html*

GD Graphics Library
> C Library: *http://www.boutell.com/gd/*
> Perl 5.0: *http://www-genome.wi.mit.edu/ftp/pub/software/WWW/GD.html*
> Tcl: *http://guraldi.hgp.med.umich.edu/gdtcl.html*

GhostScript
> *http://www.phys.ufl.edu/docs/goodies/unix/previewers/ghostscript.html*

Glimpse
> *http://glimpse.cs.arizona.edu/*

gnuplot v3.5
> *ftp://prep.ai.mit.edu/pub/gnu/gnuplot-3.5.tar.gz*

ImageMagick
> *ftp://ftp.x.org/contrib/applications/ImageMagick*

mSQL
> *http://bond.edu.au/People/bambi/mSQL/*

netpbm
> *ftp://ftp.x.org/R5contrib/netpbm-1mar1994.tar.gz*

oraperl
> *http://src.doc.ic.ac.uk/packages/perl/db/perl4/oraperl*

pgperl
> *http://www.ast.cam.ac.uk/~kgb/pgperl.html*

RDB
> *http://www.metronet.com/perlinfo/scripts/dbase/RDB.tar.z*

SWISH
> *http://www.eit.com/software/swish/swish.html*

sybperl
> *http://src.doc.ic.ac.uk/packages/perl/db/perl4/sybperl*

Online Documentation

AppleScript Guide to CGI Scripts
> *http://152.1.24.177/teaching/manuscripts/default.html*

CGI FAQ
> *http://perl.com*
> *ftp://ftp.ora.com/published/oreilly/nutshell/cgi*

CGI Security FAQ
> *http://www.cerf.net/~paulp/cgi-security/safe-cgi.txt*

Perl Reference Guide
> */doc/FAQ* in the CPAN archives

SQL-92
> *http://sunsite.doc.ic.ac.uk/packages/perl/db/refinfo/sql2/sql1992.txt*

WWW FAQ
> *http://www.boutell.com/faq*

WWW Security FAQ
> *http://www-genome.wi.mit.edu/WWW/faqs/www-security-faq.html*

Official Specifications

CGI

    http://hoohoo.ncsa.uiuc.edu/cgi/interface.html

MIME (RFC1341)

    http://www.w3.org/hypertext/WWW/Protocols/rfc1341/0_TableOfContents.html

HTML

    http://www.w3.org/hypertext/WWW/MarkUp/HTML.html

Netscape Extensions to HTML

    http://home.netscape.com/assist/net_sites/html_extensions.html

HTTP

    http://www.w3.org/hypertext/WWW/Protocols/HTTP/

URL

    http://www.w3.org/hypertext/WWW/Addressing/Addressing.html

PART III

HTTP

CHAPTER 17

HTTP Overview

The Hypertext Transfer Protocol (HTTP) is the language that Web clients and Web servers use to communicate with each other. It is essentially the backbone of the Web.

While HTTP is largely the realm of server and client programming, a firm understanding of HTTP is also important for CGI programming. In addition, sometimes HTTP filters back to the users—for example, when server error codes are reported in a browser window. In this book, we cover HTTP in four chapters:

• In the current chapter (Chapter 17), we give a brief introduction to HTTP, the structure of HTTP transactions, and a discussion of client methods.

• In Chapter 18, *Server Response Codes*, we cover the valid status codes used in HTTP server responses.

• In Chapter 19, *HTTP Headers*, we list the headers used by both clients and servers under HTTP.

• Finally, in Chapter 20, *Media Types and Subtypes*, we cover the Internet media types used under HTTP.

HTTP Basics

All HTTP transactions follow the same general format. Each client request and server response has three parts: the request or response line, a header section, and the entity body. The client initiates a transaction as follows:

1. The client contacts the server at a designated port number (by default, 80). Then it sends a document request by specifying an HTTP command called a *method*, followed by a document address, and an HTTP version number.

147

For example:

```
GET /index.html HTTP/1.0
```

uses the GET method to request the document *index.html* using version 1.0 of HTTP. HTTP methods are discussed in more detail later in this chapter.

2. Next, the client sends optional header information to inform the server of its configuration and the document formats it will accept. All header information is given line by line, each with a header name and value. Chapter 19 lists the valid HTTP headers. For example, this header information sent by the client indicates its name and version number and specifies several document preferences:

```
User-Agent: Mozilla/2.02Gold (WinNT; I)
Accept: image/gif, image/x-xbitmap, image/jpeg, image/pjpeg, */*
```

The client sends a blank line to end the header.

3. After sending the request and headers, the client may send additional data. This data is mostly used by CGI programs using the POST method. It may also be used by clients like Netscape Navigator-Gold, to publish an edited page back onto the Web server.

The server responds in the following way to the client's request:

1. The server replies with a status line containing three fields: HTTP version, status code, and description. The HTTP version indicates the version of HTTP that the server is using to respond.

   The status code is a three digit number that indicates the server's result of the client's request. The description following the status code is just human-readable text that describes the status code. For example, this status line:

   ```
   HTTP/1.0 200 OK
   ```

   indicates that the server uses version 1.0 of HTTP in its response. A status code of 200 means that the client's request was successful and the requested data will be supplied after the headers. Chapter 18 contains a listing of the status codes and their descriptions.

2. After the status line, the server sends header information to the client about itself and the requested document. HTTP headers are covered in Chapter 19. For example:

   ```
   Date: Fri, 20 Sep 1996 08:17:58 GMT
   Server: NCSA/1.5.2
   Last-modified: Mon, 17 Jun 1996 21:53:08 GMT
   Content-type: text/html
   Content-length: 2482
   ```

   A blank line ends the header.

3. If the client's request is successful, the requested data is sent. This data may be a copy of a file, or the response from a CGI program. If the client's request could not be fulfilled, additional data may be a human-readable explanation of why the server could not fulfill the request.

In HTTP 1.0, after the server has finished sending the requested data, it disconnects from the client and the transaction is over unless a `Connection: Keep Alive` header is sent. In HTTP 1.1, however, the default is for the server to maintain the connection and allow the client to make additional requests. Since many documents embed other documents as inline images, frames, applets, etc., this saves the overhead of the client having to repeatedly connect to the same server just to draw a single page. Under HTTP 1.1, therefore, the transaction might cycle back to the beginning, until either the client or server explicitly closes the connection.

Being a stateless protocol, HTTP does not maintain any information from one transaction to the next, so the next transaction needs to start all over again. The advantage is that an HTTP server can serve a lot more clients in a given period of time, since there's no additional overhead for tracking sessions from one connection to the next. The disadvantage is that more elaborate CGI programs need to use hidden input fields (as described in Chapter 10, *HTML Form Tags*) or external tools such as Netscape cookies (as described in Chapter 12, *Cookies*) to maintain information from one transaction to the next.

Client Requests

Client requests are broken up into three sections. The first line of a message always contains an HTTP command called a *method*, a URI that identifies the file or resource the client is querying, and the HTTP version number. The following lines of a client request contain header information, which provides information about the client and the data entity it is sending the server. The third part of a client request is the entity body, the data being sent to the server.

URI (Uniform Resource Identifier) is just a general term for all valid formats of addressing schemes supported on the World Wide Web. The one in common use now is URL (Uniform Resource Locator) addressing scheme. See Chapter 1, *Introduction*, for more information on URLs.

Methods

A method is an HTTP command that begins the first line of a client request. The method tells the server the purpose of the client request. There are three main methods defined for HTTP: GET, HEAD, and POST. Other methods are also defined, but are not as widely supported by servers as GET, HEAD, and POST (although the other methods will be used more often in the future, not less). Methods are case sensitive, so a "GET" is different than a "get."

The GET method

GET is a request for information located at a specified URI on the server. It is the most commonly used method by browsers to retrieve documents for viewing. The result of a GET request can be generated in many different ways. It could be a file accessible by the server, the output of a program or CGI script, the output from a hardware device, etc.

When a client uses the GET method in its request, the server responds with a status line, headers, and the requested data. If the server cannot process the request due to an error or lack of authorization, the server usually sends a textual explanation in the data portion of the response.

The entity-body portion of a GET request is always empty. GET is basically used to say "Give me this file." The file or program that the client requests is usually identified by its full path name on the server.

Here is an example of a successful GET request to retrieve a file. The client sends:

```
GET /index.html HTTP/1.0
Connection: Keep-Alive
User-Agent: Mozilla/2.02Gold (WinNT; I)
Host: www.ora.com
Accept: image/gif, image/x-xbitmap, image/jpeg, image/pjpeg, */*
```

The server responds with:

```
HTTP/1.0 200 Document follows
Date: Fri, 20 Sep 1996 08:17:58 GMT
Server: NCSA/1.5.2
Last-modified: Mon, 17 Jun 1996 21:53:08 GMT
Content-type: text/html
Content-length: 2482
```

(body of document here)

The GET method is also used to send input to programs like CGI through form tags. Since GET requests have empty entity-bodies, the input data is appended to the URL in the GET line of the request. When a <form> tag specifies the method="GET" attribute value, key-value pairs representing the input from the form are appended to the URL following a question mark (?). Pairs are separated by an ampersand (&). For example:

```
GET /cgi-bin/birthday.pl?month=august&date=24 HTTP/1.0
```

causes the server to send the *birthday.pl* CGI program the month and date values specified in a form on the client. The input data at the end of the URL is encoded to CGI specifications. For literal use of special characters, the client uses hexadecimal notation. The character encoding is described in Chapter 9, *CGI Overview*.

The GET method can also supply *extra-path information* in the same manner. This is achieved by adding the extra path after the URL, i.e., /cgi-bin/display.pl/cgi/cgi_doc.txt. The server gauges where the program's name ends (display.pl). Everything after that is read as the extra path.

The HEAD method
The HEAD method is functionally like GET except that the server will not send anything in the data portion of the reply. The HEAD method requests only the header information on a file or resource. The header information from a HEAD request should be the same as that from a GET request.

This method is used when the client wants to find out information about the document and not retrieve it. Many applications exist for the HEAD method. For example, the client may desire the following information:

- Modification time of a document, useful for cache-related queries

- The size of a document, useful for page layout, estimating arrival time, or determining whether to request a smaller version of the document

- The type of the document, to allow the client to examine only documents of a certain type

- The type of server, to allow customized server queries

It is important to note that most of the header information provided by a server is optional and may not be given by all servers. A good design for Web clients is to allow flexibility in the server response and take default actions when desired header information is not given by the server.

The following is an example HTTP transaction using the HEAD request. The client sends:

```
HEAD /index.html HTTP/1.0
Connection: Keep-Alive
User-Agent: Mozilla/2.02Gold (WinNT; I)
Host: www.ora.com
Accept: image/gif, image/x-xbitmap, image/jpeg, image/pjpeg, */*
```

The server responds with:

```
HTTP/1.0 200 Document follows
Date: Fri, 20 Sep 1996 08:17:58 GMT
Server: NCSA/1.5.2
Last-modified: Mon, 17 Jun 1996 21:53:08 GMT
Content-type: text/html
Content-length: 2482
```

(No entity body is sent in response to a HEAD request.)

The POST method

The POST method allows data to be sent to the server in a client request. The data is directed to a data handling program that the server has access to (e.g., a CGI script). The POST method can be used for many applications. For example, it can be used to provide input for:

- Network services, such as newsgroup postings

- Command-line interface programs

- Annotation of documents on the server

- Database operations

The data sent to the server is in the entity-body section of the client's request. After the server processes the POST request and headers, it passes the entity-body to the program specified by the URI. The encoding scheme most commonly used with POST is URL-encoding, which allows form data to be translated into a list of variables and values for CGI processing. Chapter 9 provides details on CGI and URL-encoded data.

Here is a quick example of a client request using the POST method to send birth-date data from a form:

```
POST /cgi-bin/birthday.pl HTTP/1.0
User-Agent: Mozilla/2.02Gold (WinNT; I)
Accept: image/gif, image/x-xbitmap, image/jpeg, image/pjpeg, */*
Host: www.ora.com
Content-type: application/x-www-form-urlencoded
Content-length: 20

month=august&date=24
```

Other methods
The following methods are also defined, although not as frequentlly used.

LINK
> Requests that header information is associated with a document on the server.

UNLINK
> Requests dissociation of header information from a document on the server.

PUT
> Requests that the entity-body of the request be stored at the specified URI.

DELETE
> Requests the removal of data at a URI on the server.

OPTIONS
> Requests information about communications options available on the server. The request URI can be substituted with an asterisk (*) to indicate the server as a whole.

TRACE
> Requests the request entity body be returned intact. Used for debugging.

Server Responses

The server's response to a client request is grouped into three parts. The first line is the server response line, which contains the HTTP version number, a number indicating the status of the request, and a short phrase describing the status. The response line is followed by the header information and an entity body if there is one.

The server response codes are covered in Chapter 18. Server response headers are covered in Chapter 19.

CHAPTER 18

Server Response Codes

The first line in an HTTP server response indicates whether the client request was successful or not, and why. The status is given with a three-digit *server response code* (also known as a *status code*) and a descriptive message.

Status codes are usually generated by Web servers, but they might also be generated by CGI scripts that bypass the server's precooked headers and supply their own. Status codes are grouped as follows:

Code Range	Response Meaning
100-199	Informational
200-299	Client request successful
300-399	Client request redirected, further action necessary
400-499	Client request incomplete
500-599	Server errors

HTTP defines only a few specific codes in each range, although servers may define their own as needed. If a client receives a code that it does not recognize, it should understand its basic meaning from its numerical range. While most Web browsers handle codes in the 100-, 200-, and 300- range silently, some error codes in the 400- and 500- range are commonly reported back to the user (e.g., "404 Not Found").

Informational

A response in the range of 100-199 is informational, indicating that the client's request was received and is being processed.

100 Continue
> The initial part of the request has been received and the client may continue with its request.

101 Switching Protocols

The server is complying with a client request to switch protocols to the one specified in the Upgrade header field.

Client Request Successful

A response in the range of 200-299 means that the client's request was successful.

200 OK

The client's request was successful, and the server's response contains the requested data.

201 Created

This status code is used whenever a new URI is created. With this result code, the Location header (described in Chapter 19, *HTTP Headers*) is given by the server to specify where the new data was placed.

202 Accepted

The request was accepted but not immediately acted upon. More information about the transaction may be given in the entity body of the server's response. There is no guarantee that the server will actually honor the request, even though it may seem like a legitimate request at the time of acceptance.

203 Non-Authoritative Information

The information in the entity header is from a local or third-party copy and not from the original server.

204 No Content

A status code and header is given in the response, but there is no entity body in the reply. Browsers should not update their document view upon receiving this response. This is a useful code for an imagemap handler to return when the user clicks on useless or blank areas of an image.

205 Reset Content

The browser should clear the form used for this transaction for additional input. Appropriate for data-entry CGI applications.

206 Partial Content

The server is returning partial data of the size requested. Used in response to a request specifying a Range header. The server must specify the range included in the response with the Content-Range header.

Redirection

A response code in the 300-399 range indicates that the request was not performed and the client needs to take further action for a successful request.

300 Multiple Choices

The requested URI refers to more than one resource. For example, the URI could refer to a document that has been translated into many languages. The entity body returned by the server could have a list of more specific data about how to choose the correct resource.

301 Moved Permanently
The requested URI is no longer used by the server, and the operation specified in the request was not performed. The new location for the requested document is specified in the Location header. All future requests for the document should use the new URI.

302 Moved Temporarily
The requested URI has moved, but only temporarily. The Location header points to the new location. Immediately after receiving this status code, the client should use the new URI to resolve the request, but the old URI should be used for all future requests.

303 See Other
The requested URI can be found at a different URI (specified in the Location header) and should be retrieved by a GET on that resource.

304 Not Modified
This is the response code to an If-Modified-Since header, where the URI has not been modified since the specified date. The entity body is not sent, and the client should use its own local copy.

305 Use Proxy
The requested URI must be accessed through the proxy in the Location header.

Client Request Incomplete

A response code in the range of 400-499 means that the client's request was incomplete, and may indicate further information is required from the client.

400 Bad Request
This response code indicates that the server detected a syntax error in the client's request.

401 Unauthorized
The result code is given along with the WWW-Authenticate header to indicate that the request lacked proper authorization, and the client should supply proper authorization when requesting this URI again.

402 Payment Required
This code is not yet implemented in HTTP.

403 Forbidden
The request was denied for a reason the server does not want to (or has no means to) indicate to the client.

404 Not Found
The document at the specified URI does not exist.

405 Method Not Allowed
This code is given with the Allow header and indicates that the method used by the client is not supported for this URI.

406 Not Acceptable
The URI specified by the client exists, but not in a format preferred by the client. Along with this code, the server provides the Content-Language, Content-Encoding, and Content-Type headers.

407 Proxy Authentication Required
The proxy server needs to authorize the request before forwarding it. Used with the Proxy-Authenticate header.

408 Request Time-out
This response code means the client did not produce a full request within some predetermined time (usually specified in the server's configuration), and the server is disconnecting the network connection.

409 Conflict
This code indicates that the request conflicts with another request or with the server's configuration. Information about the conflict should be returned in the data portion of the reply.

410 Gone
This code indicates that the requested URI no longer exists and has been permanently removed from the server.

411 Length Required
The server will not accept the request without a Content-Length header supplied in the request.

412 Precondition Failed
The condition specified by one or more If . . . headers in the request evaluated to false.

413 Request Entity Too Large
The server will not process the request because its entity body is too large.

414 Request-URI Too Long
The server will not process the request because its request URI is too large.

415 Unsupported Media Type
The server will not process the request because its entity body is in an unsupported format.

Server Errors

Response codes in the range of 500-599 indicate that the server encountered an error and may be unable to perform the client's request.

500 Internal Server Error
This code indicates that a part of the server (for example, a CGI program) has crashed or encountered a configuration error.

---

501 Not Implemented
: This code indicates that the client requested an action that cannot be performed by the server.

502 Bad Gateway
: This code indicates that the server (or proxy) encountered invalid responses from another server (or proxy).

503 Service Unavailable
: This code means that the service is temporarily unavailable, but should be restored in the future. If the server knows when it will be available again, a Retry-After header may also be supplied.

504 Gateway Time-out
: This response is like 408 (Request Time-out) except that a gateway or proxy has timed out.

505 HTTP Version not supported
: The server will not support the HTTP protocol version used in the request.

CHAPTER 19

HTTP Headers

HTTP headers are used to transfer all sorts of information between client and server. There are four different categories of headers:

General   Information not related to the client, server, or HTTP

Request   Preferred document formats and server parameters

Response   Information about the server sending the response

Entity   Information on the data being sent between the client and server

General headers and entity headers are the same for both the server and client.

All headers in HTTP messages contain the header name followed by a colon (:), then a space, and the value of the header. Header names are case-insensitive (thus, Content-Type is the same as Content-type). The value of a header can extend over multiple lines by preceding each extra line with at least one space or tab.

This chapter covers the most recent draft of the HTTP 1.1 specification that was available at publication time (draft 7), as well as some headers not in the spec but which are in common use regardless.

General Headers

General headers are used in both client requests and server responses. Some may be more specific to either a client or server message.

Cache-Control: *directives* Specifies caching directives in a comma-separated list.	**Cache-Control**
	→

Cache- Control ←	***Cache request directives***

Cache request directives

`no-cache`
Do not cache.

`no-store`
Remove information promptly after forwarding.

`max-age` = *seconds*
Do not send responses older than *seconds*.

`max-stale` [= *seconds*]
Send expired data. If *seconds* are specified, only send data expired by less than the specified number of seconds.

`min-fresh` = *seconds*
Send data only if still fresh after the specified number of seconds.

`only-if-cached`
Do not retrieve new data. Only return data already in the cache. Useful unless the network connection is down.

Cache response directives

`public`
Cachable by any cache.

`private`
Not cachable by a shared cache.

`no-cache`
Do not cache.

`no-store`
Remove information promptly after forwarding.

`no-transform`
Do not convert data.

`must-revalidate`
Client must revalidate the data.

`proxy-revalidate`
Client must revalidate data except for private client caches.

`max-age`=*seconds*
The document should be considered stale in the specified number of seconds.

Connection: *options*

Specifies options desired for this connection but not for further connections by proxies. The `close` connection option signifies that either the client or server wishes to end the connection (i.e., this is the last transaction).

Connection

Date: *dateformat*

Indicates the current date and time. The preferred date format is RFC 1123. For example:

```
Mon, 06 May 1996 04:57:00 GMT
```

For backwards compatibility, however, the RFC 850 and ANSI C *asctime()* formats are also acceptable:

```
Monday, 06-May-96 04:57:00 GMT
Mon May 6 04:57:00 1996
```

Date

MIME-Version: *version*

Specifies the version of MIME used in the HTTP transaction. If a message's entity-body does not conform to MIME, this header can be omitted. If the transaction involves MIME-encoded data, but this header is omitted, the default value is assumed to be 1.0.

MIME-Version

Pragma: no-cache

Specifies directives to a proxy system. This header is ignored by the target server. HTTP defines one directive for this header: no-cache. In HTTP 1.0, this tells the proxy to request the document from the server instead of the local cache. HTTP 1.1 prefers using `Cache Control: no-cache` instead.

Pragma

Transfer-Encoding: *encoding_type*

Indicates what type of transformation has been applied to the message body for safe transfer. Currently only the chunked encoding type is defined by HTTP.

Transfer-Encoding

Upgrade: *protocol/version*

Specifies the preferred communication protocols. Used in conjunction with response code 101 `Switching Protocols`. For example:

```
Upgrade: HTTP/1.2
```

Upgrade

Via	`Via:` *protocol host* [*comment*] ... Used by gateways and proxies to indicate the protocols and hosts that processed the transaction between client and server.

Client Request Headers

Client header data communicates the client's configuration and preferred document formats to the server. Request headers are used in a client message to provide information about the client.

Accept	`Accept:` *type/subtype* [; `q=`*qvalue*] Specifies media types that the client prefers to accept. Multiple media types can be listed separated by commas. The optional *qvalue* represents on a scale of 0 to 1 an acceptable quality level for accept types. See Chapter 20, *Media Types and Subtypes*, for a listing of some commonly-accepted media types.
Accept-Charset	`Accept-Charset:` *character_set* [; `q=`*qvalue*] Specifies the character sets that the client prefers. Multiple character sets can be listed separated by commas. The optional *qvalue* represents on a scale of 0 to 1 an acceptable quality level for non-preferred character sets.
Accept-Encoding	`Accept-Encoding:` *encoding_types* Specifies the encoding schemes that the client can accept, such as `compress` or `gzip`. Multiple encoding schemes can be listed, separated by commas. If no encoding types are listed, then none are acceptable to the client.
Accept-Language	`Accept-Language:` *language* [; `q=`*qvalue*] Specifies the languages that the client prefers. Multiple languages can be listed separated by commas. The optional *qvalue* represents on a scale of 0 to 1 an acceptable quality level for non-preferred languages. Languages are written with their two-letter abbreviations (e.g., *en* for English, *de* for German, *fr* for French, etc.).

Authorization: *scheme credentials*

Provides the client's authorization to access data at a URI. When a requested document requires authorization, the server returns a WWW-Authenticate header describing the type of authorization required. The client then repeats the request with the proper authorization information.

The authorization scheme generally used in HTTP is BASIC, and under the BASIC scheme the credentials follow the format *username:password* encoded in base64. For example, for the username of "webmaster" and a password of "zrma4v," the authorization header would look like this:

```
Authorization: BASIC d2VibWFzdGVyOnpycmE1hNHY=
```

The value decodes into `webmaster:zrma4v`.

Authorization

Cookie: *name=value*

Contains a name/value pair of information stored for that URL. Multiple cookies can be specified, separated by semicolons. For browsers supporting Netscape persistent cookies; not included in the HTTP standard. See Chapter 12, *Cookies*, for more information.

Cookie

From: *email_address*

Gives the email address of the user executing the client.

From

Host: *hostname[:port]*

Specifies the host and port number of the URI. Clients must supply this information in HTTP 1.1, so servers with multiple hostnames can easily differentiate between ambiguous URLs.

Host

If-Modified-Since: *date*

Specifies that the URI data is to be sent only if it has been modified since the date given as the value of this header. This is useful for client-side caching. If the document has not been modified, the server returns a code of 304, indicating that the client should use the local copy. The specified date should follow the format described under the Date header.

If-Modified-Since

If-Match	`If-Match:` *entity_tag*
	A conditional requesting the entity only if it matches the given entity tags (see the `ETag` entity header). An asterisk (`*`) matches any entity, and the transaction continues only if the entity exists.
If-None-Match	`If-None-Match:` *entity_tag*
	A conditional requesting the entity only if it does not match any of the given entity tags (see the `ETag` entity header). An asterisk (`*`) matches any entity; if the entity doesn't exist, the transaction continues.
If-Range	`If-Range:` *entity_tag* | *date*
	A conditional requesting only the portion of the entity that is missing if it has not been changed, and the entire entity if it has. Must be used in conjunction with a `Range` header. Either an entity tag or a date can be used to identify the partial entity already received; see the `Date` header for information on the format for dates.
If-Unmodified-Since	`If-Unmodified-Since:` *date*
	Specifies that the URI data is to be sent only if it has not been modified since the given date. The specified date should follow the format described under the `Date` header.
Max-Forwards	`Max-Forwards:` *n*
	Limits the number of proxies or gateways that can forward the request. Useful for debugging with the TRACE method, avoiding infinite loops.
Proxy-Authorization	`Proxy-Authorization:` *credentials*
	Used for a client to identify itself to a proxy requiring authorization.
Range	`Range: bytes=`*n–m*
	Specifies the partial range(s) requested from the document. Multiple ranges can be listed, separated by commas. If the first digit in the comma-separated byte range(s) is missing, the range is assumed to count from the end of the document. If the second digit is missing, the range is byte *n* to the end of the document. The first byte is byte 0.

`Referer:` *url* Gives the URI of the document that refers to the requested URI (i.e., the source document of the link).	**Referer**
`User-Agent:` *string* Gives identifying information about the client program.	**User-Agent**

Server Response Headers

The response headers described here are used in server responses to communicate information about the server and how it may handle requests.

`Accept-Ranges:` `bytes│none` Indicates the acceptance of range requests for a URI, specifying either the range unit (e.g., `bytes`) or `none` if no range requests are accepted.	**Accept-Ranges**
`Age:` *seconds* Indicates the age of the document in seconds.	**Age**
`Proxy-Authenticate:` *scheme realm* Indicates the authentication scheme and parameters applicable to the proxy for this URI and the current connection. Used with response 407 (`Proxy Authentication Required`).	**Proxy-Authenticate**
`Public:` *methods* Indicates methods supported by the server as a comma-separated list. Intended for declaration of non-standard methods supported at this site. For methods applicable only to an individual URI, use the `Allow` header. See Chapter 17, *HTTP Overview*, for a discussion of request methods.	**Public**
`Retry-After:` *date│seconds* Used with response code 503 (`Service Unavailable`). It contains either an integer number of seconds or a GMT date and time (as described by the `Date` header formats). If the value is an integer, it is inter-	**Retry-After**

$\rightarrow$

HTTP

Retry-After ←	preted as the number of seconds to wait after the request was issued. For example: ```\nRetry-After: 3600\nRetry-After: Sat, 18 May 1996 06:59:37 GMT\n```
Server	`Server:` *string* Contains the name and version number of the server. For example: ```\nServer: NCSA/1.3\n```
Set-Cookie	`Set-Cookie:` *name=value* [; *options*] Contains a name/value pair of information to retain for this URL. For browsers supporting Netscape persistent cookies; not included in the HTTP standard. See Chapter 12 for more information. Options are: *expires=date* The cookie becomes invalid after the specified date. *path=pathname* The URL range for which the cookie is valid. *domain=domain_name* the domain name range for which the cookie is valid. *secure* Return the cookie only under a secure connection.
Vary	`Vary:` *	*headers* Specifies that the entity has multiple sources and may therefore vary according to specified list of request header(s). Multiple headers can be listed, separated by commas. An asterisk (*) means that another factor other than the request headers may affect the document that is returned.
Warning	`Warning:` *code host*[:*port*] "*string*" Indicates additional information to that in the status code, for use by caching proxies. The *host* field contains the name or pseudonym of the server host, with an optional port number. The two-digit warning codes and their recommended descriptive strings are: `10 Response is stale` The response data is known to be stale.

11 Revalidation failed The response data is known to be stale because the proxy failed to revalidate the data. 12 Disconnected operation The cache is disconnected from the network. 13 Heuristic expiration The data is older than 24 hours and the cache heuristically chose a freshness lifetime greater than 24 hours. 14 Transformation applied The proxy has changed the encoding or media type of the document, as specified by the Content-Encoding or Content-Type headers. 99 Miscellaneous warning Arbitrary information to be logged or presented to the user.	**Warning**
WWW-Authenticate: *scheme realm* Used with the 401 (Unauthorized) response code. It specifies the authorization scheme and realm of authorization required from a client at the requested URI. Many different authorization realms can exist on a server. A common authorization scheme is BASIC, which requires a username and password. For example: WWW-Authenticate: BASIC realm="Admin" When returned to the client, this header indicates that the BASIC type of authorization data in the appropriate realm should be returned in the client's Authorization header.	**WWW-Authenticate**

HTTP

Entity Headers

Entity headers are used in both client requests and server responses. They supply information about the entity body in an HTTP message.

Allow: *methods* Contains a comma-separated list of methods that are allowed at a specified URI. In a server response it is used with code 405 (Method Not Allowed) to inform the client of valid methods available for the requested information. See Chapter 17 for more information on HTTP methods.	**Allow**

Content-Base	`Content-Base:` *uri* Specifies the base URI for resolving relative URLs. The base URI must be written as an absolute URI.
Content-Encoding	`Content-Encoding:` *encoding_schemes* Specifies the encoding scheme(s) used for the transferred entity body. Values are `gzip` (or `x-gzip`) and `compress` (or `x-compress`). If multiple encoding schemes are specified (in a comma-separated list), they must be listed in the order in which they were applied to the source data.
Content-Language	`Content-Language:` *languages* Specifies the language(s) that the transferred entity body is intended for. Languages are represented by their 2-digit code (e.g., *en* for English, *fr* for French).
Content-Length	`Content-Length:` *n* This header specifies the length of the data (in bytes) of the transferred entity body. Due to the dynamic nature of some requests, the content length is sometimes unknown and this header is omitted.
Content-Location	`Content-Location:` *uri* Supplies the URI for the entity, in cases where a document has multiple entities with separately accessible locations. The URI can be either an absolute or relative URI.
Content-MD5	`Content-MD5:` *digest* Supplies a MD5 digest of the entity, for checking the integrity of the message upon receipt.
Content-Range	`Content-Range: bytes` *n–m/length* Specifies where the accompanying partial entity body should be inserted, and the total size of the full entity body. For example: `Content-Range: bytes 6143-7166/15339`

`Content-Transfer-Encoding:` *scheme*	**Content-Transfer-E**...
Specifies any transformations that are applied to the entity body for transport over a network. Common values are: `7bit`, `8bit`, `binary`, `base64`, and `quoted-printable`.	
`Content-Type:` *type/subtype*	**Content-Type**
Describes the media type and subtype of an entity body. It uses the same values as the client's `Accept` header, and the server should return media types that conform with the client's preferred formats.	
`ETag:` *entity_tag*	**ETag**
Defines the entity tag for use with the `If-Match` and `If-None-Match` request headers.	
`Expires:` *date*	**Expires**
Specifies the time when a document may change or its information becomes invalid. After that time, the document may or may not change or be deleted. The value is a date and time in a valid format as described for the `Date` header.	
`Last-Modified:` *date*	**Last-Modified**
Specifies when the specified URI was last modified. The value is a date and time in a valid format as described for the `Date` header.	
`Location:` *uri*	**Location**
Specifies the new location of a document, usually with response codes 201 (`Created`), 301 (`Moved Permanently`), or 302 (`Moved Temporarily`). The URI given must be written as an absolute URI.	
`URI:` *<uri>*	**URI**
Specifies the new location of a document, usually with response codes 201 (`Created`), 301 (`Moved Permanently`), or 302 (`Moved Temporarily`). An optional `vary` parameter may also be used in this header indicating multiple documents at the URI in the following categories: `type`, `language`, `version`, `encoding`, `charset`, and `user-agent`. Sending these parameters in a server response	

HTTP

→

URI	
←	prompts the client to specify its preferences appropriately in the new request. The URI header is deprecated in HTTP 1.1 in favor of the Location, Content-Location, and Vary headers.

CHAPTER 20

Media Types and Subtypes

Media types are used to communicate the format of the content in HTTP transactions. Clients use media types in their `Accept` headers to indicate what formats they prefer to receive data in. Servers use media types in their `Content-Type` headers to tell the client what format the accompanying entity is in—i.e., whether the enclosed text is HTML that needs to be formatted, GIF or JPEG to be rendered, or PDF format that requires opening an external viewer or using a plug-in.

See Chapter 19, *HTTP Headers*, for more information on the `Accept` and `Content-Type` headers.

Internet media types used by HTTP closely resemble MIME types. MIME (Multipurpose Internet Mail Extension) was designed as a method for sending attachments in mail over the Internet. Like MIME, media types follow the format *type/subtype*. Asterisks (*) represent a wildcard—for example, the following client header means that documents of all formats are accepted:

```
Accept: */*
```

The following client header means that all `text` format types are accepted, regardless of the subtype:

```
Accept: text/*
```

Servers and CGI programs are expected to examine the accept types reported by the `Accept` header and return data of an acceptable type when possible. Most servers determine the format of a document from its filename suffix—for example, a file ending with *.htm* or *.html* is assumed to be HTML format, so the server will send the document with a `Content-Type` of `text/html`. When calling a CGI program, servers cannot know the format of the data being returned, so the CGI program is responsible for reporting the content type itself. For that reason, every CGI program needs to include a Content-Type header such as:

```
Content-Type: text/html
```

The following table lists commonly-used media types along with the filename suffixes recognized by most servers. Most servers can be easily configured to recognize additional suffixes as well.

Type/Subtype	Usual Extension
application/activemessage	
application/andrew-inset	
application/applefile	
application/atomicmail	
application/cals-1840	
application/commonground	
application/cybercash	
application/dca-rft	
application/dec-dx	
application/eshop	
application/iges	
application/mac-binhex40	
application/macwriteii	
application/mathematica	
application/msword	
application/news-message-id	
application/news-transmission	
application/octet-stream	bin
application/oda	oda
application/pdf	pdf
application/postscript	ai, eps, ps
application/remote-printing	
application/riscos	
application/rtf	rtf
application/sgml	
application/slate	
application/vnd.framemaker	
application/vnd.koan	
application/vnd.mif	
application/vnd.ms-artgalry	
application/vnd.ms-excel	
application/vnd.ms-powerpoint	
application/vnd.ms-project	
application/vnd.ms-tnef	
application/vnd.ms-works	
application/vnd.music-niff	
application/vnd.svd	
application/vnd.truedoc	
application/wita	
application/wordperfect5.1	
application/x-bcpio	bcpio
application/x-cpio	cpio

Type/Subtype	Usual Extension
`application/x-csh`	csh
`application/x-dvi`	dvi
`application/x-gtar`	gtar
`application/x-hdf`	hdf
`application/x-latex`	latex
`application/x-mif`	mif
`application/x-netcdf`	nc, cdf
`application/x-sh`	sh
`application/x-shar`	shar
`application/x-sv4cpio`	sv4cpio
`application/x-sv4crc`	sv4crc
`application/x-tar`	tar
`application/x-tcl`	tcl
`application/x-tex`	tex
`application/x-texinfo`	texinfo, texi
`application/x-troff-man`	man
`application/x-troff-me`	me
`application/x-troff-ms`	ms
`application/x-troff`	t, tr, roff
`application/x-ustar`	ustar
`application/x-wais-source`	src
`application/x400-bp`	
`application/zip`	zip
`audio/32kadpcm`	
`audio/basic`	au, snd
`audio/x-aiff`	aif, aiff, aifc
`audio/x-wav`	wav
`image/cgm`	
`image/g3fax`	
`image/gif`	gif
`image/ief`	ief
`image/jpeg`	jpeg, jpg, jpe
`image/naplps`	
`image/tiff`	tiff, tif
`image/vnd.dwg`	
`image/vnd.dxf`	
`image/vnd.svf`	
`image/x-cmu-raster`	ras
`image/x-portable-anymap`	rpnm
`image/x-portable-bitmap`	pbm
`image/x-portable-graymap`	pgm
`image/x-portable-pixmap`	ppm
`image/x-rgb`	rgb
`image/x-xbitmap`	xbm
`image/x-xpixmap`	xpm
`image/x-xwindowdump`	xwd
`message/external-body`	
`message/http`	
`message/news`	
`message/partial`	

Type/Subtype	Usual Extension
message/rfc822	
multipart/alternative	
multipart/appledouble	
multipart/digest	
multipart/form-data	
multipart/header-set	
multipart/mixed	
multipart/parallel	
multipart/related	
multipart/report	
multipart/voice-message	
text/enriched	
text/html	html, htm
text/plain	txt
text/richtext	rtx
text/sgml	
text/tab-separated-values	tsv
text/x-setext	etx
video/mpeg	mpeg, mpg, mpe
video/quicktime	qt, mov
video/vnd.vivo	
video/x-msvideo	qvi
video/x-sgi-movie	movie

PART IV

JavaScript

CHAPTER 21

JavaScript Quick Reference

JavaScript is an evolving scripting language that can be used to extend the capabilities of HTML pages on the World Wide Web. At the end of this chapter is a concise summary of the various JavaScript objects, and the properties, methods, and event handlers defined for them. If you're already writing JavaScript code, this section should help refresh your memory about specific names and syntaxes. For newcomers, we also provide an overview of JavaScript and its capabilities. But if you want to learn JavaScript, you'll have to consult a book devoted to it, such as *JavaScript: The Definitive Guide*, by David Flanagan, published by O'Reilly & Associates.

JavaScript is being developed by Netscape Communications Corporation for use in their Netscape Web browser (client-side JavaScript) and their Web server products (server-side JavaScript). The core JavaScript language has become fairly stable in Netscape 3.0. However, the final JavaScript specification is still pending and plenty of features are still being tuned and added. (In Netscape 2.0, the version of JavaScript is much more limited.) Despite the beta status of JavaScript, tremendous numbers of people are already using it, and Netscape is offering it freely to the market in an attempt to create a standard.

But what is JavaScript and what does it actually do? It may be natural to assume that JavaScript is a simplified version of Java, the programming language from Sun Microsystems, but this is not the case. As a matter of fact, other than an incomplete syntactic resemblance and the ability of both languages to deliver "executable content" over networks, JavaScript and Java are entirely unrelated.

However, Java and JavaScript do provide complimentary capabilities, and thus work very well together. JavaScript can control browser behavior and content but cannot draw graphics or perform networking. Java has no control over the browser as a whole, but can do graphics, networking, and multithreading. In Netscape 3.0, JavaScript can communicate with the Java interpreter built into the browser and can work with and control any Java applets in a Web page.

JavaScript Overview

JavaScript is a simple, interpreted programming language. Client-side JavaScript is JavaScript embedded into HTML Web pages. It allows "executable content" to be distributed over the Internet. (Currently the only JavaScript-enabled browsers are Netscape versions 2.0 and 3.0, and Microsoft Internet Explorer version 3.0.) An example of a client-side JavaScript application appears later in this chapter.

Server-side JavaScript provides an alternative to CGI scripts but goes a step beyond: the code is embedded directly within HTML pages and allows executable server-side scripts to be intermixed with Web content. Server-side JavaScript dynamically generates HTML that is displayed by the client. But its most powerful features come from the server-side objects it has access to. The File object, for example, allows a server-side script to read and write files on the server. Keep in mind, however, that (as of this printing) Netscape's server-side JavaScript product, LiveWire, is still in beta testing, and no other vendors have yet developed products incorporating this technology.

Here's an overview of some of the things you can do with JavaScript:

- Control the appearance and content of HTML documents. You can write arbitrary HTML code into a document as the document is being parsed by the browser. You can also use the JavaScript Document object to generate documents entirely from scratch.

- Control the behavior of the browser. For example, the Window object supports methods (a function/subroutine in JavaScript parlance) to pop up dialog boxes, to create and open/close entirely new browser windows, etc.

- Interact with document content. The JavaScript Document object, and the objects it contains, allow programs to read, and sometimes interact with, portions of the document. It is not possible to read the actual text itself, but, for example, it is possible to obtain a list of all hypertext links in a document. By far the most important capability for interacting with document contents is provided by the Form object, and by the Form element objects it can contain: the Button, Checkbox, Hidden, Password, Radio, Reset, Select, Submit, Text, and Textarea objects. These objects allow you to read and write the values of any input element in any form in the document.

- Interact with the user. An important feature of JavaScript is the ability to define "event handlers"—arbitrary pieces of code to be executed when a particular event occurs (usually a user action). JavaScript can trigger any kind of action in response to user events. For example, code could be written to display a special message in the status line when the user positions the mouse over a hypertext link, or to pop up a confirmation dialog box when the user submits an important form.

- Read and write cookie values, and dynamically generate HTML based on the value of cookies. See Chapter 12, *Cookies*, for more information on cookies.

- Perform arbitrary (mathematical) computation. It also simplifies the process of computing and working with dates and times. (See the section entitled "Date Object" later in this chapter.)

These are just a few of JavaScript's many capabilities. JavaScript can be used to greatly enhance your HTML code.

Client-Side JavaScript Examples

The following example shows a simple JavaScript program, or "script," embedded in a Web page. When loaded into a JavaScript-enabled browser, it produces the output shown in Figure 21-1. Notice that the `<script>` and `</script>` tags are used to embed client-side JavaScript code within an HTML file.

```
<html>
<body>
<script language="JavaScript">;
document.write("<h2>Table of Factorials</h2>");
for(i = 1, fact = 1; i < 10; i++, fact *= i) {
    document.write(i + "! = " + fact);
    document.write("<br>");
}
</script>
</body>
</html>
```

Figure 21-1: A Web page generated with JavaScript

As the example shows, the `document.write()` method can be used, in client-side JavaScript, to dynamically output HTML text that will be parsed and displayed by the Web browser. Besides allowing control over the appearance and content of Web pages, JavaScript provides control over the behavior of the browser, and also over the behavior and content of HTML forms that appear in a Web page.

The use of event handlers can also be powerful. Event handlers specify code to be executed when a particular event occurs. The HTML fragment shown below produces a simple form with a button. The onClick attribute of the <input> button type (an HTML extension added by Netscape specifically for client-side JavaScript) defines an event handler that will be executed when the user clicks the button. As shown in Figure 21-2, the alert() function called by the event handler causes a dialog box to be displayed.

```
<form>
<input type="button"
       value="Click here"
       onClick="alert('You clicked the button')">
</form>
```

Figure 21-2: A JavaScript response to an event

The previous examples highlight only the simplest features of client-side JavaScript. They don't touch on its ability to access the hierarchy of objects that are based on the Web content.

The JavaScript Reference Pages

The following entries summarize the various JavaScript objects and independent functions. The properties, constants, arrays, methods, functions, and event handlers for each object are described in the entry for that object. Thus, if you want to read about the write() method of the Document object (Document.write), look it up in the entry for Document.

If you can't remember what object a method or property, etc., goes with, the following table should help. The left column lists the names of all the functions, properties, etc., and the right column gives the name of the object(s) with which they are associated. Since this table serves as something of a table of contents for this section, object names themselves also appear in the left hand column.

We've tried to cram as much useful information as possible into this chapter. But JavaScript has many intricacies to which we cannot do justice in so short a format. For more complete reference information, as well as an excellent guide to using the language, see *JavaScript: The Definitive Guide*.

For	See Object	For	See Object
abs()	Math	cookie	Document
acos()	Math	cos()	Math
action	Form	current	History
alert()	Window	Date	Date
alinkColor	Document	defaultChecked	Checkbox
Anchor	Anchor		Radio
anchor()	String	defaultSelected	Option
anchors[]	Document	defaultStatus	Window
appCodeName	Navigator	defaultValue	Text
applets[]	Document		Textarea
appName	Navigator	description	MimeType
appVersion	Navigator		Plugin
arguments[]	Function	Document	Document
Array	Array	document	Window
asin()	Math	domain	Document
assign()	Object	E	Math
atan()	Math	Element	Element
atan2()	Math	elements[]	Form
back()	History	embeds[]	Document
bgColor	Document	enabledPlugin	MimeType
big()	String	encoding	Form
blink()	String	escape()	escape()
blur()	FileUpload	eval()	eval()
	Password		Object
	Text	exp()	Math
	Textarea	fgColor	Document
	Window	FileUpload	FileUpload
bold()	String	filename	Plugin
Boolean	Boolean	fixed()	String
border	Image	floor()	Math
Button	Button	focus()	FileUpload
caller	Function		Password
ceil()	Math		Text
charAt()	String		Textarea
Checkbox	Checkbox		Window
checked	Checkbox	fontcolor()	String
	Radio	fontsize()	String
clear()	Document	Form	Form
clearTimeout()	Window	form	Button
close()	Document		Checkbox
	Window		Element
closed	Window		FileUpload
complete	Image		Hidden
confirm()	Window		Password

JavaScript

For	See Object	For	See Object
form *(cont'd)*	Radio	length *(cont'd)*	JavaArray
	Reset		Select
	Select		String
	Submit		Window
	Text	Link	Link
	Textarea	link()	String
forms[]	Document	linkColor	Document
forward()	History	links[]	Document
Frame	Frame	LN10	Math
frames[]	Window	LN2	Math
Function	Function	location	Document
getClass()	getClass()	Location	Location
getDate()	Date	location	Window
getDay()	Date	log()	Math
getHours()	Date	LOG10E	Math
getMinutes()	Date	LOG2E	Math
getMonth()	Date	lowsrc	Image
getSeconds()	Date	Math	Math
getTime()	Date	max()	Math
getTimezoneOffset()	Date	MAX_VALUE	Number
getYear()	Date	method	Form
go()	History	MimeType	MimeType
hash	Location	mimeTypes	Navigator
height	Image	mimeTypes[]	Plugin
Hidden	Hidden	min()	Math
History	History	MIN_VALUE	Number
history	Window	name	Button
host	Location		Checkbox
hostname	Location		Element
href	Location		FileUpload
hspace	Image		Hidden
Image	Image		Image
images[]	Document		MimeType
index	Option		Password
indexOf()	String		Plugin
isNaN()	isNaN()		Radio
italics()	String		Reset
java	java		Select
	Packages		Submit
JavaArray	JavaArray		Text
JavaClass	JavaClass		Textarea
javaEnabled()	Navigator		Window
JavaObject	JavaObject	NaN	Number
JavaPackage	JavaPackage	Navigator	Navigator
join()	Array	navigator	navigator
lastIndexOf()	String	NEGATIVE_INFINITY	Number
lastModified	Document	netscape	netscape
length	Array		Packages
	History	next	History

For	See Object	For	See Object
Number	Number	previous	History
Object	Object	prompt()	Window
onabort()	Image	protocol	Location
onblur()	FileUpload	prototype	Function
	Text	Radio	Radio
	Textarea	random()	Math
	Window	referrer	Document
onchange()	FileUpload	reload()	Location
	Select	replace()	Location
	Text	Reset	Reset
	Textarea	reset()	Form
onclick()	Button	reverse()	Array
	Checkbox	round()	Math
	Link	scroll()	Window
	Radio	search	Location
	Reset	Select	Select
	Submit	select()	Text
onerror()	Image	selected	Option
	Window	selectedIndex	Select
onfocus()	FileUpload	self	Window
	Text	setDate()	Date
	Textarea	setHours()	Date
	Window	setMinutes()	Date
onload()	Image	setMonth()	Date
	Window	setSeconds()	Date
onmouseout()	Link	setTime()	Date
onmouseover()	Link	setTimeout()	Window
onreset()	Form	setYear()	Date
onsubmit()	Form	sin()	Math
onunload()	Window	small()	String
open()	Document	sort()	Array
	Window	split()	String
opener	Window	sqrt()	Math
Option	Option	SQRT1_2	Math
options[]	Select	SQRT2	Math
Packages	Packages	src	Image
parent	Window	status	Window
parse()	Date	strike()	String
parseFloat()	parseFloat()	String	String
parseInt()	parseInt()	sub()	String
Password	Password	Submit	Submit
pathname	Location	submit()	Form
PI	Math	substring()	String
Plugin	Plugin	suffixes	MimeType
plugins	Document	sun	Packages
	Navigator		sun
port	Location	sup()	String
POSITIVE_INFINITY	Number	taint()	taint()
pow()	Math	taintEnabled()	Navigator

JavaScript

For	See Object	For	See Object
tan()	Math	UTC()	Date
target	Form	value	Button
	Link		Checkbox
text	Option		Element
Text	Text		FileUpload
Textarea	Textarea		Hidden
title	Document		Option
toGMTString()	Date		Password
toLocaleString()	Date		Radio
toLowerCase()	String		Reset
top	Window		Submit
toString()	Boolean		Text
	Function		Textarea
	Number	valueOf()	Object
	Object	vlinkColor	Document
toUpperCase()	String	vspace	Image
type	Element	width	Image
	Select	Window	Window
unescape()	unescape()	window	Window
untaint()	untaint()	write()	Document
URL	Document	writeln()	Document
userAgent	Navigator		

Anchor Object

Represents a named position (of an HTML document) that may be the target or destination of a hypertext link. A hypertext link may refer to an anchor by using its name after a # character in a URL. In Netscape 2.0, the elements of the `document.anchor[]` array are set to `null`, so it is not possible to actually obtain an Anchor object. See also Document.Link.

```
document.anchors.length       // number of anchors in the document
document.anchors[i]           // one of the Anchor objects
```

An Anchor object is created by any standard HTML `<a>` tag that contains a `<name>` attribute:

```
<a
  name="anchor_name"          links may refer to this anchor by this name
  [ href=URL ]                an anchor may also be a link
  [ target="window_name" ]    links may refer to other windows
>
anchor HTML text
</a>
```

Array Object

Creates and initializes an array. Along with the usual array capabilities that all JavaScript objects have, the Array object provides additional array functionality: a constructor function for initializing arrays, an automatically updated `length` field that stores the size of the array, and `join()`, `reverse()`, and `sort()` methods that manipulate the elements of an array. Available in Netscape 3.0. See also Object.

`new Array()`	*with no arguments, length field is set to 0*
`new Array(size)`	*size = number of elements; sets length*
`new Array(element0, element1, ..., elementn)`	
	length set to number of elements

Properties

`length`

Read/write integer specifying the number of elements in the array, or, when the array does not have contiguous elements, a number one larger than the index of the last element in the array. The length property of a new array is initialized when the array is created with the `Array()` constructor method. Adding new elements to an array created with the `Array()` constructor updates the `length`, if necessary:

`a = new Array();`	*a.length initialized to 0*
`b = new Array(10);`	*b.length initialized to 10*
`c = new Array("one", "two", "three");`	*c.length initialized to 3*
`c[3] = "four";`	*c.length updated to 4*
`c[10] = "blastoff";`	*c.length becomes 11*

You can also set the value of the `length` property to change the size of an array (i.e., truncate elements or add "undefined" ones).

Methods

`join`

Converts each of the elements of an array to a string, and then concatenates those strings, inserting the specified *separator* string between the elements. Returns the resulting string. You can split a string up into array elements—with the `split()` method of the String object.

```
array.join()
array.join(separator)   if no separator, the empty string is used
```

`reverse`

Reverse, in place (i.e., without creating a new array), the order of the elements of an array.

`sort`

With no arguments, sorts alphabetically (by character encoding); elements are first converted to strings, if necessary, so that they can be compared. To sort the array elements in some other order, you must supply a function that compares two values and returns a number indicating their relative order.

```
array.sort()
array.sort(orderfunc)     orderfunc - optional comparison function
```

The comparison function should take two arguments, *a* and *b*, and should:

- Return a value less than zero if, according to your sort criteria, *a* is less than *b*, and should appear before *b* in the sorted array.

- Return zero if *a* and *b* are equivalent for the purposes of this sort.

- Return a value greater than zero if *a* is greater than *b* for the purposes of the sort.

Boolean Object

An object wrapper around the boolean value; exists solely to provide a `toString()` method to convert boolean values to strings. When the `toString()` method is invoked to convert a boolean value to a string (and it is often invoked implicitly by JavaScript), JavaScript internally converts the boolean value to a transient Boolean object, on which the method can be invoked.

You can create Boolean objects that are not transient by calling the `Boolean()` constructor method:

```
new Boolean(value)
```

The argument is the *value* to be held by the Boolean object. This will be converted to a boolean value, if necessary. The values 0, `null`, and the empty string `""` are all converted to `false`. All other values, including the string "false," are converted to `true`. Available in Netscape 3.0. See also Object.

Methods

`toString()`
> Returns `true` or `false`, depending on the boolean value represented by the Boolean object.

`valueOf()`
> Returns the boolean value represented by the Boolean object.

Button Object

Represents a graphical pushbutton in a form within an HTML document. Use a Button object whenever you want to allow the user to trigger some action on your Web page. Note that the Submit and Reset objects are types of Button objects that submit a form and reset a form's values. Often these default actions are sufficient for a form, and you do not need to create any other types of buttons. Available in Netscape 2.0; enhanced in 3.0. See also Element, Form, Reset, Submit.

```
form.button_name
form.elements[i]
form.elements['button_name']
```

Properties

form

Read-only reference to the Form object that contains the specified *button* object.

name

Set by the name attribute of the HTML <input> tag that creates the button, this read-only string property provides the name of the button.

```
form.button_name
form.elements['button_name']
```

type

See the type property of the Element object (Element.type).

value

Set by the value attribute of the HTML <input> tag that creates the button, this read-only string property provides text displayed in the Button object.

Event Handlers

onClick()

Invoked when the button is clicked; defined by the onClick attribute of the HTML <input> tag. Value may be any number of JavaScript statements, separated by semicolons, that are executed when the user clicks the button.

```
<INPUT TYPE="button"          a definition of the handler
       value="button-text"
       onClick="handler-statements">


button.onclick                a reference to the handler
button.onclick()              an explicit invocation of the handler
```

HTML syntax

A Button object is created with a standard HTML <input> tag, with the addition of the onClick attribute:

```
<form>
   ...
  <input
    type="button"             specifies that this is a button
    value="label"             the text that is to appear within the button;
                              specifies the value property
    [ name="name" ]           a name that can later be used to refer to the button;
                              specifies the name property
    [ onClick="handler" ]     JavaScript statements to be executed
                              when the button is clicked
  >
   ...
</form>
```

JavaScript

Checkbox Object

Represents a single graphical checkbox in an HTML form. Note that the text that appears next to the checkbox is not part of the Checkbox object itself, and must be specified external to the Checkbox's HTML <input> tag. The onClick event handler allows you to specify JavaScript code to be executed when the Checkbox is checked or "un-checked." The value of the checked property gives the state of the Checkbox; it can also be set to change the state. Available but buggy in Netscape 2.0; enhanced in 3.0. See also Element, Form, Radio.

A Checkbox object with a unique name may be referenced in any of these ways:

```
form.checkbox_name
form.elements[i]
form.elements['checkbox_name']
```

When a form contains a group of checkboxes with the same name, they are placed in an array, and may be referenced as follows:

```
form.checkbox_name[j]
form.checkbox_name.length
form.elements[i][j]
form.elements[i].length
form.elements['checkbox_name'][j]
form.elements['checkbox_name'].length
```

Properties

checked
> Read/write Boolean property that specifies whether the Checkbox is checked (true) or not (false). Setting the checked property changes the appearance of the Checkbox but does not cause the onclick() event handler to be invoked.

defaultChecked
> Read-only Boolean property that represents the Checkbox's initial state. May be specified using the checked attribute in the HTML <input> tag. Can be used to reset a Checkbox to its default state.

form
> Read-only reference to the Form object that contains the Checkbox.

name
> Read-only string, set by the HTML name attribute, that specifies the name of the Checkbox object (or array of Checkbox objects).

type
> See the type property of the Element object (Element.type).

value
> Read/write string that specifies the text that is passed to the Web server if the Checkbox is checked when the form is submitted. The initial value of value is specified by the HTML value attribute. If no value attribute is specified, then the default value string is "on."

Event handlers

onclick()

Invoked when the user clicks on a Checkbox; it is defined by the HTML onClick attribute. The value of this attribute may be any number of JavaScript statements, separated by semicolons, which are executed when the user clicks on the Checkbox.

```
<INPUT type="checkbox"              a definition of the handler
       onClick="handler-statements">
```

```
checkbox.onclick                    a reference to the handler
checkbox.onclick();                 an explicit invocation of the handler
```

HTML syntax

A Checkbox object is created with a standard HTML `<input>` tag, with the addition of the new `onClick` attribute. Multiple Checkbox objects are often created in groups by specifying multiple `<input>` tags which have the same `name` attribute.

```
<form>
    ...
  <input
    type="checkbox"         specifies that this is a Checkbox
    [ name="name" ]         a name that can later be used to refer to this Checkbox
                            or to the group of Checkboxes with this name;
                            specifies the name property
    [ value="value" ]       the value returned when this Checkbox is selected;
                            specifies the value property
    [ checked ]             specifies that the Checkbox is initially checked
                            Specifies the defaultChecked property
    [ onClick="handler" ]   JavaScript statements to be executed when the
                            Checkbox is clicked
  >
  label                     the HTML text that should appear next to the Checkbox
    ...
</form>
```

Date Object

With no arguments, the `Date()` method creates a `Date` object set to the current date and time. Otherwise, the arguments to `Date()` specify the date, and, optionally, the time, for the new object. The Date object is built into JavaScript and does not have an HTML analog. Most of the Date object methods are invoked through an instance of the Date object. For example:

```
d = new Date();            //get today's date and time
system.write('Today is: " + d.toLocaleString());// and print it out
```

This syntax for creating Date objects assumes that date and time values are specified in local time. When your code must work the same way regardless of the time zone in which it is run, you should specify all your hard-coded dates in the GMT (or UTC) time zone. The most common use of the Data object is to subtract the millisecond representations of the current time from some other time to determine the difference.

Buggy to the point of uselessness in Netscape 2.0. See also Date.parse, Date.UTC(). (Note that the `Date.parse()` and `Date.UTC()` functions, though related to Date, do not operate on the Date object.)

To create a Date object, use one of the following five syntaxes. In the third through fifth syntaxes, the specified times are interpreted as local (not GMT) times.

```
new Date();
new Date(milliseconds)              milliseconds between date and 12AM 1/1/70
new Date(date_string);              date_string = month_name dd, yy [hh:mm[:ss]]
new Date(year, month, day);         year minus 1900; month 0-11; day 1-31
new Date(year, month, day, hours, minutes, seconds)   24-hour clock
```

Methods

getDate()
> Returns the day of the month of a Date object. Return values are between 1 and 31.

getDay()
> Returns the day of the week of a Date object. Return values are between 0 (Sunday) and 6 (Saturday).

getHours()
> Returns the hours field of a Date object. Return values are between 0 (midnight) and 23 (11 PM).

getMinutes()
> Returns the minutes field of a Date object. Return values are between 0 and 59.

getMonth()
> Returns the month field of a Date object. Return values are between 0 (January) and 11 (December).

getSeconds()
> Returns the seconds field of a Date object. Return values are between 0 and 59.

getTime()
> Returns the internal, millisecond representation of a Date object (i.e., the number of milliseconds between midnight GMT on 1/1/1970 and the specified date).

getTimezoneOffset()
> Returns the difference in minutes between this date (in the local time zone) and GMT. Tells you what time zone the JavaScript code is running in. Since getTimezoneOffset is invoked through a Date object, but doesn't reference the Date object, it should actually be its own function.

getYear()
> Returns the year field of a Date object. Return value is the year minus 1900 (e.g., 96 for 1996).

parse()
>   Parses a string representation of a date and returns it in millisecond format.

setDate()
>   Sets the day of the month field of a Date object.

>   *date*.setDate(*day_of_month*) //*day_of_month* is 1-31

setHours()
>   Sets the hour field of a Date object.

>   *date*.setHours(*hours*) //*hours* is integer betw 0 (midnight)
>   and 23 (11pm)

setMinutes()
>   Sets the minutes field of a Date object.

>   *date*.setMinutes(*minutes*) //*minutes* is integer betw 0 and 59

setMonth()
>   Sets the month field of a Date object.

>   *date*.setMonth(*month*) //*month* is integer betw 0 (Jan) and 11 (Dec)

setSeconds()
>   Sets the seconds field of a Date object.

>   *date*.setSeconds(*seconds*) //*seconds* is integer betw 0 and 59

setTime()
>   Sets a Date object in the milliseconds between the desired date/time and midnight GMT on January 1, 1970. Representing a date in this millisecond format makes it independent of time zone.

>   *date*.setTime(*milliseconds*)

setYear()
>   Sets the year field of a Date object.

>   *date*.setYear(*year*)   //*year* is year minus 1900; e.g. 96 for 1996

toGMTString()
>   Converts a Date to a string, using the GMT time zone; format of string varies slightly according to platform.

toLocaleString()
>   Converts a Date to a string, using the local time zone; uses local conventions for data and time formatting.

UTC()
>   Converts a numeric date and time specification to millisecond format.

Date.parse() Method

`Date.parse()` is a function that is related to the Date object, but it is not a method of (or invoked on) the Date object. `Date.parse()` parses a date/time string and returns the number of milliseconds between the specified date/time and midnight, January 1st, 1970, GMT. This number can be used directly, used to create a new Date object, or to set the date in an existing Date object with `Date.setTime()`.

`Date.parse()` understands the IETF standard date format used in email and other Internet communications (e.g., Wed, 8 May 1996 17:41:46 -0400), as well as partial dates of this format; it also understands the GMT time zone, and the standard abbreviations for the time zones of the U.S. Buggy in Netscape 2.0. See also Date, Date.UTC().

    date.parse(date_string)

Date.UTC() Method

`Date.UTC()` is a function that is related to the Date object, but is not a method of the Date object or invoked on it; it is always invoked as `Date.UTC()`, not as `date.UTC()`, on some object *date*.

`Date.UTC` converts time in UTC (Universal Coordinated Time) format (i.e., in the GMT zone) to milliseconds. It returns the number of milliseconds between midnight on January 1st, 1970, UTC and the time specified by the arguments. This can be used by the `Date()` constructor method and by the `Date.setTime()` method.

For arguments, use: *year* minus 1900 (e.g., 96 for 1996); *month* 0 (January) through 11 (December); 24-hour clock for hour (0-23). In Netscape 2.0, `Date.UTC()` does not compute the correct number of milliseconds. See also Date, Date.parse.

    date.UTC(year, month, day, [, hours [, minutes [, seconds]]]);

To create a Date object using a UTC time specification, you can use code like this:

    d = new Date(Date.UTC(96, 4, 8, 16, 30));

Document Object

The currently displayed HTML document. An instance of the Document object is stored in the document field of the Window object. As a special case, when referring to the Document object of the current window (i.e., the window in which the JavaScript code is executing), you can omit the *window* reference and simply use document. Available in Netscape 2.0. See also Form, Frame, Window.

```
window.document
document                    // to refer to Document obj of current window
```

Properties

Note that for all attributes to set a color, the value can be one of the standard color names recognized by JavaScript, or an RGB value in six hexadecimal digits (*RRGGBB*).

alinkColor

> String that specifies the color of activated links (i.e., links being selected by user). Can be set directly in the document <head>, or inherited from the alink attribute in the <body>.

anchors[]

> An array of Anchor objects, one for each anchor (i.e., hypertext target) in the document.

anchors.length

> Read-only integer specifying the number of elements in the anchors[] array.

applets[]

> An array of Java objects, one for each <applet> that appears in the document.

applets.length

> A read-only integer specifying the number of elements in the applets[] array.

bgColor

> String that specifies the background color of the document. Can be set directly at any point in document, or inherited from the bgcolor attribute in the <body>. Buggy in Netscape 2.0.

cookie

> A string that is the value of a cookie associated with this document. String property that allows you to read, create, modify, and delete the cookie(s) that apply to the current document. A "cookie" is a small amount of named data stored by the Web browser so that it can use data input on one page in another page, or recall user preferences across Web-browsing sessions.

> document.cookie

> The read and write values of the cookie property generally differ. In a JavaScript expression, the cookie property returns a string containing all the cookies from the current document, in *name=value* pairs (separated by semicolons). Use String.indexOf() and String.substring() to determine the value of a particular cookie. Since cookies cannot contain any semicolons, commas, or whitespace, they are commonly encoded using escape() before storing and decoded using unescape() after retrieving.

To associate a cookie value with the current document for the current Web browsing session, set *document*.cookie to a string of the form *name=value*. To create a cookie that can last across browser sessions, include an expiration date by setting *document*.cookie to a string of the form:

   name=value; expires=*date*

date should be a date specification in the format written by Date.toGMT-String().

domain
   String that specifies the Internet domain which the document is from; used for security purposes.

embeds[]
   An array of Java objects, one for each <embed> tag in the document.

embeds.length
   Read-only integer that specifies the number of elements in the embeds[] array.

fgColor
   String that specifies the default color of document text. Can be set directly in the document <head>, or inherited from the text attribute in the <body>.

forms[]
   An array of Form objects, one for each <form> that appears in the document.

forms.length
   Read-only integer specifying the number of elements in the forms[] array.

images[]
   An array of Image objects, one for each image embedded in the document with the <img> tag.

images.length
   The number of elements in the images[] array.

lastModified
   Read-only string that contains the (local) date and time at which *document* was most recently modified (derived from the HTTP header).

linkColor
   String that specifies the color of unvisited links. Can be set directly in the document <head>, or inherited from the link attribute in the <body>.

links[]
   An array of Link objects, one for each hypertext link in the document.

links.length
   Read-only integer specifying the number of elements in the links[] array.

location
   Synonym for the URL property. Use URL instead because it is less likely to be confused with the Window.location property.

plugins[]
   Synonym for the embeds[] array.

`plugins.length`

The number of elements in the `plugins[]` or `embeds[]` array.

`referrer`

Read-only string that contains the URL of the document from which the current *document* was reached.

`title`

Read-only string that specifies the `<title>` of the document.

URL

Read-only string that specifies the URL of the document that contained the link that referred to the current document.

`vlinkColor`

String that specifies the color of visited links. Can be set directly in the document `<head>`, or inherited from the `vlink` attribute in the `<body>`.

Methods

`clear()`

Clears the window or frame that contains *document*.

`close()`

Displays any output to *document* that has been written but not yet displayed, and closes the output stream.

`open()`

Opens a stream to *document*, so that subsequent *document*.`write()` calls can append data to the document.

`write()`

Appends each of its arguments, in order, to *document*. Numeric values are converted to a string representation; boolean values are appended as either "true" or "false." When invoked in scripts that are run while the document is loading, you can call `document.write()` to insert dynamically generated HTML text into the document.

> *document*.write(*value,...*)

When invoked within a `<script>` tag on an HTML document that is being parsed, arguments are appended at the location of the tag; when invoked on a document that is not being parsed, the document must first be opened with `Document.open()`.

`writeln()`

Identical to `write()`, except that it appends a newline character to the output.

Event handlers

The following event handlers are, strictly speaking, properties of Window, not Document:

`onload`

Invoked when the document is fully loaded. Specified by the `onLoad` attribute of `<body>`.

onUnload
>   Invoked when the document is unloaded. Specified by the `onUnload` attribute of `<body>`.

The Document object obtains values for a number of its properties from attributes of the HTML `<body>` tag. Further, the HTML contents of a document appear within the `<body>` and `</body>` tags.

```
<body
    [ BACKGROUND="imageURL" ]       a background image for the document
    [ BGCOLOR="color" ]             a background color for the document
    [ text="color" ]                the foreground color of the document's text
    [ LINK="color" ]                the color for unvisited links
    [ alink="color" ]               the color for activated links
    [ VLINK="color" ]               the color for visited links
    [ onLoad="handler" ]            JavaScript to run when the document is loaded
    [ onUnload="handler" ]          JavaScript to run when the document is unloaded
>

        HTML document contents go here

</body>
```

Element Object

Technically speaking, there is no single Element object in JavaScript. Each of the various types of form elements are types of Element objects. Available in Netscape 2.0. See also Button, Checkbox, FileUpload, Form, Hidden, Password, Radio, Reset, Select, Submit, Text, Textarea.

```
form.elements[i]
form.name
```

Properties

form
    Read-only reference to Form object that contains this element.

name
    Read-only string (from the HTML name attribute) that specifies the name of this element. The name of a form element is used for two purposes. First, it is used when the form is submitted. Data for each element in the form is usually submitted in the format:

```
name=value  // name and value are encoded as necessary
                   for transmission
```

If a name is not specified for a form element, then the data for that element cannot be meaningfully submitted to a Web server. The second use of the name property is to refer to a form element in JavaScript code.

type

Read-only string property (Netscape 3.0 and later) that specifies the type of the form element. The value depends on the input element:

Object Type	HTML Tag	type Property
Button	`<input type=button>`	"button"
Checkbox	`<input type=checkbox>`	"checkbox"
FileUpload	`<input type=file>`	"file"
Hidden	`<input type=hidden>`	"hidden"
Password	`<input type=password>`	"password"
Radio	`<input type=radio>`	"radio"
Reset	`<input type=reset>`	"reset"
Select	`<select>`	"select-one"
Select	`<select multiple>`	"select-multiple"
Submit	`<input type=submit>`	"submit"
Text	`<input type=text>`	"text"
Textarea	`<textarea>`	"textarea"

value

Read/write string property that specifies the value to be sent to the server for this element when the form is submitted; initial value specified by the HTML value attribute. For Button, Submit, and Reset objects, the value property specifies the text to appear within the button.

escape() Function

The built-in `escape()` function creates and returns a new string that contains an encoded version of *s* to allow transmission of data. A common use of `escape()` is to encode cookie values, which have restrictions on the punctuation characters they may contain. Available in Netscape 2.0. See also String, unescape().

escape(*s*)   *s is the string to be "escaped" or encoded*

All spaces, punctuation, and accented characters are converted to the form %*xx*, where *xx* is two hexadecimal digits that represent the ISO-8859-1 (Latin-1) encoding of the character. For example:

```
escape("Hello World!");
```

yields the string:

```
Hello%20World%21
```

eval() Function

A built-in JavaScript function; not a method of any object. Executes the code in its string argument *code*, which may contain one or more JavaScript statements (separated by semicolons). You can also use `eval()` to evaluate a JavaScript expression rather than execute a statement. Returns the value of the last expression in *code* that it evaluates. `eval()` allows a JavaScript program to dynamically modify the code that it executes.

Crashes Netscape 2.0 on 16-bit Windows (version 3.1) platforms. A possible workaround: use `Window.setTimeout()` with a zero-millisecond delay. In 3.0, `eval` has become a method of the Object object. See also Object, Window.

```
eval(code)
```

FileUpload Object

Represents a file upload input element in a form. It looks like a text input field, with the addition of a Browse... button that opens a directory browser. Entering a filename into a FileUpload object (either directly or through the browser) causes Netscape to submit the contents of that file along with the form (which must use "multipart/form-data" encoding and the post method). The FileUpload object does not recognize the HTML `value` attribute to specify an initial value for the input field. For security reasons, only the user may enter a filename; JavaScript may not enter text into the FileUpload field in any way. Available in Netscape 2.0; enhanced in 3.0. See also Element, Form, Text.

```
form.name
form.elements[i]
form.elements['name']
```

Properties

`form`
> Read-only reference to the Form object that contains the FileUpload object.

`name`
> Read-only string, set by the HTML `name` attribute, that specifies the name of the FileUpload object. This *name* can also be used to reference the FileUpload object as a property of its form. (For example, if the `name` property of a File-Upload object in form `foo` is "info," then `foo.info` refers to the FileUpload object.)

`type`
> Read-only string that specifies the type of this form element. For FileUpload objects, it has the value "file." Available in Netscape 3.0 and later.

`value`
> Read-only string that specifies the value contained in the input field (which is also the value sent to the server when the form is submitted). In Netscape 2.0, this field is always blank. In 3.0 any filename specified by the user may be read, but the property still may not be set.

Methods

blur()

Removes the keyboard focus from the FileUpload object. Until focus is granted to some other form element, the user's keystrokes may be ignored by all elements. Due to a bug in Netscape 2.0, the `blur()` method invokes the `onblur()` event handler.

focus()

Sets the keyboard focus to the FileUpload object. When focus is set, all keystrokes are automatically entered into this object.

Event handlers

onblur()

Defined by the HTML onBlur attribute, the value of which may be any number of JavaScript statements, separated by semicolons; these statements are executed whenever the FileUpload object loses keyboard focus because of a user action. `onblur` should only be invoked by direct user actions, but a bug in Netscape 2.0 causes it to be invoked by the `FileUpload.blur()` method.

onchange()

Invoked when the user changes the value in the FileUpload object and moves the keyboard focus elsewhere. This event handler is not invoked for every keystroke in the FileUpload object, but only when the user completes an edit.

onfocus()

Invoked when a user action causes the FileUpload object to gain the keyboard focus.

HTML syntax

A FileUpload object is created with a standard HTML `<input>` tag, with the addition of optional attributes for event-handlers:

```
<form ENCtype="multipart/form-data" method=post>  required attributes
    ...
    <input
        type="file"                 specifies that this is a FileUpload object
        [ name="name" ]             a name that can later be used to refer to this object;
                                    specifies the name property
    [ size=integer ]                how many characters wide the object is
    [ maxlength=integer ]           max allowed number of input characters
    [ onBlur="handler" ]            the onblur() event handler
    [ onChange="handler" ]          the onchange() event handler
    [ onFocus="handler" ]           the onfocus() event handler
    ...
```

JavaScript

Form Object

Represents an HTML `<form>` in a document. Each form in a document is represented as an element of the `Document.forms[]` array. Named forms are also represented by the *form_name* property of their document, where *form_name* is the name specified in the name attribute of the <form> tag. Available in Netscape 2.0. See also Button, Checkbox, Element, FileUpload, Hidden, Password, Radio, Reset, Select, Submit, Text, Textarea.

```
document.form_name
document.forms[form_number]
document.forms.length
```

The elements of a form (buttons, input fields, check boxes, and so on) are collected in the Form.elements[] array. Named elements, like named forms, can also be referenced directly by name—the element name is used as a property name of the Form object. Thus, to refer to a Text object element named "phone" within a form named "questionnaire," you might use the JavaScript expression:

```
document.questionnaire.phone
```

Properties

action
> Read/write string specifying the URL to which the form is to be submitted. Initially specified by the action attribute of the <form> HTML tag.

elements[]
> An array of input elements that appear in the form. Each element is a Button, Checkbox, Hidden, Password, Radio, Reset, Select, Submit, Text, or Textarea object.

elements.length
> The number of items in the elements[] array.

encoding
> Read/write string that specifies the encoding method used for form data. Initially specified by the enctype attribute of the <form> HTML tag. The default encoding of "application/x-www-form-urlencoded" is almost always appropriate.

method
> Read/write string that specifies the technique for submitting the form. It should have the value "get" or "post". Initially specified by the method attribute.

target
> Read/write string that specifies the name of the frame or window in which the results of submitting a form should be displayed. Initially specified by the target attribute. The special names "_top", "_parent", "_self", and "_blank" are also supported for the target property and the target attribute.

Methods

reset()
> Resets each of the input elements of the form to their default values.

submit()
> Method that submits a form.

Event Handlers

onreset

> Invoked just before the elements of the form are reset. Specified by the onReset attribute.

onsubmit

> Invoked just before the form is submitted. Specified by the onSubmit attribute of the <form> tag. This event handler allows form entries to be validated before being submitted.

HTML syntax

A Form object is created with a standard HTML <form> tag. JavaScript adds the optional onSubmit event handler attribute to this tag. The form contains any input elements created with the <input> tag between <form> and </form>.

```
<form
    [ name="form_name" ]          to name the form in JavaScript
    [ target="window_name" ]      the name of the window for responses
    [ action="url" ]              the URL to which the form is submitted
    [ method=(get|post) ]         the method of form submission
    [ enctype="encoding" ]        how the form data is encoded
    [ onSubmit="handler" ]        a handler invoked when form is submitted
>

                                  form text and <input> tags go here

</form>
```

Frame Object

Though the Frame object is sometimes referred to, there is, strictly speaking, no such object. All frames within a browser window are instances of the Window object, and they contain the same properties and support the same methods, and event handlers as the Window object does. See the Window object, and its properties, methods, and event handlers for details.

Note, however, that there are a few practical differences between Window objects that represent top-level browser windows and those that represent frames within a browser window:

- When the defaultStatus property is set for a frame, the specified status message is only visible when the mouse is within that frame.

- The top and parent properties of a top-level browser window always refer to the top-level window itself. These properties are only really useful for frames.

- The close() method is not useful for Window objects that are frames.

Available in Netscape 2.0.

```
window.frames[i]
window.frames.length
frames[i]
frames.length
```

Function Object

An object wrapper around the basic function data type; this object type exists so that functions can have properties and methods associated with them. When a function value is used in an "object context," i.e., when you attempt to invoke a method or read a property of a function, JavaScript internally converts the function value into a temporary Function object, so that the method can be invoked or the property value read.

```
function functionname(argname1 [, . . . argname_n)]
{
        body                 // body of function
}
```

To create a new function, use the Function() constructor method:

```
new Function([argname1 [, ..., argname_n]], body)
```

Functions defined in this way are sometimes called "anonymous" because they are not given a name when they are created. Just as JavaScript converts from a function value to a Function object whenever necessary, so it will convert from a Function object (created with the Function() constructor) to a function value whenever you use the object in a function value context—i.e., whenever you invoke it with the () operator. This conversion from Function object to function value is done by the valueOf() method.

Since there is no special keyword in JavaScript that refers to the Function object of the currently executing function, you must refer to Function objects by name, as in:

```
function myfunc()
{
    if (myfunc.arguments.length == 0) return;
        ...
}
```

Enhanced in Netscape 3.0. See also the Object Object.

Properties

arguments[]
:   An array of arguments that were passed to the function. Can only be accessed from within the body of a function. Note that the arguments[] property is actually just a reference to the Function object itself. Thus, instead of using function.arguments[i] and function.arguments.length, you can use function[i] and function.length.

arguments.length
:   The number of elements in the arguments[] array.

caller
> A reference to the Function object that invoked this one, or `null` if the function is invoked at the top level. Can only be accessed from within the body of a function. You can print out the `caller` for debugging purposes, and you can even invoke that function through the `caller` property.

prototype
> An object which, for constructor functions, defines properties and methods that will be shared by all objects created with that constructor function. Any objects created through a constructor function will "inherit" the properties and methods defined in that prototype.

Methods

toString()
> Converts the Function object to a string by returning the function definition (a string of valid JavaScript code).

valueOf()
> Returns the function value contained in a Function object. See the Object.valueOf() method.

---

getClass() Function

A function that takes a `JavaObject` object and returns the JavaClass object of that JavaObject. Available in Netscape 3.0. See also JavaArray, JavaClass, JavaObject, JavaPackage, and Packages.

```
getClass(javaobj)
```

Usage

Don't confuse the JavaScript `getClass()` function with the `getClass` method of all Java objects. Similarly, don't confuse the JavaScript JavaClass object with the Java *java.lang.Class* class.

Consider the Java rectangle object created with the following line:

```
var r = new java.awt.Rectangle();
```

r is a JavaScript variable that holds a JavaObject object. Calling the JavaScript function `getClass()` returns a JavaClass object that represents the *java.awt.Rectangle* class:

```
var c = getClass(r);
```

You can see that this is so by comparing this JavaClass object to `java.awt.Rectangle`:

```
if (c == java.awt.Rectangle) ...
```

The Java `getClass()` method is invoked differently and performs an entirely different function:

```
c = r.getClass();
```

After executing the above line of code, c is a JavaObject that represents a *java.lang.Class* object. This *java.lang.Class* object is a Java object that is a Java representation of the `java.awt.Rectangle` class. See your Java documentation for details on what you can do with the `java.lang.Class` class.

To summarize, you can see that the following expression will always evaluate to `true` for any JavaObject o:

```
(getClass(o.getClass()) == java.lang.Class)
```

Hidden Object

An invisible form element that allows arbitrary data to be transmitted to the server when the form is submitted. You can use a Hidden object when you want to transmit additional information, besides the user's input data, to the server. (Cookies can also be used to transmit data from client-to-server; however, cookies are persistent on the client side.)

When an HTML document is generated on the fly by a server, another use of Hidden form elements is to transmit data from the server to the client for later processing by JavaScript on the user's side.

Hidden objects can also be useful for communication between CGI scripts, even without the intervention of JavaScript on the client side. In this usage, one CGI script generates a dynamic HTML page containing hidden data, which is then submitted back to a second CGI script. This hidden data can communicate state information, such as the results of submission of a previous form. Enhanced in Netscape 3.0. See also Element, Form, Document.

```
form.name
form.elements[i]
form.elements['name']
```

Properties

`form`
> Read-only reference to the Form object that contains the Hidden object.

`name`
> Read-only string, set by the HTML name attribute, that specifies the name of the Hidden object. This is also the *name* that can be used to reference the Hidden object as a property of its form.

`type`
> Read-only string that specifies the type of this form element. For Hidden objects, it has the value "hidden." Available in Netscape 3.0 and later.

value

Read/write string, initially set by the HTML **value** attribute, which specifies arbitrary data to be transmitted to the server when the form is submitted. This data is never visible to the user.

HTML syntax

A Hidden object is created with a standard HTML **<input>** tag:

```
<form>
   . . .
  <input
    type="hidden"              specifies that this is a Hidden object
    [ name="name" ]            a name that can later be used to refer to this object;
                               specifies the name property
    [ value="value" ]          the value transmitted when the form is submitted;
                               specifies the initial value of the value property

  >
   . . .
</form>
```

History Object

Read-only array of strings that specify the URLs that have been previously visited by the browser. The contents of this list are equivalent to the URLs listed in Netscape's Go menu. You can use the History object to implement your own Forward and Back buttons, or other navigation controls, within a window.

In Netscape 2.0, and in 3.0 without data tainting, JavaScript can use the **length** property to determine the number of entries on the History object's URL list, and can use the **back()**, **forward()**, and **go()** methods to cause the browser to revisit any of the URLs on the list, but it cannot directly or indirectly read the URLs stored in the array.

In 3.0 and later, when the data tainting security model is enabled, the elements of the array are available and may be read (but not changed). Additional properties (described below) are also available. See also Location.

```
window.history
frame.history
history
```

Properties

current

Read-only string that specifies the URL of the current document. Only available with data tainting enabled in Netscape 3.0.

length

The number of URLs that are saved in the History object. (Note that the History object does not provide a property that specifies the position of the current URL in the history list, and because there is no method to move to an absolute position in the history list, only methods to move relative to the current position.)

next
> Read-only string that specifies the URL of the document after this one in the history list. Only available with data tainting enabled in Netscape 3.0.

previous
> Read-only string that specifies the URL of the document before this one in the history list. Only available with data tainting enabled in Netscape 3.0.

Methods

back()
> Go backwards to a previously visited URL (if any). Has the same effect as a user's click on the Netscape Back button; it's also equivalent to:
>
> ```
> history.go(-1);
> ```

forward()
> Go forward to a previously visited URL (if any). Calling this method has the same effect as a user's click on the Netscape Forward button; it's also equivalent to:
>
> ```
> history.go(1);
> ```

go()
> Go to a previously visited URL (if any).
>
> ```
> history.go(relative_position);
> history.go(target_string);          //* buggy in 2.0 */
> ```
>
> The first form of the History.go() method takes an integer argument (positive argument=forward; negative argument=back) and causes the browser to visit the URL that is the specified number of positions distant in the history list maintained by the History object. Thus history.go(-1) is equivalent to history.back() (and produces the same effect as a user click on the Netscape Back button). Similarly, history.go(3) is equivalent to calling history.forward() three times. In the second syntax, the *target_string* argument is supposed to make the browser revisit the first (i.e., most recent) URL that contains the specified string. Caveat: This form of the method is buggy in Netscape 2.0 and may cause the browser to crash.

toString()
> Returns a string of HTML text. When this string is formatted by a browser (i.e., written with document.write()) it displays the browser history as a table of URLs, each with an appropriate hyperlink. Only available with data tainting enabled in Netscape 3.0.

Image Object

The Image objects in the document.images[] array represent the images embedded in an HTML document using the <img> tag. Only two properties are writeable: src and lowsrc. When you set src, the browser will load the image specified by the new value of the src property, or by the lowsrc property, for low-resolution monitors. (Note that lowsrc must be set before src because the latter starts the download of the new image.) Setting src can be used to change the graphics on a page in response to user actions (e.g., changing the image on a button to indicate that it is or is not available for selection based on whether the user has input certain information).

Available in Netscape 3.0. (Note that because of a bug in Netscape 2.0, all images in a page that contains JavaScript must have width and height attributes specified, even though the Image object is not available in 2.0.) See also Document.

```
document.images[i]
document.images.length
document.image-name
```

You can dynamically create Image objects using the Image() constructor method:

```
new Image([width, height]);
```

Properties

border
> Read-only integer that specifies the width, in pixels, of the border around an image. Its value is set by the border attribute.

complete
> Read-only boolean that specifies whether the image is completely loaded yet; if an error occurs or the loading is aborted, the complete property will be set to true.

height
> Read-only integer that specifies the height, in pixels, of the image. Its value is set by the height attribute.

hspace
> Read-only integer that specifies the amount of extra horizontal space, in pixels, inserted on the left and right of the image. Its value is set by the hspace attribute.

lowsrc
> Read/write string that specifies the URL of an alternate image, suitable for display at low resolutions. Its initial value is set by the lowsrc attribute. Setting this property has no immediate effect; however, if src is set, a new image will be loaded, and on low-resolution systems, the current value of lowsrc will be used instead of the newly updated value of src.

name

Read-only string, specified by the HTML `name` attribute, that gives the name of the image. When an image is given a name with the `name` attribute, a reference to the image is placed in the *image-name* property in addition to the `document.images[]` array. Image objects created with the `Image()` constructor function do not have names, and cannot have names assigned.

srcRead/write string that specifies the URL of the image to be displayed. Its initial value is set by the `src` attribute.

vspace

Read-only integer that specifies the amount of extra vertical space, in pixels, inserted above and below the image. Its value is set by the `vspace` attribute.

width

Read-only integer that specifies the width, in pixels, of the image. Its value is set by the `width` attribute.

Event handlers

onabort

Invoked if the user aborts the download of an image. Defined by the `onAbort` attribute, the value of which may be any number of JavaScript statements (separated by semicolons) that will be executed when the user aborts loading.

```
<img src="url
    onAbort="handler          a definition of the handler
    ...>
image.onabort                 a reference to the handler
image.onabort()               an explicit invocation of the handler
```

onerror

Invoked if an error occurs while downloading the image. Defined by the `onError` attribute, the value of which may be any number of JavaScript statements (separated by semicolons) that will be executed when an error occurs during loading.

```
<img src="url
    onError="handler          a definition of the handler
    ...>
image.onerror                 a reference to the handler
image.onerror()               an explicit invocation of the handler
```

onload

Invoked when the image successfully finishes loading. Defined by the `onLoad` attribute, the value of which may be any number of JavaScript statements (separated by semicolons) that will be executed when the image is completely loaded.

```
<img src="url
    onLoad="handler           a definition of the handler
    ...>
image.onload                  a reference to the handler
image.onload()                an explicit invocation of the handler
```

HTML syntax

The Image object is created with a standard HTML `<img>` tag, with the addition of event handlers. Some `<img>` attributes have been omitted from the syntax below, because they are not used by or accessible from JavaScript.

```
<img src="url"                      the image to display
    width=pixels                    the width of the image
    height=pixels                   the height of the image
    [ name="image-name" ]           a property name for the image
    [ lowsrc="url" ]                alternate low-resolution image
    [ border=pixels ]               width of image border
    [ hspace=pixels ]               extra horizontal space around image
    [ vspace=pixels ]               extra vertical space around image
    [ onLoad=handler ]              invoked when image is fully loaded
    [ onError=handler ]             invoked if error in loading
    [ onAbort=handler ]             invoked if user aborts load
>
```

---

isNaN() Function

Tests whether an argument (*x*) is "not a number"; specifically determines whether it is the reserved value NaN, which represents an illegal number (such as the result of dividing zero by zero). This function is required because it is not possible to express the NaN value as a literal in JavaScript. Commonly used to test the results of `parseFloat()` and `parseInt()` to see if they represent legal numbers, or to check for arithmetic errors, such as division by zero. Not implemented on all platforms for Netscape 2.0. See also parseFloat, parseInt.

    isNaN(x)

JavaArray Object

A representation of a Java array, which allows JavaScript to read and write the elements of the array using familiar JavaScript array syntax. When reading and writing values from array elements, data conversion between JavaScript and Java representations is handled by the system. Note that Java arrays differ from JavaScript arrays in the following ways. First, Java arrays have a fixed length that is specified when they are created; thus, the JavaArray `length` field is read-only. Second, Java arrays are *typed* (i.e., their elements must all be of the same data type); attempting to set an array element to a value of the wrong type will result in a JavaScript error. Available in Netscape 3.0. See also getClass, JavaClass, JavaObject, JavaPackage, Packages.

    javaarray.length   the length of the array
    javaarray[index]   read or write an array element

Properties

`length`
> Read-only integer that specifies the number of elements in the Java array represented by the JavaArray object.

Usage

If `java.awt.Polygon` is a JavaClass object, you can create a JavaObject representing an instance of the class using:

```
p = new java.awt.Polygon();
```

This object p has properties `xpoints` and `ypoints`, which are JavaArray objects representing Java arrays of integers. You could initialize the contents of these arrays with JavaScript code like the following:

```
for(int i = 0; i < p.xpoints.length; i++)
    p.xpoints[i] = Math.round(Math.random()*100);
for(int i = 0; i < p.ypoints.length; i++)
    p.ypoints[i] = Math.round(Math.random()*100);
```

JavaClass Object

JavaScript representation of a Java class. Its properties represent the public static fields and methods (also called class fields and methods) of the represented class; these properties can be used to read and write the static fields and to invoke the static methods of Java classes. Use a `for/in` loop to enumerate the properties for any given class.

Note that the JavaClass object does not have properties representing the *instance* fields of a Java class, which are represented by the JavaObject object. However, the JavaClass object does allow for the creation of Java objects (represented by a JavaObject object) using the new keyword and invoking the constructor method of a JavaClass. For primitive data types, conversion between JavaScript values and Java values is handled automatically by the system. Note that Java is a *typed* language (i.e., each of the fields of an object must adhere to a specific data type). Available in Netscape 3.0. See also getClass, JavaArray, JavaObject, JavaPackage, Packages.

`javaclass.static_field`	*read or write a static Java field*
`javaclass.static_method(...)`	*invoke a static method*
`new javaclass(...)`	*create a new Java object*

Usage

`java.lang.System` is a JavaClass object that represents the java.lang.System class in Java. The following code reads a static field of this class:

```
var java_console = java.lang.System.out;
```

Invoke a static method of this class with a line such as:

```
var version = java.lang.System.getProperty("java.version");
```

The JavaClass object allows you to create a new Java object like this:

```
var java_date = new java.lang.Date();
```

JavaObject Object

JavaScript representation of a Java object. Its properties represent the public instance fields and methods defined for the Java object; these properties can be used to read and write the public instance fields and to invoke the public instance methods of a Java object. (The static/class fields and methods are represented by the JavaClass object.) Use the for/in loop to enumerate the properties of any given JavaObject.

For primitive data types, conversion between JavaScript values and Java values is handled automatically by the system. Note that Java is a *typed* language (i.e., each of the fields of an object must adhere to a specific data type). Available in Netscape 3.0. See also getClass, JavaArray, JavaClass, JavaPackage, Packages.

javaobject.field	*read or write an instance field*
javaobject.method(...)	*invoke an instance method*

Usage

java.lang is the name of a JavaPackage that contains the JavaClass java.lang.System. This class has the property out, which is a JavaObject. This JavaObject has a property println, which is a method that can be invoked like this:

```
java.lang.System.out.println("Hello from Java!");
```

The previous line of code will write a message on the Java console. java.awt.Rectangle is a JavaClass that represents the *java.awt.Rectangle* class. The following line creates a JavaObject that represents an instance of this class:

```
var r = new java.awt.Rectangle(0,0,4,5);
```

Then access the public fields of this JavaObject r using code such as:

```
var perimeter = 2*r.width + 2*r.height;
```

JavaPackage Object

A JavaScript representation of a Java package. A package in Java is a collection of related classes. In JavaScript, a JavaPackage can contain classes (represented by the JavaClass object) and it can also contain other JavaPackage objects.

The property naming scheme for the JavaPackage hierarchy mirrors the naming scheme for Java packages. However, the JavaPackage object named `java` does not actually represent a package in Java, but is simply a convenient placeholder for other JavaPackages that do represent *java.lang, java.net, java.io*, and other important Java classes. Think of the JavaPackage object as representing a Java package representing a directory in the Java class hierarchy.

The `java` JavaPackage object is actually a property of every Window object, which makes it a "global" variable in client-side JavaScript. Since every JavaScript expression is evaluated in the context of one window or another, you can always just use `java` and know that you will be referring to the JavaPackage object you want. There are other global JavaPackage objects as well (`sun`, `netscape`). The `Packages` property is a JavaPackage object that contains references to each of these `java`, `sun`, and `netscape` JavaPackages.

Available in Netscape 3.0. See also JavaArray, JavaClass, JavaObject, Packages.

> `package.package_name`   *refers to another JavaPackage*
> `package.class_name`   *refers to a JavaClass object*

Properties
The properties of a JavaPackage object are the names of the JavaPackage objects and JavaClass objects that it contains. These properties will be different for each individual JavaPackage. Note that it is not possible to use the JavaScript `for/in` loop to iterate over the list of property names of a Package object; consult a Java reference manual, or examine the Java class hierarchy, to determine the packages and classes contained within any given package.

Usage

You can use JavaPackage objects to refer to any Java class. The *java.lang.System* class, for example, is:

> `java.lang.System`

Or:

> `Packages.java.lang.System`

Similarly, the *netscape.javascript.JSObject* class is:

> `Packages.netscape.javascript.JSObject`

Link Object

Represents a hypertext link or a clickable area of a client-side image map in an HTML document. A subclass of the Location object; however, Link differs in that it does not load a new URL automatically (i.e., it changes the URL that the link refers to, but the URL is not displayed until the user selects it). Note that in JavaScript, a hypertext link is a Link object, and a named link destination is an Anchor object. Enhanced in Netscape 3.0. See also Anchor, Location.

```
document.links[]
document.links.length
```

Properties

hash
> The hash portion of the HREF URL, including the leading hash (#) mark. This portion specifies the name of an anchor within the object referred to by the URL.

host
> The combination of the hostname and port portions of the HREF URL.

hostname
> The hostname portion of the HREF URL.

href
> The complete URL specified by the HREF property.

pathname
> The path portion of the HREF URL.

port
> The port portion of the HREF URL.

protocol
> The protocol portion of the HREF URL, including the trailing colon.

search
> The search or query portion of the HREF URL, including the leading question mark.

target
> The name of a Window object (i.e., a frame or a top-level browser window) in which the HREF URL should be displayed.

Event handlers

The values of the following attributes may be any number of JavaScript statements separated by semicolons.

onclick()
> Statements invoked when the user clicks on the link. Defined by the onClick attribute of the HTML <a> or <area> tag that defines the hypertext link. The onclick() event handler is invoked before the browser follows the clicked hypertext link.

`<a onClick="handler-statements">`	*a definition of the handler*
`link.onclick`	*a reference to the handler*
`link.onclick();`	*an explicit invocation of the handler*

onmouseout()
> Statements invoked when the user moves the mouse off of the link. Defined by the onMouseOut attribute of the HTML <a> or <area> tag that defines the hypertext link. Available in 3.0 and later.

```
<a onMouseOut="handler-statements">    a definition of the handler
<area onMouseOut="handler-statements">    another definition
link.onmouseout                        a reference to the handler
link.onmouseout();                     an explicit invocation of the handler
```

onmouseover()

Statements invoked when the user moves the mouse over the link. The status property of the current window may be set here. Defined by the
onMouseOver attribute of the HTML <A> or <area> tag that defines the
hypertext link.

```
<a onMouseOver="handler-statements">    a definition of the handler
<area onMouseOver="handler-statements">    another definition
link.onmouseover                        a reference to the handler
link.onmouseover();                     an explicit invocation of the handler
```

HTML syntax

A Link object is created with standard <a> and </a> tags, with the addition of the
onClick, onMouseOver, and onMouseOut event-handler attributes. The HREF
attribute is required for all Link objects. If the name attribute is also specified, then
an Anchor object is also created:

```
<A HREF="url"
    [ name="anchor_tag" ]          creates an Anchor object
    [ target="window_name" ]       where the HREF should be displayed
    [ onClick="handler" ]          invoked when link is clicked
    [ onMouseOver="handler" ]      invoked when mouse is over link
    [ onMouseOut="handler" ]       invoked when mouse leaves link
>
link text or image                 the visible part of the link
</A>
```

In Netscape 3.0 and later, a Link object is also created by each <area> tag within
a client-side image map; standard HTML with the addition of event-handler tags:

```
<MAP name="map_name">
    <area SHAPE="area_shape"
        COORDS=coordinates
        HREF="url"
        [ target="window_name" ]       where the HREF should be displayed
        [ onClick="handler" ]          invoked when area is clicked
        [ onMouseOut="handler" ]       invoked when mouse leaves area
>
    . . .
</MAP>
```

Location Object

Represents a URL. Each of the properties of the Location object is a read/write
string that contains one or more portions of the URL described by the object. The
location property of the Window object is a Location object that specifies the
URL of the document. Changing properties of a Location object of a Window

causes the browser to read in the changed URL. To load a new URL, you usually set the `location` property to a string; or you can set any of the properties of the Location object instead. The `href` property is commonly used. If you just set the hash property of the `window.location` object, the browser will jump to the newly specified anchor.

When you set the `location` or `location.href` properties to a URL that you have already visited, the browser will either load that URL from the cache, or will check with the server to see if the document has changed and reload it if necessary. In Netscape 2.0, it will always check with the Web server. In 3.0, the action it takes depends on the `Verify Document` setting in Netscape's `Network Preferences`.

See also Document, Link, Window.

```
location
window.location
document.links[]
```

Properties
The fields of a Location object refer to the various portions of a URL, which has the following general format:

```
protocol://hostname:port/pathname?search#hash
```

hash
> The hash portion of the URL, including the leading hash mark (#). This portion specifies the name of an anchor within a single HTML file.

```
location.hash
window.location.hash
document.links[i].hash
```

host
> A combination of the hostname and port portions of the URL.

```
location.host
window.location.host
document.links[i].host
```

hostname
> The hostname portion of the URL.

```
location.hostname
window.location.hostname
document.links[i].hostname
```

href
> The complete URL.

```
location.href
window.location.href
document.links[i].href
```

pathname

The path portion of the URL.

```
location.pathname
window.location.pathname
document.links[i].pathname
```

port

The port portion of the URL.

```
location.port
window.location.port
document.links[i].port
```

protocol

The protocol portion of the URL, including the trailing colon.

```
location.protocol
window.location.protocol
document.links[i].protocol
```

search

The search or query portion of the URL, including the leading question mark.

```
location.search
window.location.search
document.links[i].search
```

Methods

reload()

Reloads the current document from the cache or server. The optional *force* argument is a boolean that specifies whether the document should be reloaded even if it hasn't been modified; if omitted or `false`, the method will reload the full page only if it has been changed since it was last loaded.

```
location.reload()
location.reload(force)
```

replace()

Replaces the current document with a new one, without generating a new entry in the browser's session history.

```
location.replace(url)
```

Math Object

Read-only reference to a placeholder object that contains mathematical functions and constants. Math is itself an object, not a class of objects, so its constants and methods are invoked directly through it. Math is actually a global property of the Window object, and as such, is usually referred to as Math, rather than as *window*.Math. random() function added in 3.0. See also Number.

```
Math.constant
Math.function()
```

Invoke functions and constants as follows:

```
y = Math.sin(x);
area = radius * radius * Math.PI;
```

Constants

E
> The constant e (the base of natural logarithms)

LN10
> The natural logarithm of 10

LN2
> The natural logarithm of 2

LOG10E
> The base-10 logarithm of e

LOG2E
> The base-2 logarithm of e

PI
> The constant π

SQRT1_2
> The reciprocal of the square-root of 2

SQRT2
> The square-root of 2

Methods (Functions)

abs
> Computes an absolute value.
>
> ```
> Math.abs(x)          //x is any numeric value or expression
> ```

acos
> Computes an arc cosine (inverse cosine). Return value is between 0 and π radians.
>
> ```
> Math.acos(x)         //x is a numeric value or expression
>                      between -1.0 and 1.0 radians
> ```

asin
> Computes an arc sine (inverse sine). The return value is between $-\pi/2$ and $\pi/2$ radians.
>
> ```
> Math.asin(x)         //x is a numeric value or expression
>                      between -1.0 and 1.0 radians
> ```

atan

Computes an arc tangent (inverse tangent) in radians. The return value is between $-\pi/2$ and $\pi/2$ radians.

```
Math.atan(x)            //x is any numeric value or expression
```

atan2

Computes the counter-clockwise angle from the positive X axis to a point (x, y). Performs half of the conversion between Cartesian coordinates and polar coordinates; computes and returns the angle theta of an (*x*, *y*) point.

```
Math.atan2(x, y)        //x, y are the coordinates of the point
```

ceil

Rounds a number up to the closest integer (i.e., computes the ceiling function); negative numbers are rounded up to 0.

```
Math.ceil(x)            //x is any number or numeric expression
```

cos

Computes a cosine; the return value will be between -1.0 and 1.0 radians.

```
Math.cos(x)             //x is any number or numeric
                          expression, in radians
```

exp

Computes an exponent of e.

```
Math.exp(x)             //x is a number or numeric expression
                          to be used as exponent
```

floor

Rounds a number down to the closest integer (i.e., computes the floor function); negative numbers are rounded to be more negative.

```
Math.floor(x)           //x is any numeric value or expression
```

log

Computes a natural logarithm.

```
Math.log(x)         //x is any numeric value or expression
                      greater than 0
```

max

Returns the larger of two values.

```
Math.max(a, b)    //a, b are any two numeric values or expressions
```

min

Returns the smaller of two values.

```
Math.min(a, b)    //a, b are any two numeric values or expressions
```

pow

Computes x^y. (Raises its first argument to the power of its second argument and returns the result.)

```
Math.pow(x, y)
```

random

Computes a random number; available in 3.0 and later.

round

Rounds to the closest integer. In Netscape 2.0, `Math.round()` does not correctly round very large numbers.

```
Math.round(x)          //x is any numeric value or expression
```

sin

Computes a sine.

```
Math.sin(x)            //x is an angle, in radians
```

sqrt

Computes a squareroot.

```
Math.sqrt(x)           //x is any numeric value or expression
                         greater than or equal to 0
```

tan

Computes a tangent.

```
Math.atan(x)           //x is an angle, in radians
```

MimeType Object

Represents a MIME datatype supported by the browser (or through a "helper application" or a plug-in for embedded data). Available in Netscape 3.0. See also Netscape, Plugin.

```
navigator.mimeTypes[i]
navigator.mimeTypes["name"]
navigator.mimeTypes.length
```

Properties

description

Read-only English description of the content and encoding of the type.

enabledPlugin

Reference to the Plugin object that supports this MIME type, or `null`, if no installed and enabled plug-in supports it. If a MIME type is supported by a plug-in, it can be embedded in a Web page with the <embed> tag; otherwise it must be output in some other way.

name
> Read-only name of the MIME datatype (e.g., "text/html"). Value of this property can be used as an index into the `navigator.mimeTypes[]` array.

suffixes
> Read-only comma-separated list of the common filename extensions associated with this MIME type (e.g., for "text/html" the suffixes are "html, htm").

Usage

The `navigator.mimeTypes[]` array may be indexed numerically, or with the name of the desired MIME type (which is the value of the **name** property). To check which MIME types are supported by the browser, you can loop through each element in the array numerically. Or, if you just want to check whether a specific type is supported, you can write code like the following:

```
var show_movie = (navigator.mimeTypes["video/mpeg"] != null);
```

Navigator Object

Contains properties that describe the Web browser in use; these can be used to perform platform-specific customization. There is only a single instance of the Navigator object, which you can reference through the `navigator` property of any Window object. Enhanced in Netscape 3.0. See also MimeType, Plugin.

```
navigator
```

Properties

appCodeName
> Read-only string specifying the code name of the browser.

appName
> Read-only string specifying the name of the browser.

appVersion
> Read-only string specifying version information for the browser.

mimeTypes[]
> An array of MimeType objects describing the MIME types recognized and supported by the browser. Added in Netscape 3.0.

mimeTypes.length
> The number of elements in the `mimeTypes[]` array.

plugins[]
> An array of Plugin objects describing the installed plugins. Added in Netscape 3.0.

plugins.length
> The number of elements in the `plugins[]` array.

`userAgent`
>Read-only string passed by the browser as the user-agent header in HTTP requests. In Netscape 2.0 and 3.0, this property is the value of `navigator.appCodeName` followed by a slash and the value of `navigator.appVersion` (e.g., Mozilla/2.01 (Win16; I). In Microsoft Internet Explorer 3.0b1 running on Windows 95, this property has the value "Mozilla/2.0 (compatible; MSIE 3.0A; Windows 95)".

Methods

`javaEnabled()`
>Tests whether Java is supported and enabled in the current browser.

`taintEnabled()`
>Tests whether the data-tainting security model is supported and enabled in the current browser (`true` if enabled). Added in Netscape 3.0.

Number Object

Numbers are a basic, primitive data type in JavaScript. In Netscape 3.0, JavaScript also supports the Number object, an object type that represents a primitive numeric value. JavaScript automatically converts between the primitive and object forms as necessary. In JavaScript 3.0, you can explicitly create a Number object with the Number() constructor, although there is rarely any need to do so. Available in Netscape 3.0. See also Math, Number().

>`Number.constant`

The `Number()` constructor:

>`new Number(value)`

is actually more commonly used as a placeholder for five useful numeric constants. Note that these values are properties of the `Number()` constructor function itself, not of individual number objects. For example, you use the `MAX_value` property as follows:

>`biggest = Number.MAX_value`

not like this:

>`n = new Number(2);`
>`biggest = n.MAX_value`

Constants

`MAX_value`
>The largest representable number.

`MIN_value`
>The smallest (i.e., closest to zero, not most negative) number representable in JavaScript.

NaN

Special Not-a-Number value. JavaScript prints the `Number.NaN` value as NaN. Note that the `NaN` value always compares unequal to any other number, including itself. Thus, you cannot check for the not-a-number value by comparing to `Number.NaN`. Use the `isNaN()` function instead.

NEGATIVE_INFINITY

Special negative infinite value; returned on overflow. JavaScript displays the `NEGATIVE_INFINITY` value as `-Inf`. This value behaves mathematically like an infinity.

POSITIVE_INFINITY

Special infinite value; returned on overflow. JavaScript displays the `POSI-TIVE_INFINITY` value as `Inf`. This value behaves mathematically like an infinity.

Methods

toString()

Converts a number to a string, using a specified radix (base).

```
number.toString(radix)  //radix is an integer between 2 and 16
```

By contrast, the `toString()` method of the Number object is a method of each Number object, not of the `Number()` constructor function. You can use the `toString` method with a variable that holds a number, even though that value is not actually an object:

```
value = 1234;
binary_value = n.toString(2);
```

JavaScript implicitly invokes the `Number()` constructor to convert the number to a temporary Number object for which the `toString()` method can be invoked.

Object Object

A built-in datatype of the JavaScript language; serves as the "superclass" for all other JavaScript objects, and therefore methods of the Object object are also methods of all other object types. The behavior of the Object object is also shared by all other object types. When an Object object is newly created, it has no properties defined; you can add a property definition to an object simply by assigning a value to the property. Objects can also be used as associative arrays.

A number of the Object methods can be defined for any object, and will be invoked by the JavaScript system at appropriate times, to perform some sort of operation on the object (e.g., `toString`). JavaScript allows object syntax to be used to refer to properties and methods of primitive datatypes, such as JavaScript strings. JavaScript creates a temporary object "wrapper" for the primitive value so that the method can be invoked or the property accessed.

Enhanced in Netscape 3.0. See also Array, Boolean, Function, Number, String, Window.

```
new Object();
new Object(value);                    // Netscape 3.0 and later
```

In Netscape 3.0 and later, the optional *value* argument may specify a value of any primitive JavaScript type: a number, a boolean, a string, or a function. If no *value* argument is passed, this constructor returns a newly created object, which has no properties defined. If a *value* argument is specified, then the constructor creates and returns a Number, Boolean, String, or Function object wrapper around the primitive value.

Methods

assign()

If defined, used to implement the JavaScript assignment operator (=).

```
object.assign(value)      //value is the value to be assigned
```

eval()

Evaluates a string of JavaScript code in the context of the given object. Prior to Netscape 3.0, eval() is a standalone function; in 3.0, it is a method of Object. However, in 2.0 (client-side JavaScript) it behaves as if it were a method of the Window object.

```
eval(code)                      // Netscape 3.0
window.eval(code)               // Netscape 3.0
```

toString()

If defined, used to convert an object to a string.

valueOf()

Returns the primitive value of the object, if any. For objects of type Object, this method simply returns the object itself. For other object types, such as Number and Boolean, this method returns the primitive value associated with the object. This method was added in Netscape 3.0.

Example

Defining the toString(), method, and also the less frequently used assign() and valueOf() methods of an object, is most efficiently done in a constructor method for your object type, or with the prototype object of your object.

```
// define a constructor for the Complex object type
function Complex(x,y) { this.x = x; this.y = y; }

// give it a toString() method
Complex.prototype.toString =
    new Function("return '{' + this.x + ',' + this.y + '}';");

// Create an object of this new Complex type
c = new Complex(2, 2);

// Convert the object to a string, implicitly invoking the
```

```
// toString() method, and display the string.
alert("c = " + c);
```

Option Object

Describes a single option displayed within a Select object. Note that although the text displayed by this option is specified outside of the <option> tag, that text must be plain, unformatted text, without any HTML tags. This is so that the text can be properly displayed in list boxes and drop-down menus that do not support HTML formatting. Enhanced in Netscape 3.0. See also Select.

> *select*.options[*i*]

You can dynamically create new Option objects for display in a Select object with the Option() constructor. Once a new Option object is created, it can be appended to the list of options in a Select object by assigning it to options[options.length]. See Select.options[].

Properties

defaultSelected
> Read-only boolean that specifies whether this option is selected by default. Set by the selected attribute.

index
> Read-only integer that specifies the index of this option within the array of options. The first Option object in the array is at index 0 and has its index property set to 0. The second Option has an index of 1, and so on.

selected
> Read/write boolean that specifies whether this option is currently selected. Its initial value is specified by the selected attribute. Can be used to test whether a given option is selected; or to select (by setting it to true) or deselect (by setting it to false) a given option. The Select.onchange() event handler is not invoked.

text
> The text that describes the option. It is the plain text (not formatted HTML text) that follows the <option> tag. In 2.0, this property is read-only. In 3.0 it is read/write.

value
> Read/write string that specifies the value to be passed to the server if this option is selected when the form is submitted. The initial value is specified by the value attribute.

HTML syntax
An Option object is created by an <option> tag within a <select> which is itself within a <form>. Multiple <option> tags typically appear within the <select>.

```
<form ...>
  <select  ...>
    <option
        [ value="value" ]          the value returned when the form is submitted
        [ selected ] >             specifies whether this option is initially selected
      plain_text_label             the text to display for this option
        ...
  </select>
        ...
</form>
```

Packages Object

An object that contains references to other JavaPackage objects and to JavaClass
objects. Each JavaPackage object represents a node in the tree of package names.
The Packages property refers to a JavaPackage object that is the root of this
package name hierarchy.

The Packages object is a "global" variable in JavaScript; a read-only reference to a
JavaPackage object, it is defined as a property of all Window objects. Thus, you
can always refer to it simply as Packages, rather than explicitly accessing it
through a particular Window object.

Note that the Window object also contains "global" properties named java,
netscape, and sun, all of which are synonyms for the properties of the Packages object. So instead of writing Packages.java.lang.Math, for example,
you can just write java.lang.Math.

Available in Netscape 3.0. See also JavaClass, JavaObject, JavaPackage.

Properties

java
> Reference to a JavaPackage object that represents the top node of the java.*
> package hierarchy.

netscape
> Reference to a JavaPackage object that represents the top node of the
> netscape.* package hierarchy.

sun
> Reference to a JavaPackage object that represents the top node of the sun.*
> package hierarchy.

parseFloat() Function

Parses and returns the first number that occurs in s (i.e., converts a string to a
number). Parsing stops, and the value is returned, when parseFloat() encounters a character in s that is not a valid part of the number (i.e., a sign, digit, decimal point, exponent, etc.). If s does not begin with a number parseInt() can
parse, the function returns NaN, a reserved value that represents "not-a-number."

`parseFloat()` is a built-in JavaScript function; not a method of any object. Buggy in Netscape 2.0. See also isNaN(), parseInt().

```
parseFloat(s) //s is the string to be parsed and coverted to a number
```

---

parseInt() Function

Parses and returns the first number that occurs in the string *s* (i.e., it converts a string to an integer). Parsing stops, and the value is returned, when `parseInt()` encounters a character in *s* that is not a valid numeral for the specified *radix*. If *s* does not begin with a number that `parseInt()` can parse, then the function returns NaN, a reserved value that represents "not-a-number."

Specifying a *radix* of 10 makes the `parseInt()` parse a decimal number. The value 8 specifies that an octal number (using digits 0 through 7) is to be parsed. The value 16 specifies a hexadecimal value, using digits 0 through 9 and letters A through F. *radix* can be any value between 2 and 36.

If *radix* is 0, or if it is not specified, `parseInt()` tries to determine the radix of the number from *s*. If *s* begins with 0x, then `parseInt()` parses the remainder of *s* as a hexadecimal number. If *s* begins with a 0, then `parseInt()` parses the number in octal. Otherwise, if *s* begins with a digit 1 through 9, then `parseInt()` parses it as a decimal number.

`parseInt` is a built-in JavaScript function, not a method of any object. Buggy in Netscape 2.0. See also isNaN(), parseFloat().

```
parseInt(s)
parseInt(s, radix) //s is the string to be parsed
    //radix is the integer base of the number to be parsed
```

Password Object

A text input field intended for input of sensitive data, such as passwords. As the user types characters, only asterisks appear. The `value` property is a read/write string that initially contains the value specified by the `value` attribute; it specifies the data to be transmitted if the user does not type anything. For security reasons, this default value is the only thing that JavaScript has access to. The user's input is transmitted to the server when the form is submitted, but that input does not appear in this property, and setting this property has no effect on the value transmitted. Enhanced in Netscape 3.0. See also Element, Form, Text.

```
form.name
form.elements[i]
form.elements['name']
```

Properties

form
> Read-only reference to the Form object that contains the Password object.

name
> Read-only string, set by the HTML name attribute, that specifies the name of the Password object. This is also the *name* that can be used to reference the Password object as a property of its form.

type
> Read-only string that specifies the type of this form element. For Password objects, it has the value "password." Available in Netscape 3.0 and later.

value
> Read/write string, initially set by the HTML value attribute. For security, the user's input is not available through this property, and setting this property does not affect the data transmitted with the form.

Methods

blur()
> Removes the keyboard focus from the Password object.

focus()
> Sets the keyboard focus to the Password object. When focus is set, all keystrokes are automatically entered into this object.

HTML syntax

A Password object is created with a standard HTML <input> tag:

```
<form>
   ...
  <input
    type="password"          specifies that this is a Password object
    [ name="name" ]          a name that can later be used to refer to this object;
                             specifies the name property
    [ value="default" ]      the default value transmitted when the form is submitted
    [ size=integer ]         how many characters wide the object is
  >
   ...
</form>
```

Plugin Object

Represents a plug-in application that has been installed in the browser. Available in Netscape 3.0. See also Netscape, MimeType.

```
navigator.plugins[i]
navigator.plugins['name']
navigator.plugins.length
```

Properties

`description`
> Read-only string that contains a human-readable description of the plug-in, specified by the plug-in itself. This property may specify a full product name, information about the vendor and version, and so on.

`filename`
> Read-only string that specifies the name of the disk file that contains the plug-in code.

`mimeTypes[]`
> Read-only array of MimeType objects, one for each MIME type supported by the plug-in.

`mimeTypes.length`
> The number of elements in the `mimeTypes[]` array.

`name`
> Read-only string that specifies the name of the plug-in. This is generally a much shorter string than `description`. The value of this property may be used as an index into the `navigator.plugins[]` array.

Usage

The `navigator.plugins[]` array may be indexed numerically when you want to loop through the complete list of installed plug-ins, looking for one that meets your needs. The `navigator.plugins[]` array can also be indexed by plug-in name, however. That is, if you want to check whether a specific plug-in is installed in the user's browser, you might use code like this:

```
document.write( navigator.plugins("Shockwave") ?
            "<EMBED src="movie.dir' height=100 WIDTH=100>" :
            "You don't have the Shockwave plugin!" );
```

The name used as an array index with this technique is the same name that appears as the value of the `name` property.

Radio Object

Represents a single graphical radio button in an HTML form. Note that the text that appears next to a Radio button is not part of the Radio object itself, and must be specified externally to the `<input>` tag. The Radio button object is always used in groups of mutually-exclusive options that have the same name. To references on Radio objects within a group, use the syntax below.

Note that only one Radio object in a group may contain the `checked` attribute, which sets the initial values of the `checked` and `defaultChecked` properties (`true` for that object and `false` for all other Radio buttons in the group). If none of the objects have the `checked` attribute, then the first one in the group will be checked (and `defaultChecked`) by default.

In Netscape 2.0, there is a bug in how Radio objects in a group are assigned to an array. The workaround is to always assign an event-hander, if only a dummy one, to all of your Radio objects that will be manipulated with JavaScript. Enhanced in Netscape 3.0. See also Checkbox, Element, Form.

```
form.radio_name[j]
form.radio_name.length
form.elements[i][j]
form.elements[i].length
form.elements['radio_name'][j]
form.elements['radio_name'].length
```

Properties

checked
> Read/write boolean value that specifies whether the button is checked or not; can be examined to determine the button's state, or be set to select or deselect the button. Setting checked changes the appearance of the button, but does not invoke onClick.

defaultChecked
> Read-only Boolean that specifies the initial state of the radio button.

form
> Read-only reference to the Form object that contains the Radio object.

name
> Read-only string, set by the HTML name attribute, that specifies the name of the Radio button.

type
> Read-only string that specifies the type of this form element. For Radio objects, it has the value "radio." Available in Netscape 3.0 and later.

value
> Read/write string, initially set by the HTML value attribute, which specifies the value passed to the server if the Radio button is selected when the form is submitted. Each Radio object in a group should specify a distinct value.

Event handlers

onClick
> Invoked when the Radio button is clicked; allows you to specify JavaScript code to be executed when the button is checked or "un-checked."

```
<input type="radio"               a definition of the handler
      onClick="handler-statements">
radio.onclick                     a reference to the handler
radio.onclick();                  an explicit invocation of the handler
```

HTML syntax

A Radio object is created with a standard HTML <input> tag, with the addition of the new onClick attribute. Radio objects are created in groups by specifying multiple <input> tags that have the same name attribute (mandatory if the radio is part of a form that will submit data to a CGI script). Specifying a name attribute sets the *name* property, and also allows you to refer to the button by name (instead of as a member of the form elements array).

```
<form>
   ...
   <input
      type="radio"              specifies that this is a radio button
      [ name="name" ]           a name that can later be used to refer to this button
                                or to the group of buttons with this name;
                                specifies the name property
      [ value="value" ]         the value returned when this button is selected;
                                specifies the value property
      [ checked ]               specifies that the button is initially checked;
                                specifies the defaultChecked property
      [ onClick="handler" ]     JavaScript statements to be executed
                                when the button is clicked
   >
   label                        the HTML text that should appear next to the button
   ...
</form>
```

Reset Object

The Reset object has the same properties and methods as the Button object, but is used only to reset a form's values (to their defaults). For most elements this means to the value specified by the HTML value attribute. If no initial value was specified, then a click on the Reset button will "clear" any user input from those objects. If no value attribute is specified for a Reset object, it will be labeled "Reset." Enhanced in Netscape 3.0. See also Button, Element, Form.

```
form.name
form.elements[i]
form.elements['name']
```

Properties

form
> Read-only reference to the Form object that contains the Reset object.

name
> Read-only string, set by the HTML name attribute, that specifies the name of the Reset object. This is also the *name* that can be used to reference the Reset object as a property of its form.

type
> Read-only string that specifies the type of this form element. For Reset objects, it has the value "reset." Available in Netscape 3.0 and later.

`value`

Read-only string, set by the HTML `value` attribute, that specifies the text to appear in the button. If no `value` is specified, then (in Netscape) the button will be labelled "Reset" by default.

Event handlers

`onclick()`

Invoked when the Reset button is clicked. Defined by the `onClick` attribute of the HTML `<input>` tag that defines the Reset button. The value of this attribute may be any number of JavaScript statements, separated by semicolons; these statements will be executed when the user clicks on the Reset button. In Netscape 2.0, there is no way for the `onclick()` event handler to prevent the fields from being reset. However, in 3.0, the event handler may return `false` to prevent the Reset object from resetting the form.

```
<input type="reset"              a definition of the handler
      onClick="handler-statements">
reset.onclick                    a reference to the handler
reset.onclick();                 an explicit invocation of the handler
```

HTML syntax

A Reset object is created with a standard HTML `<input>` tag, with the addition of the `onClick` attribute:

```
<form>
  ...
  <input
    type="reset"                 specifies that this is a Reset button
    [ value="label" ]            the text that is to appear within the button;
                                 specifies the value property.
    [ name="name" ]              a name that can later be used to refer to the button;
                                 specifies the name property
    [ onClick="handler" ]   JavaScript statements to be executed when button clicked
  >
  ...
</form>
```

Select Object

Represents a graphical list of choices from which the user may select. If the `multiple` attribute is present in the HTML definition of the object, then the user may select any number of options from the list. If that attribute is not present, then the user may select only one option, and options have a "radio button" (i.e., mutually exclusive toggle) behavior.

If the `size` attribute has a value greater than 1, or if the `multiple` attribute is present, Select objects are displayed in a list box that is `size` lines high in the browser window. If `size` is smaller than the number of options, then the list box will include a scrollbar so that all the options are accessible. On the other hand, if `size` is specified as 1, and `multiple` is not specified, then the currently selected option is displayed on a single line and the list of other options is made available through a drop-down menu.

Enhanced in Netscape 3.0. See also Element, Form, Option.

```
form.name
form.elements[i]
form.elements['name']
```

Properties

form
> Read-only reference to the Form object that contains the Select object.

length
> Read-only integer that specifies the number of elements in the options[] array (i.e., the number of options that appear in the Select object).

name
> Read-only string, set by the HTML name attribute, that specifies the name of the select object. This is also the *name* that can be used to reference the Select object as a property of its form.

options[]
> An array of Option objects, each of which describes one of the options displayed within the Select object. The options.length property specifies the number of elements in the array, as does the *select*.length property. See the Option object for further details.

selectedIndex
> Read-only (read/write in 3.0) integer that specifies the index of the selected option within the Select object. If the Select object has its multiple attribute set and allows multiple selections, then this property only specifies the index of the first selected item or -1 if none are selected.

type
> Read-only string that specifies the type of this form element. For Select objects, it has the value "select-one" or "select-multiple." Available in Netscape 3.0 and later.

Event handlers

onchange()
> Invoked when the user selects or deselects an item. Defined by the onChange attribute of the HTML <select> tag that defines the Select object. The value of this attribute may be any number of JavaScript statements, separated by semicolons; these statements will be executed whenever the user selects or deselects an option. Buggy to the point of uselessness in Netscape 2.0.

```
<select onChange="handler-statements">   a definition of the handler
select.onchange                          a reference to the handler
reset.onchange();                        an explicit invocation of the handler
```

HTML syntax

A Select object is created with a standard HTML `<select>` tag, with the addition of the new onChange, onBlur, and onFocus event-handler attributes. Options to appear within the Select object are created with the `<option>` tag:

```
<form>
    ...
<SELECT
    name="name                 name identifying this object; specifies name property
    [ SIZE=integer ]           number of visible options in select object
    [ MULTIPLE ]               multiple options may be selected, if present
    [ onChange="handler" ]     invoked when the selection changes
    [ onBlur="handler" ]       invoked when object loses focus
    [ onFocus="handler" ]      invoked when object gains focus
>
<option value="value1" [selected]> option_label1
<option value="value2" [selected]> option_label2
    .
    .   other options here
    .
</select>
    ...
</form>
```

String Object

Exists to provide methods for operating on string values (a basic JavaScript data type). The String class defines a number of methods, most of which simply make a copy of the string with HTML tags added before and after.

The string datatype and the String object are not the same, but in Netscape 2.0 are indistinguishable. In Netscape 3.0, you can use the typeof operator to distinguish them (a string has type "string" and a String object has type "object"); however, you can use them interchangeably because JavaScript converts between these two types whenever necessary. When you invoke a String object method on a string value, JavaScript converts that value to a temporary String object, allowing the method to be invoked. In Netscape 3.0, you can use the String object constructor method to create String objects that are not temporary, and that can actually be used by your programs:

```
new String(value)        // Netscape 3.0 only
```

Enhanced in Netscape 3.0.

Properties

length
: The number of characters in the string. For any string *s*, the index of the last character is s.length-1.

prototype
: See Function prototype.

Methods

anchor()

Returns a copy of the string, enclosed within `<a name="`*name*`">` and `</a>` HTML tags. The `name` attribute of the `</a>` tag is set to the *name* argument. If the resulting string is appended to an HTML document (with `Document.write()` for example), it defines an anchor, with a name of *name*, which can be the target of a hypertext link.

big()

Returns a copy of the string, enclosed between `<big>` and `</big>` HTML tags.

blink()

Returns a copy of the string, enclosed between `<blink>` and `</blink>` HTML tags.

bold()

Returns a copy of the string, enclosed between `<b>` and `</b>` HTML tags.

charAt()

Extracts the *n*th character from a string. The first character of the string is numbered 0. If *n* is not between 0 and `string.length-1`, then this method returns an empty string. Note that JavaScript does not have a character datatype that is distinct from the string type, so the returned character is a string of length 1.

```
string.charAt(n) //n is the index of the character to be returned
```

fixed()

Returns a copy of the string, enclosed between `<tt>` and `</tt>` HTML tags.

fontcolor()

Returns a copy of the string, enclosed between `<font color="`*color*`">` and `</font>` HTML tags. The *color* argument is a string specifying the color name or value to be used as the value of the `color` attribute in the `<font>` HTML tag. Colors are specified either as one of the standard color names recognized by JavaScript, or as red, green, and blue color values, expressed as six hexadecimal digits (*RRGGBB*).

```
string.fontcolor(color)
```

fontsize()

Returns a copy of the string, enclosed between `<font size="`*size*`">` and `</font>` HTML tags. The *size* argument is an integer between 1 and 7 or a string that begins with a + or - sign followed by a digit between 1 and 7. If an integer is specified, it is an absolute font size specification. If a string is specified, the font specification is relative to the `<basefont>` size.

```
string.fontsize(size)
```

indexOf()

Searches the string for an occurrence of *substring*. The search begins at position *start* within *string*, or at the beginning if no *start* is specified.

---

start is an integer between 0 and string.length-1. Returns the position of the first occurrence of *substring* after the *start* position, or -1 if no occurrence is found.

```
string.indexOf(substring)
string.indexOf(substring, start)
```

italics()
Returns a copy of the string, enclosed between <i> and </i> HTML tags.

lastIndexOf()
Searches the string backwards for an occurrence of *substring*. The search begins at position *start* within *string*, or at the end, if no *start* is specified. start is an integer between 0 and string.length-1. Returns the position of the first occurrence of *substring* before the *start* position, or -1 if no occurrence is found.

```
string.lastIndex(substring)
string.lastIndex(substring, start)
```

link()
Returns a copy of the string, enclosed between <a href="*size*"> and </a> HTML tags. *href* specifies the URL target of the hypertext link that is to be added to the string. This string argument specifies the value of the HREF attribute of the <a> HTML tag.

```
string.link(href)
```

small()
Returns a copy of the string, enclosed between <small> and </small> HTML tags.

split()
Converts a string to an array of strings, using a specified delimiter character/string at which the string will be split. If no delimiter is specified, then the returned array has only one element, the string itself. Note that the String.split() method is the inverse of the Array.join() method.

```
string.split()
string.split(delimiter)
```

strike()
Returns a copy of the string, enclosed within <strike> and </strike> HTML tags.

sub()
Returns a copy of the string, enclosed within _{and} HTML tags.

substring()
Extracts a substring of a string. *from* is a value between 0 and string.length-1. *to* is an optional integer that is one greater than the position within *string* of the last character of the desired substring. *to* must be between 1 and string.length. The character at position *from* is included in the substring, while the character at position *to* is not. The

returned string contains characters copied from positions *from* to *to-1* of *string*.

> *string*.substring(*from*, *to*)

sup()
> Returns a copy of the string, enclosed within \^{and \} HTML tags.

toLowerCase()
> Returns a copy of the string, with all characters converted to lowercase.

toUpperCase()
> Returns a copy of the string, with all characters converted to uppercase.

valueOf()
> Returns the string value contained in the String object; Netscape 3.0 and later. See Object.valueOf().

Usage

A number of the String methods are used for creating HTML:

```
link_text = "My Home Page".bold();
document.write(link_text.link("http://www.djf.com/~david"));
```

The code above code embeds the following string into the HTML document that is currently being parsed:

```
<A HREF="http://www.djf.com/~david"><B>My Home Page</B></A>
```

The following code extracts the 3rd through 5th characters of a string and converts them to upper-case letters:

```
s.substring(2,5).toUpperCase();
```

Submit Object

When a Submit button is clicked on, it submits the data in the form that contains the button to the server specified by the form's `action` attribute, and loads the resulting HTML page sent back by that server. The Submit object has the same properties and methods as the Button object. If no `value` attribute is specified for a Submit object, it will be labelled "Submit Query."

Form data may also be submitted by invoking the `Form.submit()` method. The `Submit.onclick()` event handler can define additional JavaScript statements to be executed when a Submit button is clicked; to cancel a form submission, use `Form.onsubmit()`.

Enhanced in Netscape 3.0. See also Button, Element, Form.

```
form.name
form.elements[i]
form.elements['name']
```

Properties

`form`

> Read-only reference to the Form object that contains the Submit object.

`name`

> Read-only string, set by the HTML `name` attribute, that specifies the name of the Submit object. This is also the *name* that can be used to reference the Submit object as a property of its form.

`type`

> Read-only string that specifies the type of this form element. For Submit objects, it has the value "submit." Available in Netscape 3.0 and later.

`value`

> Read-only string, set by the HTML `value` attribute, that specifies the text to appear in the button. If no `value` is specified, then (in Netscape) the button will be labelled "Submit Query" by default.

Event handlers

`onclick()`

> Invoked when the Submit button is clicked. Defined by the `onClick` attribute of the HTML `<input>` tag that defines the Submit button. The value of this attribute may be any number of JavaScript statements, separated by semicolons; these statements will be executed when the user clicks on the Submit button. In Netscape 2.0, there is no way for the `onclick()` event handler to cancel the submit action; use the `Form.onsubmit()` event handler to perform input validation and to cancel form submission if necessary.

```
<input type="submit"           a definition of the handler
      onClick="handler-statements">
submit.onclick                 a reference to the handler
submit.onclick();              an explicit invocation of the handler
```

HTML syntax

A Reset object is created with a standard HTML `<input>` tag, with the addition of the `onClick` attribute:

```
<form>
   ...
   <input
     type="submit"         specifies that this is a Submit button
     [ value="label" ]     the text that is to appear within the button;
                           specifies the value property
     [ name="name" ]       a name that can later be used to refer to the button;
                           specifies the name property
     [ onClick="handler" ] JavaScript statements to be executed when button clicked
   >
   ...
</form>
```

taint() Function

Taints a value or window (when the data tainting security model is in effect). `taint()` does not taint the value it is passed; instead, it returns a tainted copy of that value, or a tainted reference to that value for object types. (Note that taint is associated with primitive values and with references to objects, not with the objects themselves.)

Sometimes taint is carried not by data values, but by the control flow of a program. In this case, you may want to add taint to the entire window in which JavaScript code runs by calling `taint()` with no arguments. Available in Netscape 3.0. See also untaint().

```
taint()
taint(value)
```

Text Object

Represents a text input field in a form. The `size` attribute specifies the width, in characters, of the input field as it appears on the screen, and the `maxlength` attribute specifies the maximum number of characters the user will be allowed to enter. You can read the `value` property to obtain the user's input, or you can set it to display arbitrary (unformatted) text in the input field. Use the Password object instead of the Text object when the value you are asking the user to enter is sensitive information. Use a Textarea object to allow the user to enter multiple lines of text.

When a form contains only one Text or Password object, then the form will automatically be submitted if the user strikes the Return key in that Text or Password object. Enhanced in Netscape 3.0. See also Element, Form, Password, Textarea.

```
form.name
form.elements[i]
form.elements['name']
```

Properties

defaultValue
: Read-only string that specifies the initial value to appear in the input field. Specified by the `value` attribute of the `<input>` tag.

form
: Read-only reference to the Form object that contains the Text object.

name
: Read-only string, set by the HTML `name` attribute, that specifies the name of the Text object. This is also the *name* that can be used to reference the Text object as a property of its form.

type
: Read-only string that specifies the type of this form element. For Text objects, it has the value "text." Available in Netscape 3.0 and later.

value
: Read/write string that specifies the value contained in the input field (which is also the value sent to the server when the form is submitted). The initial value of this property is specified by the value attribute of the <input> tag.

Methods

blur()
: Removes the keyboard focus from the text object. In Netscape 2.0, the blur() method invokes the onblur() event handler of the Text object. This is inconsistent with the behavior of other event handlers, which are only invoked in response to user actions.

focus()
: Sets the keyboard focus to the Text object. When focus is set, all keystrokes are automatically entered into this object.

select()
: Highlights all the text in the Text object, and enters a special mode so that future input replaces the highlighted text.

Event handlers

The value of the following event handlers may be any number of JavaScript statements, separated by semicolons, which are executed when the handler is invoked.

onblur()
: Invoked when a user action causes the Text object to lose the keyboard focus. Defined by the onBlur attribute of the HTML <input> tag that defines the Text object.

```
<input type="text onblur"          a definition of the handler
    onClick="handler-statements">
text.onblur                        a reference to the handler
text.onblur();                     an explicit invocation of the handler
```

onchange()
: Invoked when the user changes the value in the Text object and then "commits" those changes by moving the keyboard focus elsewhere. Defined by the onChange attribute of the HTML <input> tag that defines the Text object. This event handler is not invoked when the value property of a Text object is set by JavaScript.

```
<input type="text onchange"        a definition of the handler
    onChange="handler-statements">
text.onchange                      a reference to the handler
text.onchange();                   an explicit invocation of the handler
```

onfocus()
: Invoked when a user action causes the Text object to gain the keyboard focus. Defined by the onFocus attribute of the HTML <input> tag that

JavaScript

defines the Text object. Note that the `onfocus` event handler is not invoked by the `Text.focus()` method.

```
<input type="text onfocus"          a definition of the handler
       onFocus="handler-statements">
text.onfocus                        a reference to the handler
text.onfocus();                     an explicit invocation of the handler
```

HTML syntax

A Text object is created with a standard HTML `<input>` tag, with the addition of optional attributes for event handlers:

```
<form>
  ...
  <input
     type="text"              specifies that this is a Text object
     [ name="name" ]          a name that can later be used to refer to this object;
                              specifies the name property
     [ value="default" ]      the default value transmitted when form is submitted;
                              specifies the defaultValue property
     [ size=integer ]         how many characters wide the object is
     [ maxlength=integer ]    max allowed number of input characters
     [ onBlur="handler" ]     the onblur() event handler
     [ onChange="handler" ]   the onchange() event handler
     [ onFocus="handler" ]    the onfocus() event handler
  >
  ...
</form>
```

Textarea Object

Represents a (multi-line) text input field in a form. The name attribute specifies a name for the object. This is mandatory if the form is to be submitted, and also provides a convenient way to refer to the Textarea object from JavaScript code.

Read the value property to obtain the user's input, or set it to display arbitrary (unformatted) text in the Textarea. The initial value of the value property (and the permanent value of the defaultValue property) is the text that appears between the `<textarea>` and `</textarea>` tags.

If you need only a single line of input text, use the Text object. If the text to be input is sensitive information, such as a password, use the Password object. Enhanced in Netscape 3.0. See also Element, Form, Password, Text.

```
form.name
form.elements[i]
form.elements['name']
```

Properties

defaultValue

Read-only string that specifies the initial value to appear in the input field. This default value is whatever plain text appears between the `<textarea>` and `</textarea>` tags.

form

Read-only reference to the Form object that contains the Textarea object.

name

Read-only string, set by the HTML `name` attribute, that specifies the name of the Textarea object. This is also the *name* that can be used to reference the Textarea object as a property of its form.

type

Read-only string that specifies the type of this form element. For Textarea objects, it has the value "textarea." Available in Netscape 3.0 and later.

value

Read/write string that specifies the value contained in the Textarea (which is also the value sent to the server when the form is submitted). The initial value of this property is the same as the `defaultValue` property.

Methods

blur()

Removes the keyboard focus from the text object.

focus()

Sets the keyboard focus to the Textarea object. When focus is set, all key-strokes are automatically entered into this object.

Event handlers

The value of the following event handlers may be any number of JavaScript state-ments, separated by semicolons, which are executed when the handler is invoked.

onblur()

Invoked when a user action causes the Textarea object to lose the keyboard focus. Defined by the `onBlur` attribute of the HTML `<textarea>` tag that defines the Textarea object. Note that the `onblur()` event handler is not invoked by the `Textarea.blur()` method.

```
<textarea onblur="handler-statements">     a definition of the handler
</textarea>
text.onblur                 a reference to the handler
text.onblur();              an explicit invocation of the handler
```

onchange()

Invoked when the user changes the value in the Textarea object and then "commits" those changes by moving the keyboard focus elsewhere. Defined by the `onChange` attribute of the HTML `<textarea>` tag that defines the Text object. This event handler is not invoked when the `value` property of a Text object is set by JavaScript.

```
<textarea onchange="handler-statements">  a definition of the handler
</textarea>
text.onchange              a reference to the handler
text.onchange();           an explicit invocation of the handler
```

This event handler is not invoked for every keystroke in the Textarea object, but only when the user completes an edit.

onfocus()

Invoked when a user action causes the Textarea object to gain the keyboard focus. Defined by the onFocus attribute of the HTML <textarea> tag that defines the Textarea object. Note that the onfocus event handler is not invoked by the Text.focus() method.

```
<textarea onfocus="handler-statements">  a definition of the handler
</textarea>
text.onfocus               a reference to the handler
text.onfocus();            an explicit invocation of the handler
```

HTML syntax

A Textarea object is created with standard HTML <textarea> and </textarea> tags, with the addition of optional attributes for event-handlers. Note that the wrap attribute, which specifies how long lines should be handled, has three legal values: off specifies that they should be left as is; virtual specifies that they should be displayed with line breaks but transmitted without; physical specifies that they should be displayed and transmitted with line breaks inserted.

```
<form>
    ...
  <textarea
    [ name="name" ]                  a name that can later refer to this object
    [ rows=integer ]                 how many lines tall the object is
    [ cols=integer ]                 how many characters wide the object is
    [ wrap=off|virtual|physical ]    how word wrapping is handled
    [ onBlur="handler" ]             the onblur() event handler
    [ onChange="handler" ]           the onchange() event handler
    [ onFocus="handler" ]            the onfocus() event handler
  >
    plain_text                       The initial text; specifies defaultValue
  </textarea>
    ...
</form>
```

---

unescape() Function

The unescape() function is a built-in part of JavaScript; it is not a method of any object. unescape() decodes a string encoded with escape() and returns the decoded copy.

```
unescape(s)     // s is the string to be decoded or "unescaped"
```

Available in Netscape 2.0. See also escape(), String.

Usage

unescape decodes s by finding and replacing character sequences of the form %*xx*, where *xx* is two hexadecimal digits. Each such sequence is replaced by the single character represented by the hexadecimal digits in the Latin-1 encoding. Thus, unescape() decodes the string:

```
Hello%20World%21
```

to:

```
Hello World!
```

untaint() Function

Untaints a value or window (when the data tainting security model is in effect). untaint() does not remove the taint of the value it is passed; instead, it returns an untainted copy of that value, or an untainted reference to that value for object types. (Note that taint is associated with primitive values and with references to objects, not with the objects themselves.)

JavaScript automatically associates taint with data values that are potentially private, and that should not be "stolen" by scripts. If you need to allow these values to be exported by scripts, you must use untaint() to make untainted copies.

Sometimes taint is carried not by data values, but by the control flow of a program. In this case, you may need to remove taint from an entire window in which JavaScript code runs. You can do this by calling untaint() with no arguments. Note, however, that you can only do this if the window carries only the taint of the script that calls untaint(). If the window has also been tainted by other scripts, then it cannot be untainted. Available in Netscape 3.0. See also taint().

```
untaint()
untaint(value)
```

Window Object

Represents a Web browser window or frame. Since JavaScript code is evaluated in the context of the Window object in which it is running, the Window object must contain references (or references to references) to all the other JavaScript objects of interest (i.e., it is the root of a JavaScript "object hierarchy"). Many of the properties of the Window object are references to other important JavaScript objects. Most of these properties refer to an object particular to the window. The location property of a Window, for example, refers to the Location object of the window. Still other Window properties (e.g., navigator) refer to "global" objects, while a couple refer only to the window itself.

In client-side JavaScript, no special syntax is required to refer to the current window, and you can use the properties of that window object as if they were variables (e.g., you can write document rather than *window*.document). Similarly, you can use the methods of the current window object as if they were functions (e.g., `alert()` instead of *window*.`alert()`).

`self`	*the current window*
`window`	*the current window*

To refer to a frame within a window, use:

```
frames[i]              // or self.frames[i]
window.frames[i]
```

To refer to the parent window (or frame) of a frame, use:

```
parent                 // or self.parent, window.parent
window.parent          // parent of specified frame
```

To refer to the top-level browser window from any frame contained within it, use:

```
top                    // or self.top, window.top
```

New top-level browser windows are created with the `Window.open()` method. When you call this method, save the return value of the `open()` call in a variable, and use that variable to reference the new window.

Enhanced in Netscape 3.0. See also Frame.

Properties

`closed`
> Read-only boolean that specifies whether a window has been closed. Available in Netscape 3.0.

`defaultStatus`
> Read/write string that specifies the default message to appear in the status line.

`document`
> Reference to the Document object contained in the window.

`frames[]`
> An array of the frames contained by this window. The `frames.length` property contains the number of elements in the `frames[]` array, as does the *window*.`length` property.
>
> ```
> window.frames[i]
> window.frames.length
> ```

`history`
> Reference to the History object for this window.

`java`
> Reference to the JavaPackage object that is the top of the package name hierarchy for the core *java.** packages that comprise the Java language. Available in Netscape 3.0.

length

The number of elements in the `frames[]` array. Same as `frames.length`. Read-only.

location

Reference to the Location object for this window.

Math

Reference to an object holding various mathematical functions and constants. Available in Netscape 3.0.

name

String that contains the name of the window. The name is optionally specified when the window is created with the `open()` method. In Netscape 2.0, this property is read-only; in 3.0 and later, it is read/write.

navigator

Reference to the Netscape object that applies to this and all other windows.

netscape

Reference to the JavaPackage object that is the top of the package name hierarchy for the core *netscape.** Java packages from Netscape. Available in Netscape 3.0.

opener

Read-only property that refers to the Window object that contained the document that called `open()` to create this window. Available in Netscape 3.0.

Packages

Reference to the JavaPackage object that represents the top of the Java package name hierarchy. Available in Netscape 3.0.

parent

Reference to the parent window or frame of the current window. Only useful when the current window is a frame rather than a top-level window.

self

Reference to the window itself. A synonym for `window`.

status

Read/write string that specifies the current contents of the status line.

sun

Reference to the JavaPackage object that is the top of the package name hierarchy for the *sun.** Java packages from Sun Microsystems. Available in Netscape 3.0.

top

Reference to the top-level window that contains the current window. Only useful when the current window is a frame rather than a top-level window.

window

Reference to the window itself. A synonym of `self`.

JavaScript

Methods

alert()
> Displays a simple message in a dialog box. The box has an OK button, and is non-modal (i.e., doesn't interrupt program execution).

> *window*.alert(*message*)

blur()
> Takes keyboard focus from the top-level browser window; this sends the window to the background on most platforms.

clearTimeout()
> Cancels a pending timeout operation. The *timeoutId* argument is a value returned by the call to setTimeout() and identifies which block of deferred code to cancel.

> *window*.clearTimeout(*timeoutId*)

close()
> Closes a window.

confirm()
> Asks a yes-or-no question using a dialog box. Returns true if the user clicks the OK button, false if the user clicks Cancel.

> *window*.confirm(*question*)

focus()
> Gives the top-level browser window keyboard focus; this brings the window to the front on most platforms.

open()
> Looks up an existing window or opens up a new one. Buggy in Netscape 2.0.

> *window*.open([*url*, [*name*, [*features*]]])

> If the *name* argument specifies the name of an existing window, then a reference to that window is returned. The returned window will display the specified *url*, but the *features* will be ignored. If *url* is the empty string, a blank window is opened.

> If *name* does not refer to an existing window, it specifies the name of the new window; *name* can be used as the value of a target attribute of an <a> or <form> tag to force documents to be displayed in the window.

> *features* is a comma-separated list of features to appear in the window; if this argument is empty or not specified, then all features will be present in the window. If *features* specifies any one feature, then any feature that does not appear in the list will not appear in the window. The string should not contain any whitespace; each element has the form:

> *feature*[=*value*]

The available features are:

`toolbar`
> The browser toolbar

`location`
> The input field for entering URLs into the browser

`directories`
> Directory buttons, such as "What's New" in Netscape

`status`
> The status line

`menubar`
> The browser menubar

`resizable`
> If this feature is present and not set to no, then the window will not have resize handles around its border

`width`
> Must be followed by a value that specifies the width of the window in pixels

`height`
> Must be followed by a value that specifies the height of the window in pixels

`prompt()`
> Displays the specified (plain text) *message* in a dialog box that also contains a text input field and three buttons (OK, Clear, and Cancel). It should ask the user to enter the information you want. The optional *default* is a string or integer that will initially be displayed in the input field. If the *default* argument is not passed, or if its value is null, then `prompt()` displays the string "<undefined>". Pass the empty string ("") to make `prompt()` display an empty input box.

> > *window*.prompt(*message*)
> > *window*.prompt(*message, default*)

> Selecting the Cancel button causes `prompt()` to return `null`; OK returns the text value in the input field; Clear erases the field.

`scroll()`
> Scrolls the document displayed in the Window so that the specified *x* and *y* coordinates appear in the upper-left corner. `scroll(0,0)` specifies the top-left corner of the document.

> > *window*.scroll(*x, y*)   // x, y are coords to scroll to

```
setTimeout()
```
Executes string of JavaScript *code* after a specified amount of time
(*delay* milliseconds) elapses. Returns an opaque value (a "timeout
id") that can be passed to the `clearTimeout()` method to cancel the
execution of *code*.

```
window.setTimeout(code, delay)
```

Event handlers
The value of the following event handlers may be any number of JavaScript statements, separated by semicolons, which are executed when the handler is invoked.

```
onblur()
```
Invoked when a top-level window loses focus. Defined by specifying the
onBlur attribute of the `<body>` or `<frameset>` tags of the document or
frameset that occupies the top-level window. May also be defined by assigning
a function to the `onblur` property of the Window object.

```
<body                                a definition of the handler
    [ onBlur="JavaScript statements" ]
            . . .
>

<frameset                            another way to define the handler
    [ onBlur="JavaScript statements" ]
            . . .
>

window.onblur=handler-func           defining the handler directly
window.onblur()                      an explicit invocation of the handler
```

```
onerror()
```
Invoked when a JavaScript error occurs. The default JavaScript error handler
displays an error dialog; you can customize this behavior by providing your
own `onerror()` event handler. Define it for a window by setting the
`onerror` property of a Window object to an appropriate function; unlike
other event handlers in JavaScript, `onerror()` cannot be defined in an HTML
tag. You register an `onerror()` event handler like this:

```
window.onerror="handler-function
```

Netscape invokes the handler like this:

```
window.onerror(message, url, line)
```

message is the error message; *url* is the URL of the document in which the
error occurred; *line* is the line number at which the error occurred. When
the `onerror()` handler is invoked, it is passed these three arguments to do
with as it will. You can turn off error handling for a window by setting the
`onerror` property of the window to `null`.

```
onfocus()
```
Invoked when the top-level window receives focus. Defined by specifying the
onFocus attribute of the `<body>` or `<frameset>` tags of the document or

frameset that occupies the top-level window. May also be defined by assigning a function to the onfocus property of the Window object.

```
<body                              a definition of the handler
    [ onFocus="JavaScript statements" ]
            . . .
>

<frameset                          another way to define the handler
    [ onFocus="JavaScript statements" ]
            . . .
>
```

```
window.onfocus=handler-func        defining the handler directly
window.onfocus()                   an explicit invocation of the handler
```

onLoad()

Invoked when the document (or frameset) is fully loaded. Defined by specifying the onLoad attribute of the <body> or the <frameset> tags of that window. May also be read and invoked through the Window object. Buggy in Netscape 2.0.

```
<body                              a definition of the handler
    [ onLoad="JavaScript statements" ]
            . . .
>

<frameset                          another way to define the handler
    [ onLoad="JavaScript statements" ]
            . . .
>
```

```
window.onload=handler-func         defining the handler directly
window.onload()                    an explicit invocation of the handler
```

onUnload()

Invoked when the browser leaves the document or frameset. Defined by specifying the onUnload attribute of the <body> or <frameset> tags of that window. May also be read and invoked through the Window object.

```
<body                              a definition of the handler
    [ onUnload="JavaScript statements" ]
            . . .
>

<frameset [ rows="row sizes" ]     another way to define the handler
          [ cols="column sizes" ]
          [ onUnload="JavaScript statements" ]
            . . .
>
```

```
window.onunload=handler-func       defining the handler directly
window.onunload()                  an explicit invocation of the handler
```

PART V

Server Configuration

CHAPTER 22

Server Configuration Overview

The Web server is the software responsible for accepting browser requests, retrieving the specified file (or executing the specified CGI script), and returning its contents (or the script's results). Most Web servers on the Internet today run on UNIX machines, although the percentage of servers on other platforms (such as Windows 95, Windows NT, and the Macintosh) is steadily increasing.

Web servers are often called *httpd*, using a UNIX convention in which daemons are named with the name of the service followed by the letter "d". (A UNIX daemon is a process that sits idle waiting for other programs to make requests.)

On UNIX, there are four major flavors of Web server:

- The NCSA server, maintained by the National Center for Supercomputing Applications at the University of Illinois at Urbana-Champaign. This server is publicly available from *hoohoo.ncsa.uiuc.edu*, and is covered in Chapter 23, *Apache and NCSA Server Configuration*.

- Apache, a variation of NCSA that has grown into the most popular Web server today. The Apache server is publicly available from *www.apache.org*, and is covered alongside NCSA in Chapter 23.

- The CERN server, maintained by the World Wide Web Consortium. This server is publicly available from *www.w3.org* and is covered in Chapter 24, *CERN Server Configuration*.

- The Netscape family of servers. Although the Netscape servers are commercial products, demos are available from *www.netscape.com*. They are covered in Chapters 25, *Netscape Server Configuration*.

Server
Configuration

We cover all four of these servers, as well as:

- WebSite, a server for the Windows 95 and Windows NT server. Although Web-Site is a commercial product, demos are available from *website.ora.com*. Web-Site is covered in Chapter 26, *WebSite Server Configuration*.

The UNIX servers are configured using configuration files containing directives that control basic settings such as server name and directory paths to file access and authorization. The Netscape family of servers is configured via HTML forms but maintains its data in configuration files. The WebSite server does not use configuration files but is instead configured via a series of dialog boxes and wizards.

Typical Server Behavior

Web servers first retrieve the request using Berkeley *sockets*, a mechanism for communicating over a network. The Web server listens for requests on a particular port on the server machine, generally port 80. By default, Web browsers use port 80 for their requests.

Once the server receives the request, it locates the document being requested. It looks for the file under the *document root* directory. For example, if the document root is */usr/local/httpd/htdocs*, and the client requests the document */staff/matthew.html*, then the server retrieves */usr/local/httpd/htdocs/staff/matthew.html*.

If the URL doesn't specify a file but just a directory, the server returns the *directory index file*, generally called *index.html* or *welcome.html*.

The server sends the contents of the file back to the client, along with some *HTTP response headers* (see Chapter 19, *HTTP Headers*). Among the data in the response headers is the *media type* (also known as a *content type* or *MIME type*), i.e., the format that the file is in. The way it determines the format depends on the server, but usually it comes from the suffix of the document—e.g., *.html* is taken to be an HTML document, *.pdf* is assumed to be an Adobe Acrobat document, etc. See Chapter 20, *Media Types and Subtypes*, for a listing of common media types and the associated suffixes, if any.

Configuring the Server

Or so the theory is. Much of this behavior depends on the server configuration:

- The server might use a port other than port 80. One reason to do so is if there are multiple servers running on the same host, or to avoid needing *root* access to start and maintain the server.

- The *staff* directory might be mapped elsewhere in the file system. An administrator might set this up so different departments can manage their Web sites independently, without requiring access to the server configuration directory.

- The *staff* directory might be configured with password or host security.

- The server might be configured not to return an *index.html* file, or it might be configured to use a different default document (e.g., *default.html*).

- Instead of an HTML file, the document in question might be a CGI program. The server determines this either by the directory in which it resides, or by its suffix, depending on how the server is configured. If it is a CGI program, the server does not return it directly to the client but executes it as described in Chapter 9, *CGI Overview*. The data returned by the program is sent back to the client.

Chapters 23 through 26 cover the directives that control these issues, and many more.

Server
Configuration

CHAPTER 23

Apache and NCSA Server Configuration

Apache is the most widely used Web server on the Internet. The Apache server was developed from an early version of the NCSA server with the intent of providing further improvement while maintaining compatibility. Apache has now broken ahead as the most popular server, although many sites still use NCSA.

Although this chapter concentrates on documenting Apache, many of the directives listed here are also supported by the NCSA server. For verification of your server's support of a particular directive, we recommend the online documentation. The Apache server and documentation can be obtained from *http://www.apache.org*. The NCSA server and support information can be obtained from *http://boohoo.ncsa.uiuc.edu*.

Apache and NCSA use four separate files to configure their behavior. These are:

httpd.conf
> The server configuration file, which specifies the basics of the server's operation.

srm.conf
> The resource configuration file, which specifies how the server should treat local resources when responding to a request.

access.conf
> The access configuration file, which specifies what operations should be allowed on what files and by whom.

mime.types
> The MIME types file, which specifies what MIME types should be associated with what file suffixes (see Chapter 20, *Media Types and Subtypes*).

Example copies of each of these files are included with the server software distribution.

In addition to the directives themselves, the configuration files may contain any number of blank lines or comment lines beginning with a hash mark (#). Although directive names are not case-sensitive, we use the case conventions in the default files.

Basic Server Configuration — http.conf

The server configuration file, named *httpd.conf* by default, specifies essential information that the server needs in order to run. This includes what machine and port the server is running on, where log files should be written, and how much of the system's resources the server should claim.

The following sections contain the directives that can be used in the *httpd.conf* file for the Apache and NCSA servers.

AccessConfig	`AccessConfig` *filename* Specifies the location of the access configuration file, either as an absolute path or as a relative path from the `Server-Root` directory. For example: `AccessConfig conf/access.conf`
Action	`Action` *mime_type cgi_script* Tells the server to execute the specified CGI script whenever a file of the specified MIME type is requested, sending the requested URL as extra path information.
AgentLog	`AgentLog` *filename* Specifies the location of the log file that identifies the client program used for each request, either as an absolute path or as a relative path from the server root. For example: `AgentLog logs/agent_log`
Annotation-Server	`Annotation-Server` *servername* Specifies the name of the server to use for public annotations, as supported by the NCSA Mosaic client. This information will then be sent to clients as the value of the `Annotations-cgi` MIME header in the response. (NCSA only)
AssumeDigestS . . .	`AssumeDigestSupport` Specifies whether the server should assume MD5 message digest support on the client end.

BindAddress *hostname*	**BindAddress**
Specifies the name this server uses when multiple servers are being used for multihoming. Either the IP address or DNS name can be used. For example: `BindAddress www.ora.com`	
CacheNegotiatedDocs	**CacheNegotiat . . .**
Tells the server to allow remote proxy servers to cache negotiated documents. By default, Apache does not allow caching of negotiated documents.	
ErrorLog *filename*	**ErrorLog**
Specifies the location of the error log file, either an absolute path or relative path to the `ServerRoot` directory. The default setting is: `ErrorLog logs/error_log`	
CoreDirectory *filename*	**CoreDirectory**
Specifies the directory in which core files should be dumped, as an absolute path or a path relative to the `ServerRoot` directory. By default, these will be dumped into the `ServerRoot` directory. (NCSA only)	
DNSMode `None|Minimum|Standard|Maximum`	**DNSMode**

Controls how often and under what circumstances the server will attempt reverse DNS lookup of the client host. Possible values are:
 	
`None`
    No DNS lookup under any circumstances
 	
`Minimum`
    DNS lookup only for resolving access permissions
 	
`Standard`
    DNS lookup for every request (default)
 	
`Maximum`
    DNS lookup both to get a name for the address, and to confirm that the name can resolve back to that address
 	
(NCSA only)	

Group	Group *groupname* Specifies the group you want the server process to run as. Either a group name or group ID can be specified; a group ID should be preceded by a number sign (#).
IdentityCheck	IdentityCheck On|Off Specifies whether the server should attempt to learn the identity of the user for each request by querying the *identd* process running on the user's machine. By default identity checking is off.
KeepAlive	KeepAlive On|Off Tells the server to allow persistent connections (default=off). See also KeepAliveTimeOut and Max-KeepAliveRequests.
KeepAliveT . . .	KeepAliveTimeOut *seconds* Specifies the number of seconds to wait for the next request before closing a persistent connection. Used only when persistent connections are enabled with the KeepAlive On setting. The default is 10.
Listen	Listen [*IP_address:*]*port* Tells the server to listen for requests on the specified port for the specified IP address (if supplied). Overrides Bind-Address and Port.
LogDirGroup . . .	LogDirGroupWriteOk Specifies whether the server should be willing to start if any of the log files are in directories that are group write-able. (NCSA only)
LogDirPublic . . .	LogDirPublicWriteOk Specifies whether the server should be willing to start if any of the log files are in directories that are world write-able. (NCSA only)
LogOptions	LogOptions *options* Specifies how log information should be written to the various log files. Options are:

Separate
    Agent and referer information will be written to separate log files (specified by the `AgentLog` and `RefererLog` directives)
 	
Date
    Include a date stamp in the separate agent and referer logs
 	
Combined
    Agent and referer fields are included in the transfer log at the end of each record
 	
Servername
    The server name (from the `ServerName` directive) is included in the transfer log at the end of each record
 	
(NCSA only)
	LogOptions

`MaxClients` *number* Specifies the maximum number of slave processes. The default is 150.	MaxClients
`MaxKeepAliveRequests` *number* When persistent connections are enabled with `KeepAlive On`, the `MaxKeepAliveRequests` directive specifies the number of requests the server will allow per persistent connection. The default is 0 (no limit). (NCSA only)	MaxKeepAlive . . .
`MaxRequestsPerChild` *number* Specifies how many requests a slave process may handle during its life. For example: `MaxRequestsPerChild 300`	MaxRequests . . .
`MaxServers` *number* Defines the maximum number of consecutive slave processes. (NCSA only)	MaxServers
`MaxSpareServers` *number* Specifies the upper range for how many idle slaves the server should keep around at any given time. The default is 10.	MaxSpareServers

Server Configuration

MinSpareServers	`MinSpareServers` *number* Specifies the lower range for how many idle slaves the server should keep around at any given time. The default is 5.
PidFile	`PidFile` *filename* Specifies the location of the file into which the server should place its process ID when running in standalone mode, as an absolute path or as a relative path from the `ServerRoot` directory. The default is: `PidFile logs/httpd.pid`
Port	`Port` *number* Specifies the server's port, with a default of 80. Many non-standard ports are assigned to 8001.
ProcessName	`ProcessName` *name* Specifies what name the server should use in process listings (if configured with the SETPROCTITLE flag). (NCSA only)
RefererIgnore	`RefererIgnore` *hostname* Specifies a site to be ignored in the referer log file. (NCSA only)
RefererLog	`RefererLog` *filename* Specifies the location of the refering URL log file. It may be specified either as an absolute path or as a relative path from the `ServerRoot` directory. The default is: `RefererLog logs/referer_log`
ResourceConfig	`ResourceConfig` *filename* Specifies the location of the resource configuration file, as an absolute path or as a relative path from the `Server-Root` directory. For example: `ResourceConfig srm.conf`

`ScoreBoardFile` *filename*	**ScoreBoardFile**
Specifies the location of the server status file, used by the server to monitor the status of slave processes, as an absolute path or as a relative path from the `ServerRoot` directory. The default is: `ScoreBoardFile logs/apache_runtime_status`	
`Script` *method cgi_script*	**Script**
Specifies a CGI script to be executed when a given request method is used. The method can be GET, POST, PUT, or DELETE.	
`ServerAdmin` *email_address*	**ServerAdmin**
Specifies the email address to which complaints, suggestions, and questions regarding your server should be sent. Used when the server sends error messages in response to failed requests. This directive has no default. For example: `ServerAdmin webmaster@ora.com`	
`ServerAlias` *virtual_hostname real_hostname*	**ServerAlias**
Specifies an alternate name for a host.	
`ServerName` *hostname*	**ServerName**
Allows you to specify the preferred name for your server machine.	
`ServerPath` *pathname*	**ServerPath**
Specifies a pathname for a virtual host—that is, requests for this hostname will be automatically routed to the specified pathname. For use within `<VirtualHost>` sections.	
`ServerRoot` *directory_path*	**ServerRoot**
Specifies the directory in which all the server's associated files reside. This path is used as the root directory when relative paths are specified with other directives. For example: `ServerRoot /usr/local/etc/httpd/`	

Server Configuration

ServerType	`ServerType standalone|inetd` Specifies whether your server is to run in standalone mode or under *inetd*. The default is to run standalone.
<SRMOptions>	`<SRMOptions> ...</SRMOptions>` A sectioning directive that can be placed within a `<VirtualHost>` section in the *httpd.conf* file. Resource configuration directives specific to the virtual host are placed within a `<SRMOptions>` section. See `<VirtualHost>`. (NCSA only)
StartServers	`StartServers` *number* Specifies the initial number of slave processes at server startup. The default is 5.
TimeOut	`TimeOut` *seconds* Specifies the number of seconds to wait before closing a connection. The default is 1200.
TransferLog	`TransferLog` *filename* Specifies the location of the transfer log file, as either an absolute path or a relative path to the `ServerRoot` directory. The default is: `TransferLog logs/access_log`
TypesConfig	`TypesConfig` *filename* Specifies the location of the MIME types file. As with other configuration paths, the location may be given as either an absolute path or a relative path to the `ServerRoot` directory. The default is: `TypesConfig conf/mime.types`
User	`User` *username* Specifies the user and group you want the server process to run as. Either a user name or user ID can be specified; a user ID should be preceded by a number sign (#).

`<VirtualHost hostname>...</VirtualHost>` Used when one server services multiple hostnames. Each hostname is given its own `<VirtualHost>` directive. `<VirtualHost>` has a beginning and ending directive, with other configuration directives for the host entered in between. For Apache, most directives are valid within `<VirtualHost>` except `ServerType`, `UserId`, `GroupId`, `StartServers`, `MaxSpareServers`, `MinSpareServers`, `MaxRequestsPerChild`, `BindAddress`, `PidFile`, `TypesConfig`, and `ServerRoot`. For the NCSA server, most *httpd.conf* directives are allowed, but *srm.conf* directives need to be placed within an `<SRMOptions>` directive embedded in `<VirtualHost>`.	**\<VirtualHost\>**

Resource Configuration — srm.conf

The *srm.conf* file is for server resource management—i.e., how local resources (e.g., documents) should be handled when requested by a client.

`AccessFileName filename`
Specifies the name of directory access control files. The default is:
 	
    `AccessFileName .htaccess`
	AccessFileName

`AddAlt text filenames/suffixes ...`
Specifies alternative text for icons used with a given file listing in a directory index. The text is used as the first argument to the directive, followed by one or more file extensions or names. For example:
 	
    `AddAlt IMAGE .gif .jpg .png`
    `AddAlt LOGO logo.gif`
	AddAlt

`AddAltByEncoding text encoding_type`
Works similarly to `AddAlt`, except that it specifies alt text based on the MIME content encoding of the file being listed. For example, to specify the alt text "gzip" for a file encoded with *gzip*, the directive would be:
 	
    `AddAltByEncoding gzip x-gzip`
	AddAltByEncoding

Server Configuration

AddAltByType	AddAltByType *text mime_type*
	Works similarly to `AddAlt`, except that it specifies alt text based on the media type of the file being listed. For example, to use the alt text "IMAGE" for all image files, the directive would be:
	`AddAltByType IMAGE image/*`
AddDescription	AddDescription *text suffixes* ...
	Used to associate a descriptive text phrase with a particular type of file. The text appears to the right of the file name in a directory index. The descriptive text must be surrounded by quotes and be fairly short. Files can be associated by extension or name. For example:
	`AddDescription "GIF Image File" .gif`
AddEncoding	AddEncoding *encoding-type suffixes* ...
	Allows you to specify which MIME encodings should be associated with documents from your server. Encodings beginning with **x-** are used for unofficial encodings. For example:
	`AddEncoding x-gzip gz`
AddIcon	AddIcon *pathname suffixes* ...
	Specifies an icon image to be displayed with a given type of file in a directory index. For example:
	`AddIcon /icons/image.gif .gif .jpg .png`
	An alternative syntax allows you to specify alt text in this directive as well:
	`AddIcon (IMAGE,/icons/image.gif) .gif .jpg .png`
	There are three special values that can be used for the file extensions in the `AddIcon` directive:
	`^^DIRECTORY^^` The icon will be used for subdirectory names.
	`..` The icon will be used for the parent directory.
	`^^BLANKICON^^` The icon is used only for spacing in the header of the page.

`AddIconByEncoding` *filename encoding_type*

Specifies an icon to be displayed with a file in a directory index based on the file's encoding. Similar to the `Add-Icon` directive, it can also specify alt text. For example:

```
AddIconByEncoding /icons/gzip.gif x-gzip
AddIconByEncoding (GZIP,/icons/gzip.gif) x-gzip
```

`AddIconByType` *filename mime_type*

Specifies an icon to be displayed with a file in a directory index based on the file's media type. The directive may also specify alt text. For example:

```
AddIconByType /icons/image.gif image/*
AddIconByType (IMAGE,/icons/image.gif) image/*
```

`AddLanguage` *language suffix*

Specifies that a certain extension should be associated with a certain language for purposes of content negotiation. For example, to associate the extension *francais* with French documents, use the following setting:

```
AddLanguage fr .francais
```

`AddType` *mime_type suffix| filename*

Specifies a MIME type and subtype to be associated with certain file extensions. For example, if you want to serve a Microsoft Word document:

```
AddType application/msword .doc
```

`AddType` directives will override any extension-to-type mappings you have in your *mime.types* file.

`Alias` *symbolic_path real_path*

Creates a virtual name or directory by mapping a virtual pathname that is used in a URL to a real path on your server. Aliasing is useful for organizing your server documents, keeping URLs simpler for users, and hiding the structure of your file system. For example, the icon directory is aliased in the default configuration file:

```
Alias /icons/ /usr/local/etc/httpd/icons
```

With this setting, a request for */icons/image.gif* is handled by sending the file */usr/local/etc/httpd/icons/image.gif.*

AddIconByEnco . . .

AddIconByType

AddLanguage

AddType

Server Configuration

Alias

DefaultIcon	`DefaultIcon` *filename* Specifies what icon to use when none has been assigned by one of the `AddIcon*` directives.
DefaultType	`DefaultType` *mime_type* Establishes a default MIME type to be returned to a browser if the mappings found in the *mime.types* file are not adequate. The default is `text/html`.
DirectoryIndex	`DirectoryIndex` *filenames* ... Specifies the file that is returned when a URL identifies a directory on your server and no filename. If more than one file is listed, the first one that is present in the directory will be returned. The default is: `DirectoryIndex index.html index.shtml index.cgi`
DocumentRoot	`DocumentRoot` *directory_path* Specifies the root of the server document tree. For example: `DocumentRoot /usr/local/etc/httpd/htdocs/`

ErrorDocument	`ErrorDocument` *code filename* | *string* | *URL*
	
	Allows you to customize the response sent by your server when an error is encountered. The error code is an HTTP status code as listed in Chapter 18, *Server Response Codes*. Possible values are:
	
	filename
	    A local file to return upon retrieving this error
	
	string
	    A message to return upon retrieving this error. The string must be surrounded by quotes.
	
	URL
	    A remote document to redirect the user to upon retrieving this error
	
	For example:
	
	`ErrorDocument 404 /errors/notfound.html`
	`ErrorDocument 408 "Sorry, the server timed out`
	`- try again later"`
	`ErrorDocument 402 http://www.ora.com/payment/`

Note: the NCSA server only supports the *filename* syntax for this directive.	**ErrorDocument**

`FancyIndexing On|Off`

Specifies that the server should create a fancy index for a directory listing, including filenames and icons representing the files' types, sizes, and last-modified dates. By default, fancy indexing is off.

FancyIndexing

`ForceType` *mime_type*

Specifies that all files in this directory should be served with the specified type. Appropriate for inclusion in *.htaccess* files or within `<Directory>` section directives.

ForceType

`HeaderName` *filename*

Specifies a file to be prepended to a file listing when generating a directory index. The example file uses the following setting:

```
HeaderName HEADER
```

The server will look for this file name first with an *.html* extension, and failing that, without an extension.

HeaderName

`ImapMenu` *option*

Under Apache, if an imagemap is called without valid coordinates, the server can return a menu of the items in the imagemap file. `ImapMenu` configures that menu. Options are:

`none`

No menu is created. The action specified with `Imap-Default` is taken.

`formatted`

A formatted menu is generated, with a listing of the possible links.

`semiformatted`

A menu with comments from the imagemap file and simple breaks is generated, with a listing of the possible links.

`unformatted`

A menu with the text of the imagemap file, unformatted. Useful if map files are written as HTML.

ImapMenu

Server
Configuration

ImapDefault	`ImapDefault` *option* | *URL*
	Specifies the default action for imagemap files, if there is no `default` directive in the imagemap file itself. A URL can be specified, or one of the following options:
	`error` Fails with a server response code of 500 (see Chapter 18).
	`nocontent` Sends a server response code of 204, telling the client to keep the same page displayed (see Chapter 18).
	`map` Uses the URL of the imagemap file, without coordinates (so a menu is generated unless specified otherwise).
	`referer` Uses the referring document, or the server root if a `Referer` header is not specified.
ImapBase	`ImapBase` *option* | *URL*
	Specifies the default base for imagemap files, if there is no `base` directive in the imagemap file itself. A URL can be specified, or one of the following options:
	`map` Uses the URL of the imagemap file, without coordinates (so a menu is generated unless specified otherwise).
	`referer` Uses the referring document, or the server root if a `Referer` header is not specified.
IndexIgnore	`IndexIgnore` *filenames* …
	Tells the server to ignore certain files when building a directory index on the fly. The files are specified as full server paths, and you can use the wildcards * and ? with their usual meanings. Thus, to ignore all hidden files (i.e., files whose names begin with a period) at every level, you could use the following setting:
	`IndexIgnore */.?*`
	Any number of `IndexIgnore` directives may be included.

`IndexOptions` *options* ...

Specifies a number of options to use when creating a directory index on the fly. Possible options are:

`None`

Generate only plain directory indexes.

`FancyIndexing`

Equivalent to `FancyIndexing On`. Unless fancy indexing is turned on by either method, the other index options (except `None`) are ignored.

`IconsAreLinks`

Make the icons link to the documents (in addition to making the names link).

`ScanHTMLTitles`

Scan any HTML files in the directory, extract their titles, and use them as descriptions for the files.

`SuppressLastMod`

Omit the last-modified date from the fancy index.

`SuppressSize`

Omit the size from the fancy index.

`SuppressDesc`

Omit the description from the fancy index.

`LanguagePriority` *languages* ...

Allows you to specify a ranking of languages, which is used in the event that a user's preferences are equal among language choices. For example:

    LanguagePriority de it

specifies German before Italian.

`ReadmeName` *filename*

Specifies a file to be appended to a file listing when generating a directory index. The example file uses the following setting:

    ReadmeName README

The server will look for this filename first with an *.html* extension, and failing that, without an extension.

Server Configuration

Redirect	`Redirect` *pathname url* Tells the server to forward clients that request a given directory or document to a new location.
ScriptAlias	`ScriptAlias` *symbolic_path real_path* Creates a virtual directory of CGI programs by mapping a virtual pathname that is used in a URL to a real directory of executable CGI programs on your server. Instead of returning a document in that directory, the server will run it within a CGI environment and return the output. See Chapter 9, *CGI Overview*, for more information on CGI.

SetHandler	`SetHandler` *handler*
	
	Specifies that all files in the directory should be passed through the specified handler. Values are:
	
	`cgi-script`
	    All files treated as CGI scripts (see Chapter 9)
	
	`imap-file`
	    All files treated as imagemap files
	
	`send-as-is`
	    All files sent without additional server-supplied HTTP headers
	
	`server-info`
	    All files sent with server configuration information
	
	`server-parsed`
	    All files parsed as server-side includes (see Chapter 13, *Server Side Includes*)
	
	`type-map`
	    All files parsed as type map files for content negotiation

UserDir	`UserDir` *directory_path* Specifies the path within each user's home directory for their Web directories. The default value is `public_html`. To disable user directories, use this value: `UserDir DISABLED`

`XBitHack on|off|full`

Specifies the parsing of executable HTML documents. Options are:

`on`

> Files that are user-executable are treated as a server-parsed HTML document (SPML).

`off`

> Executable files are treated like regular files.

`full`

> Files that are both user and group executable have the last modified time altered to match that of the returned document.

XBitHack

Access Configuration — access.conf

The NCSA and Apache servers provide a system of security to sensitive documents on your server by allowing you to restrict access to directories. Access can be determined based on username/password authentication, IP address, or a combination of both. Access is controlled by the use of access configuration files (ACFs).

You may control access to any directory in your document tree with a global access configuration file. The global ACF lives in the *conf* directory and is specified by the `AccessConfig` directive in your *httpd.conf* file. The default is *access.conf*. Global ACFs have the userid and groupid of the server daemon, and therefore, the server administrator should be the only person who has access to the file. A global ACF is required.

You can also have per-directory access configuration files. These files describe access control for only the directories that they live in. Per-directory ACFs allow users who have write permission to certain directories available on the server to establish their own access rules. The name of per-directory ACFs is specified with the `AccessFileName` directive in the *srm.conf* file. The default name is *.htaccess*. Per-directory ACFs can be restricted or forbidden in the global ACF.

Both types of ACFs are constructed the same way, except for a few additional directives in global ACFs that specify directories and overrides.

Basically, an ACF does one or more of the following functions:

- Specifies the name of the password file where valid usernames and passwords are stored.

- Specifies the name of the group file where valid groups of users are listed.

- Sets the limits on who can access files in the directory and with what methods.

- Specifies which advanced features are allowed to be performed within a directory.

This is an example of a global ACF:

```
<Directory /projects>
 Options All
 AuthType Basic
 AuthUserFile /usr/local/etc/httpd/conf/.htpasswd
 AuthGroupFile /usr/local/etc/httpd/conf/.htgroup
 <Limit GET>
   order allow,deny
   allow from all
 </Limit>
</Directory>

<Directory /projects/golf>
 <Limit GET>
  order deny,allow
  deny from all
  allow from .golf.org
 </Limit>
</Directory>

<Directory /projects/golf/team>
 AuthName For Team Players Only
 <Limit GET>
  require group golfteam
 </Limit>
</Directory>

<Directory /projects/golf/team/captain>
 AuthName Captain Only
 <Limit GET>
  require user captain
 </Limit>
</Directory>
```

This example shows the various ways in which access control can be implemented. The global ACF uses the `Directory` sectioning directives to enclose access information for different directories (wildcards may also be used to designate a set of directories). The settings for each different directory apply to that directory and all of its subdirectories unless overridden in a lower directory's specifications.

Per-directory ACFs contain the same information as `<Directory>` . . . `</Directory>` sections, except without the `Directory` tags. Use of per-directory ACFs is controlled by the `AllowOverride` directive within `<Directory>` sections in the global ACF.

Password and Group Files

For user and group level authentication, a password file is needed. The location and name of the password file is specified in the `AuthUserName` directive. The easiest and most common way to create a password file is to use the *htpasswd* program that is distributed with the server. To create a new password file to store a new username and password, use this command:

```
% htpasswd -c pathname username
```

The -c option tells the program to open a file with the given pathname. The program will ask you to type the password you want to use for the given username twice, and the username and encrypted password will be stored in the new file. Other users can be added to the file by using the same command and pathname without the -c option.

Password files created with .htpasswd are similar to UNIX password files. Keep in mind, however, that there is no correspondence between valid users and passwords on a UNIX server and users and passwords on the Web server. You do not need an account on the UNIX server to have access to the Web server.

You can corral several users into a single named group by creating a group file. The location and name of the group file is specified with the AuthGroupFile directive. Each line of a group file specifies the group name, followed by a colon, followed by a list of valid usernames that belong to the group:

```
groupname: username1 username2 username3 ...
```

Each user in a group needs to be entered into the password file. When a group authentication is required, the server will accept any valid username/password from the group to allow access.

The .htpasswd user authentication scheme is known as the *basic* authentication method for HTTP servers. Apache and NCSA allow other types of authentication methods, which are configured with a similar set of directives.

Access Configuration File Directives

This is a listing of all of the directives that may be used in global and per-directory access configuration files (ACFs).

Server Configuration

allow from *hostnames* ...   **allow**

The allow directive is used within the <Limit> section of an ACF. It specifies which hosts can access a given directory with a given method. The hostname can be any of the following:

domain name
   A domain name, like *.ora.com*. Only hosts from that domain are permitted access.

host name
   A full hostname.

$\rightarrow$

allow ←	***full IP address*** An IP address of a host. ***partial IP address*** The first 1 to 3 bytes of an IP address, for subnet restriction. `all` Using the word `all` means that all hosts are allowed. There can be only one `allow` directive per `<Limit>` section. If omitted, there is no default.

AllowOverride	`AllowOverride` *options* ...
	
	Controls the extent to which you allow local per-directory access control files to override the global access defaults defined by the *access.conf* configuration file. The directive takes one or more options, which can be:
	
	`None`
	ACFs are not allowed in this directory.
	
	`All`
	ACFs are unrestricted in this directory.
	
	`Options`
	Allow use of the `Options` directive.
	
	`Indexes`
	Allow use of directory indexing directives.
	
	`FileInfo`
	Allow use of the `AddType` and `AddEncoding` directives.
	
	`AuthConfig`
	Allow use of these directives: `AuthName`, `Auth-Type`, `AuthUserFile`, `AuthGroupFile`, or any other `Auth*` directives.
	
	`Limit`
	Allow use of the `Limit` section directive.
	
	The `AllowOverride` directive can only be used for the global ACF. If omitted, the default is:
	
	`AllowOverride All`

`AuthDBMGroupFile` *filename*	**AuthDBMGroupFile**
The Apache server can be configured to use DBM authentication in addition to basic authentication. The `AuthDBMGroupFile` directive specifies the location of the DBM group file. It replaces `AuthGroupFile` when DBM is used.	
`AuthDBMUserFile` *filename*	**AuthDBMUserFile**
The Apache server can be configured to use DBM authentication in addition to basic authentication. The `AuthDBMUserFile` directive specifies the location of the DBM password file. It replaces `AuthUserFile` when DBM is used.	
`AuthGroupFile` *filename*	**AuthGroupFile**
Specifies the group filename as an absolute path. For example: `AuthGroupFile /www/Admin/.htgroup`	
`AuthName` *name*	**AuthName**
Sets the name of the authorization realm for this directory. The value is a short name describing this authorization realm; it can contain spaces.	
`AuthType` *type*	**AuthType**
Sets the type of authorization used in this directory. `Basic` authorization is the most commonly used method.	
`AuthUserFile` *filename*	**AuthUserFile**
Specifies the file that contains a list of users and passwords for user authentication. The file name is given as the absolute path of a user file created with the *htpasswd* support program. For example: `AuthUserFile /www/Admin/.htpasswd`	
`deny from` *hostnames* ...	**deny**
The `deny` directive is used within a `<Limit>` section of an ACF. It affects which hosts are denied access to a directory. The hostnames can be one of the following:	
	$\rightarrow$

Server Configuration

deny ←	**domain name** A domain name, like *.ora.com*. Hosts from that domain are denied access. **host name** A full hostname. **full IP address** The IP address of a host. **partial IP address** The first 1 to 3 bytes of an IP address, for subnet restriction. `all` Using the word `all` means that all hosts are denied access.

\<Directory\>

\<Directory\>...\</Directory\>

The `<Directory>` directive is a sectioning directive that identifies the directory or directories to which contained access-control directives apply. It is used to structure the global ACF, and cannot be used in a per-directory ACF. The start tag has the following format:

    <Directory dir>

where *dir* is the absolute pathname of the directory, which may include wildcard characters (* and ?) to designate a set of directories.

\<Limit\>

\<Limit\>...\</Limit\>

The `<Limit>` directive is a sectioning directive that identifies which clients and users can access a directory. This directive applies to both the global ACF and per-directory ACFs. The start tag has the following syntax:

    <Limit method1 method2 ...>

where *method* is one of the following:

GET
> Allows clients to retrieve documents and execute scripts with the GET request method.

POST
> Allows clients to use scripts and resources using the POST request method (mostly CGI programs).

The `order`, `deny`, `allow`, and `require` directives are the usual inhabitants of the `Limit` sectioning directive. Later versions of NCSA (1.5 and up) have three

additional directives designed for the `<Limit>` section: `referer`, `satisfy`, and `OnDeny`.	**`<Limit>`**
`<Location>`...`</Location>` A sectioning directive for specifying directives that apply to a given URL. Basically just a more specific version of `<Directory>`.	**`<Location>`**
`OnDeny` *URL* For NCSA versions 1.5 and later, the `OnDeny` directive can be used in a `<Limit>` section of an ACF to redirect the client to another URL if access to the directory has been denied.	**OnDeny**
`Options` *options* ... Controls the degree of advanced features that you wish to allow on your server. One or more options may be listed on the `Options` line, separated by spaces. Valid entries are:	**Options**

`None`
> No features are enabled in this directory.

`Indexes`
> Allows users to request indexes in this directory.

`Includes`
> Server-side includes are enabled in this directory.

`IncludesNoExec`
> Server-side includes are enabled in the directory, but the *exec* feature is disabled.

`ExecCGI`
> Execution of CGI scripts is allowed in this directory.

`FollowSymLinks`
> The server follows symbolic links in this directory.

`SymLinksIfOwnerMatch`
> The server only follows symbolic links if the target file/directory is owned by the same user ID as the link.

`All`
> All features are enabled in this directory.

→

Options ←	The Options directive can be used in both the global ACF and in per-directory ACFs. There can be only one Options directive per Directory segment. If omitted, the default is: `Options All`

order	### order *order*
	
	The order directive specifies the order in which deny and allow directives are evaluated within a <Limit> section. This directive is only available within <Limit> sections, but can be used on a global ACF or per-directory ACF basis. The order line can take one of the following forms:
	
	`order deny,allow`
	    deny directives are evaluated before allow directives (this is the default).
	
	`order allow,deny`
	    allow directives are evaluated before deny directives
	
	`order mutual-failure`
	    This setting means that any host appearing on the allow list is allowed, any host listed on the deny list is denied, and any host not appearing in either list is denied.

referer	### referer allow|deny from *URL* For NCSA version 1.5 or later, the referer directive can be used in a <Limit> section of an ACF to specify that a request in this directory must have originated from a specified location. The URL must use the service name (http:, etc.), and can be an exact match to a document name or use wildcards to designate a set of documents, directories, or servers.
require	### require *entity names* ... Specifies which authenticated users can access a given directory with a given method in a <Limit> section of an ACF. A require line requires that all of the appropriate Auth* directives are specified for the directory. *entity* is one of the following:

user

    Only the named users can access this directory with the given methods. Each name is therefore a user-name that exists in the specified password file.

group

    Only users in the named groups can access this directory with the given methods. Each name is therefore a group name that is listed in the specified group file.

valid-user

    All users listed in the AuthUserFile (specified password file) are allowed access upon providing a valid password.

satisfy all|any

For NCSA version 1.5 and later, the satisfy directive can be used in a <Limit> section of an ACF to control how access is handled when both allow and require directives are used (i.e., when both host and user/password authentication are set). The directive can take one of two values:

all

    This setting means that a user must satisfy both the allow and require directives to gain access to the directory.

any

    This setting means that a user must satisfy only one of the allow or require directives to gain access to the directory.

The following directives can also be used within the global ACF and per-directory ACFs as indicated:

DefaultType	Only per-directory ACFs
AddEncoding	All ACFs
AddDescription	Only per-directory ACFs
AddIcon	All ACFs
IndexIgnore	All ACFs
DefaultIcon	All ACFs
ReadmeName	All ACFs

These directives are a subset of those allowed in *srm.conf*, and are described earlier in this chapter.

For the Apache server, other directory-specific configuration directives may be included in `Directory` sections or per-directory ACFs in addition to those listed above. A non-applicable directive should be unaffected.

CHAPTER 24

CERN Server Configuration

The CERN server was originally developed at the European Laboratory for Particle Physics, formerly known as Counseil European pour la Recherche Nucleaire (CERN), and incidentally the birthplace of the Web. It is now maintained by the World Wide Web Consortium (W3C).

Unlike the NCSA and Apache servers, the CERN server uses a single configuration file, containing all of the information the server needs to run. There are several example configuration files included with the software, which correspond to different modes of running the server:

- The vanilla configuration file (*httpd.conf*) tells the server how to act as a normal HTTP server

- The protected configuration file (*prot.conf*) tells the server how to act as a normal HTTP server with access control

- The proxy configuration file (*proxy.conf*) tells the server how to act as an HTTP proxy server

- The caching proxy configuration file (*cache.conf*) tells the server how to act as a caching HTTP proxy server

In addition to the directives themselves, the server configuration file may contain any number of blank lines or comment lines beginning with "#". Directive names are not case-sensitive, but the case conventions used in the example files will be used here.

This section lists all of the directives available for use in a regular HTTP server setup. For easier reference, the directives are grouped into categories based on their basic functionality. Access control configuration and related directives are discussed in the last section.

Setting up the server for proxy and caching service and related directives are not discussed here. Information on these setups and the server software itself can be found at *http://www.w3.org*.

Basic Server Configuration

The directives listed in this section are used to set general server parameters.

Disable	`Disable` *method* The `Disable` directive tells the server to disallow certain HTTP request methods. By default, DELETE, PUT, CHECKIN, CHECKOUT, SHOWMETHOD, LINK, and UNLINK are all disabled.
DNSLookup	`DNSLookup On|Off` The `DNSLookup` directive controls whether the server will attempt reverse DNS lookup of the client host during requests. The default is On.
Enable	`Enable` *method* The `Enable` directive tells the server to allow certain HTTP request methods. By default, GET, HEAD, and POST are all enabled.
ErrorUrl	`ErrorUrl` *error_code filename* The document to return when the specified error is returned.
GroupId	`GroupId` *group_id* Specifies the group you want the server process to run as.
HostName	`HostName` *hostname* Allows you to specify the preferred name for your server machine.
IdentityCheck	`IdentityCheck On|Off` Specifies whether the server should attempt to learn the identity of the user for each request. By default identity checking is off.

InputTimeOut *time*	**InputTimeOut**
Specifies how long the server will wait for a request from the client after the connection has been opened. You may use any combination of hours (hours), minutes (mins), and seconds (secs). The default setting is: `InputTimeOut 2 mins`	
OutputTimeOut *time*	**OutputTimeOut**
Specifies how long the server will wait for the client to accept the response. The default setting is: `OutputTimeOut 20 mins`	
ParentGroupId *group_id*	**ParentGroupId**
Sets the group ID of the parent process right after binding to the port.	
ParentUserId *user_id*	**ParentUserId**
Sets the user ID of the parent process right after binding to the port.	
PidFile *filename*	**PidFile**
Specifies the location of the file into which the server should place its process id when running in standalone mode, either as an absolute path or as a relative path from the `ServerRoot`. This directive is needed if you plan to restart the server using the *-restart* command-line option. The default setting is: `PidFile /tmp/httpd-pid`	
Port *number*	**Port**
Specifies your server's port. The default port for standalone web servers is 80. For example, to set the port to 5234, use the following setting: `Port 5234` Specifying a port automatically sets the server to run in standalone mode, unless you have explicitly told it otherwise. If you want the server to run under *inetd*, you should set the `ServerType` directive to `inetd`, or not include a `Port` directive.	

Server Configuration

ScriptTimeOut	`ScriptTimeOut` *time* Specifies how long the server will wait for a script to produce output to be sent to a client. The value is specified using any combination of hours (hours), minutes (mins), and seconds (secs). The default setting is: `ScriptTimeOut 5 mins`
ServerRoot	`ServerRoot` *directory_path* Specifies the directory in which all the server's associated files reside. This path is used as the root directory when relative paths are specified with other directives. For example: `ServerRoot /usr/local/etc/httpd/`
ServerType	`ServerType standalone|inetd` Specifies whether your server is to run in standalone mode or under *inetd*. The default value depends on whether the `Port` directive is used. If a port is specified, the default is `standalone`; if not, the default is `inetd`.
UserId	`UserId` *user_id* Specifies the user you want the server process to run as.

Resource Configuration

The directives listed in this section are used to configure how the server handles resources requested by clients.

AddEncoding	`AddEncoding` *suffix encoding_type* Allows you to specify which MIME encodings should be associated with documents from your server. Most commonly this is used to tell browsers when a document is compressed. For example, to tell browsers that documents ending in *.gz* are encoded in gzip format, you would include the following setting: `AddEncoding .gz x-gzip` Note that the encoding begins with **x-** which marks it as an unofficial encoding.

AddLanguage *suffix language_code*

The AddLanguage directive allows you to specify which language should be associated with documents from your server. The format is the same as for AddEncoding:

```
AddLanguage .francais fr
```

This setting will associate the language French (ISO language code fr) with the extension *francais.*

AddType *suffix mime_type encoding_type quality*

The AddType directive specifies how the server should associate MIME types with documents, based on their extensions. Where other servers only associate MIME type and subtype with an extension, the CERN server also allows an encoding and a quality, although both may be omitted. For example, suppose you want to tell the server how to handle several popular image types:

```
AddType .ppm image/ppm 7bit 0.3
AddType .gif image/gif binary 0.5
AddType .jpg image/jpeg binary 0.7
AddType .png image/png binary 0.9
```

These directives tell the server to make the appropriate type associations for PPM, GIF, JPEG, and PNG images, that PPM is a basic ASCII representation while the others are binary formats, and that when forced to choose it should prefer PNG to anything, JPEG to GIF or PPM, and GIF to PPM.

If the encoding is omitted, binary is assumed. If the quality is omitted, perfect quality is assumed and a score of 1.0 is used.

MaxContentLengthBuffer *size*

When the CERN server sends a response, it tries to include a Content-Length header. If a document is too long, the server must give up and simply transmit the document without length information. The MaxContentLength-Buffer directive specifies what length is "too long." The default setting is 50K.

MetaDir *directory_name*

The subdirectory of a requested document's directory containing extra headers to send in the server response. See MetaSuffix.

MetaSuffix	**MetaSuffix** *suffix*
	Specifies the special extension used to identify an extra header information file. The server looks for a subdirectory in the requested document's directory of the same name specified with `MetaDir` directive. If that directory exists, it then looks for a file with the same name of the requested file, but with a suffix matching the name specified by `MetaSuffix`. The headers contained in this file are used in the server's response.
SuffixCaseSense	**SuffixCaseSense** On|Off
	The `SuffixCaseSense` directive determines whether suffix matching is case-sensitive. This affects not only the MIME directives, but also the directory indexing directives. The default is for suffixes to be case-insensitive.
UserDir	**UserDir** *directory_name*
	The path within each user's home directory for their Web directories.

Translation Rules

Under the CERN server, each document request is filtered through a series of translation rules to determine what local resource should be used to handle the request. The document name is matched against a filename expression in each rule; if it matches, the rule is applied. The end result may be a file to send or a CGI program to run, or it may be a redirection to another document, either locally or at another site.

The most important thing to remember about CERN translation rules is that they are applied in the order that they appear in the configuration file. So if you have a rule that disallows access to a given document, it doesn't matter if there is a rule later that allows it. The request will already have been denied.

DefProt	**DefProt** *expression setup_file*
	Associate a file or group of files with the protection setup file. Any files matching *expression* are affected. The protection setup file is a file that sets the protection parameters to be used on the specified files. See the section entitled "Access Control Configuration" at the end of this chapter.

Exec *expression script*

Specifies the pathname to your CGI program directory. This directive also tells the server to run requested documents in that directory as CGI programs and return the results. For example, suppose your main CGI directory is */www/cgi-bin/*, while your server root directory is */usr/local/etc/httpd/docs/*. To make */cgi-bin/* the server path to your actual CGI directory and to tell the server that */cgi-bin/* is a CGI directory, use the following setting:

```
Exec /cgi-bin/* /www/cgi-bin/*
```

Exec

Fail *expression*

Tells the server that the document matching *expression* may not be served. The server returns a 403 (Permission Denied) error to the user and closes the connection.

Fail

Map *expression new_path*

The Map directive tells the server to rewrite a request for a document to use a different path. It is the CERN server's way of creating virtual pathnames. The directive can specify any directory to be mapped to one relative to the ServerRoot directory. For example, to map the directory */WWW/sales/web/docs/* to the directory */sales/* under the ServerRoot directory, use this directive:

```
Map /sales/* /www/sales/web/docs/*
```

Map

Pass *expression [new_path]*

The Pass directive is used to specify directories where documents can be served from. For example, to allow documents to be served from the directory */WWW/sales/web/docs/*, use this directive:

```
Pass /WWW/sales/web/docs/*
```

Pass can also map a pathname, like the Map directive, at the same time that it permits access to the directory.

Pass

Server Configuration (sidebar)

Protect *expression setup_file uid.gid*

The Protect directive is used to declare a file or set of files to be subject to access control, and indicates a protection setup file to be used for the specified files. This directive is discussed in the *Access Control* section at the end of this chapter.

Protect

Redirect *expression url*

The Redirect directive is useful when you have had to move resources around either within the server or across servers. The

Redirect

→

Redirect ←	new path is a full URL, possibly on another server. For example, if you have moved all documents from the /www/ directory on your server to another server, use: `Redirect /www/* http://www.acme.com/products/*`

Logging

These directives are used to specify locations of log files and their configuration.

AccessLog	**AccessLog** *filename* Specifies the location of the access log file, either as an absolute path or as a relative path from the `ServerRoot` directory. There is no default setting, but a common one is: `AccessLog logs/http.log`
ErrorLog	**ErrorLog** *filename* Specifies the location of the error log file, either as an absolute path or as a relative path from the `ServerRoot` directory. There is no default setting, but a common one is: `ErrorLog logs/http.error`

LogFileDateExt	**LogFileDateExt** *suffix*
	
	This directive is used to specify the extension to be used for log file names. It can be used to specify a time/date format for the extension with the following setting:
	
	`LogFileDateExt %H:%T`
	
	providing the hour and minute separated by a colon (:), for example, `19:40`. This setting gives a date format:
	
	`LogFileDateExt %d-%m-%Y`
	
	for example, `05-30-96`. Any combination of the variables may be used. Spaces will be converted to an underscore (_) in the extension.
	
	This directive can also set a plain extension such as:
	
	`LogFileDateExt log`

LogFormat *format*

The LogFormat directive specifies whether the transfer log should be written in the common log format or the old CERN-specific log format. Acceptable values are:

Old The "old" CERN-specific log format.

Common
    The Common log format.

New Same as the Common log format.

LogTime *timezone*

The LogTime directive specifies what timestamp should be used in log files. The acceptable time zones are:

LocalTime
    Use the local time zone.

GMT Use Greenwich Mean Time instead.

NoLog *expression*

Tells the server not to log requests for the documents matched by the given expression. For example, to prevent logging of all files in the directory */top_secret/*, you would include the following setting:

    NoLog /top_secret/*

Script Configuration

The CERN server does not provide built-in support for all of the HTTP request methods. PUT and DELETE are omitted and POST is handled only in the case of a CGI program handling HTML form data. To compensate for the lack of internal support, the CERN server has several directives so that you may provide CGI programs to handle these cases.

DELETE-Script *scriptname*

The DELETE-Script directive specifies a CGI program to act as a general DELETE request handler. The program should be given as an absolute path. For example:

    DELETE-Script /www/cgi-bin/terminator

When a DELETE request is received, the program given with the directive will be executed in a CGI environment, with the

→

DELETE-Script ←	name of the requested document put into the PATH_INFO CGI variable.
POST-Script	**POST-Script** *scriptname* The POST-Script directive specifies a CGI program to act as a handler for non-CGI POST requests. The program should be given as an absolute path. For example: `POST-Script /www/cgi-bin/my_poster` When a POST request is received, unless it references a CGI program explicitly, this program will be executed in a CGI environment, with the name of the requested document put into the PATH_INFO CGI variable.
PUT-Script	**PUT-Script** *scriptname* The PUT-Script directive specifies a CGI program to act as a general PUT request handler. The program should be given as an absolute path. When a PUT request is received, the program given with the directive will be executed in a CGI environment, with the name of the requested document put into the PATH_INFO CGI variable.
Search	**Search** *scriptname* The Search directive specifies a CGI program to act as a handler for non-CGI GET requests that include a query string, making it act for GET almost as POST-Script does for POST. The purpose of this directive is to provide a search mechanism for requested documents. The program name should be given as an absolute path. As with the other script directives, this program is executed with the actual document path stored in the PATH_INFO CGI variable.

Directory Indexing

This section discusses the directives used to determine exactly how the server will respond when a user makes a directory request.

AddBlankIcon	**AddBlankIcon** *icon_path* Specifies an icon that is the same size as the other directory index icons, but is entirely transparent, i.e., a blank icon. This is used to properly align the column headings with the columns of information in the file listing.

AddDirIcon *icon_path alt_text* Specifies an icon to be used for subdirectories in a file listing. The second argument specifies alternate text for the icon. For example: `AddDirIcon /icons/directory.xbm   DIR`	**AddDirIcon**

AddIcon *icon_path alt_text mime_type*
 	
Specifies an icon and alternate text to be associated with a given MIME type or encoding of a file in a directory listing. For example, to use the icon */icons/compass.gif* and the alt text "MAP" for Netcarta webmaps (MIME type *application/webmap*), use the following setting:
 	
`AddIcon /icons/compass.gif MAP application`
`/webmap`
 	
The CERN server does have some default icon mappings (and includes the icons with the server distribution), but these are all wiped out if you use `AddIcon` directives to add mappings of your own.
	AddIcon

AddIconToStd *icon_path alt_text mime_type* The `AddIconToStd` directive acts just like `AddIcon`, except that your icons augment the mapping list rather than replace it.	**AddIconToStd**
AddParentIcon *icon_path alt_text* The `AddParentIcon` directive specifies an icon and alt text for the parent directory ("..") in a directory listing. For example: `AddParentIcon /icons/back.xbm UP`	**AddParentIcon**
AddUnknownIcon *icon_path* The `AddUnknownIcon` directive specifies an icon to be used for files of unknown type or encoding.	**AddUnknownIcon**
AlwaysWelcome On|Off Specifies whether requesting a directory without its trailing slash returns a directory listing or a "welcome" document (see the `Welcome` directive). The default is `On`, in which case the "welcome" document is returned whether or not the trailing slash is included.	**AlwaysWelcome**

Server Configuration

DirAccess	`DirAccess On|Off|Selective`
	
	Specifies whether, and under what conditions, the server should generate its own directory indices. Options are:
	
	`On` The server may build an index for any requested directory. (Default)
	
	`Off` The server may never build a directory index.
	
	`Selective`
	     Allows you to pick and choose which directory the server may index and which it will not. The server will first look in the directory for a file named *www_browsable*. If this file exists, regardless of size or contents, the server is allowed to generate an index for the directory. If the file is not present, the server generates a 403 (`Access Denied`) error. There is no provision for changing the name of this file.

DirAddHref	`DirAddHref` *filename suffix* Links a resource to the icon of specified file types in a file listing. For example, you could have an icon reference a CGI script on your server that could unpack the contents of a listed tar file and return a listing of the archive: `DirAddHref /cgi-bin/untar .tar`

DirReadme	`DirReadme Top|Bottom|None`
	
	When a directory index is generated, the server looks in the directory being indexed for a file named *README*. If this file exists, its contents are included in the directory index as an explanation of the contents of the directory. The `DirReadMe` directive specifies if and where this file should be included. Values are:
	
	`top` Include the file before the file listing
	
	`Bottom`
	     Include the file after the file listing
	
	`None`
	     Don't include the file at all

DirShowBrackets	`DirShowBrackets On|Off` Specifies whether alternate text of MIME type descriptions will have square brackets around them. The default setting is:

```
DirShowBrackets On
```

which means the descriptions will be placed within brackets. If icons are not included, this directive has no effect.

DirShowBytes On|Off

Specifies whether file size should be shown in a file listing when sizes are turned on with `DirShowSize`.

DirShowCase On|Off

Determines whether the server notices case when ordering the files for the listing. If case is noticed, then all files with uppercase names will be listed before their lowercase neighbors (i.e., normal *ls* order). If case is not noticed, upper- and lowercase names will be interleaved. The default setting is `Off`.

DirShowDate On|Off

Specifies whether the last-modified time should be included for each file.

DirShowDescription

Specifies whether a description of the file should be shown in a directory listing. The server looks for a file named *.www_descript* in the directory to act as a description database. The format of this database is one entry per line, where an entry consists of the word "DESCRIBE," the filename or template, and the description, with whitespace acting as the delimiter. Here are some example entries:

```
DESCRIBE    techspecs.html technical docs
DESCRIBE    adcopy.html    advertising copy
```

DirShowGroup On|Off

Specifies whether the group of the file should be included. The group name is used if it is available; otherwise, the group id is used. The default is `Off`.

DirShowHidden On|Off

Specifies whether hidden files (i.e., those whose names begin with ".") should be included in the file listing. The default is `Off`.

DirShowIcons	`DirShowIcons On|Off` Specifies whether icons indicating the MIME types of the files should be included on each line. The default is On.
DirShowMaxDes ...	`DirShowMaxDescrLength` *length* If descriptions of the files in a listing are shown, the length of the description is determined by the number of characters specified with the `DirShowMaxDescrLength` directive. The default is 25.
DirShowMaxLength	`DirShowMaxLength` *length* Specifies the maximum number of characters used for filenames in a listing. The file listing will always use at least the minimum number of characters (from `DirShowMinLength`), but will never show more than the maximum, truncating filenames that are too long. The default is 25.
DirShowMinLength	`DirShowMinLength` *length* Specifies the minimum number of characters used for filenames in a listing. The default is 15.
DirShowMode	`DirShowMode On|Off` Specifies whether permissions of the file should be included. The mode is written in mnemonic form, such as "`rw-rw-rw-`", rather than numeric form, such as "`666`". The default is Off.
DirShowOwner	`DirShowOwner On|Off` Specifies whether the owner of the file should be included in the directory listing. The user name is used if it is available; otherwise, the user id is used. The default is Off.
DirShowSize	`DirShowSize On|Off` Specifies whether the size should be included for each file in a listing. The default is On.
IconPath	`IconPath` *prefix* Specifies a server path prefix to be attached to all icon paths. For example, for the `Add*Icon` directives, the */icons/* part of the filenames could have been left off the

icon path by adding the following line before them in the configuration file: IconPath /icons/ Remember that this will be prefixed to every path, so only use it if you are sure that you will put all of your icons within a single directory or tree.	**IconPath**
Welcome *filename* Specifies the name of the file in a directory to use when a directory is requested rather than a specific document. If multiple Welcome directives are specified, they are searched for in order, and the first one located is returned. By default, the files are *Welcome.html, welcome.html,* and *index.html.*	Welcome

Access Control Configuration

The access control scheme used by the CERN server is a bit confusing, but it allows you to set control access to either directories or specific files based on the client's host and/or username/password authentication.

The access control scheme begins in the *httpd.conf* file with the Protect directive. This directive specifies a directory or group of directories to protect, and associates them with a specific *protection setup file.* The protection setup file specifies valid authentication schemes, the password and group files to be used for authentication, and, optionally, user, group, and host access controls for all documents in the protected tree.

When a request for a document in a protected directory is received, the server looks for a file in the directory named *.www_acl.* This is the *access control list* file (ACL). It designates which files in the directory may be accessed, with what methods, and by whom. It uses the password and group files and masks specified in its associated protection setup file to carry out access authorization.

Password File

Password files contain valid usernames and encrypted passwords for user authentication on your server. They can be created with the *adm* program that comes with your server software.

Password files are similar to the UNIX password files, but there is no correlation between valid users for your server and registered users on the UNIX machine.

Group File

The group file lists the valid groups and their members for use with access control to your system. Group members can be declared by username, previously defined group names, and host address templates. Each group declaration looks like this:

```
groupname: item1, item2 ...
```

Each item uses *group definition syntax* to declare members of the group. With this syntax, each item may be specified as:

- A single username

- A group name that has already been defined in the same group file

- A comma-separated list of usernames and group names surrounded by parentheses

- Any of the above followed by an @sign and an IP-address template

- Any of the above followed by an @sign and a comma-separated list of IP-address templates in parentheses

IP-address templates not attached to user or group names mean that all users from the specified IP are valid group members. When attached to users or groups, users are only valid from those IPs. Users and groups with no attached IP template are valid from any IP.

IP-address templates are IP addresses that may use a wildcard (*) for any part of the address for subnet restriction.

Here is a sample group file:

```
humans: mike, joel
bots: servo, crow, gypsy, cambot
mads: forrester, frank@198.112.*.*, pearl
crew: humans, bots, @198.112.108.*
deep13: mads, larry@198.113.*.*,
        (gerry, sylvia)@198.114.*.*
mst3k: crew, deep13, (glenn, jperkins, janpan)@(198.*.*.*, 36.108.*.*)
```

Group definitions can be broken across a line following a comma in the definition list.

The group definition syntax described here is also used for GetMask lines in protection setup files and for the last field of ACL entries.

Additionally, there are two predefined group names that can be used in those areas. They are:

All   All users that have an entry in the password file. Users is equivalent.

Anybody
    No restrictions are placed on access; all users are allowed without authorization. Anonymous and Anyone are equivalent.

Protection Setup File

A protection setup file is required for each protected directory or tree designated by the `Protect` directive in *httpd.conf*. The `Protect` directive specifies the pathname of the protection setup file that its directories will use. Here is a sample protection setup file:

```
AuthType      Basic
ServerId      SatelliteOfLove
PasswordFile  /WWW/Admin/passwd
GroupFile     /WWW/Admin/group
GetMask       All
ACLOverRide   On
```

The `GetMask` directive is optional. All other directives must be included.

`AuthType` *type* Indicates the type of authentication to use. `Basic` is most common. Other methods may be used if the server supports them.	**AuthType**
`ServerId` *name* This directive does not need to specify the server's actual machine name. It can be any string and is used to inform the client what password file it is using (in case the user has multiple usernames on different parts of the server).	**ServerId**
`PasswordFile` *filename* Specifies the absolute pathname of the password file.	**PasswordFile**
`GroupFile` *filename* This directive specifies the absolute pathname of the group file.	**GroupFile**
`GetMask` *list* If you want to set general restrictions on all the documents in a protected directory tree, you can set them in the protection setup file with `GetMask`. You can specify allowed users, groups, or IP addresses with the group definition syntax. This directive is optional.	**GetMask**
`ACLOverRide` `On`|`Off` Protection setups files normally do not allow any access outside of what is set in a `GetMask` directive. To override the `GetMask` rules, you can set `ACLOverRide` to `On`. The default is no overrides by the ACL.	**ACLOverRide**

Access Control List File

To control per-file access in a protected directory, you need an access control list file (ACL) named *.www_acl* in that directory. Each directory in a protected tree needs its own *.www_acl* for file-level access control. In fact, you cannot have a *.www_acl* file in a directory that is not designated in a `Protect` directive in the configuration file.

Each line of an ACL looks like this:

```
file : methods : groups
```

The first field contains the name of the file to be controlled. It can match a filename exactly or use the wildcard (`*`) to designate a group of files.

The second field lists the request methods allowed on the file. You can specify `GET`, or `POST`, or both with `GET,POST`.

The last field lists the users that are allowed access to the file. You can use users listed in the password file, groups listed in the group file, or IP-address templates. Each item should be separated by a comma. Group definition syntax can be used in this field.

Here is a sample *.www_acl* file:

```
*.html : GET : mst3k,torgo
cgi-*.pl : GET,POST : crew,mads
secret*.html : GET : bots,frank
```

There is no order to rules matching here. In the example, user `torgo`, who is not a member of the `bots` or `mst3k` groups, is allowed to access the "secret" files.

Access Configuration Directives

Protect	**Protect** *expression setup_file uid.gid*
	In the server configuration file (*httpd.conf*), the `Protect` directive specifies a set of directories to be protected and gives the name of the protection setup file to be used for access control in those directories. The directive looks like this:
	`Protect /WWW/mst3k/* /WWW/Admin/httpd.setup`
	This sets access control for all directories under */WWW/mst3k*. The directory names must be an absolute pathname, and may use the wildcard character (`*`). An optional third argument can specify the user and group name (separated by a period) of the protected

directory's owner, if the permissions are different from the server daemon's. For example:	**Protect**

```
Protect /WWW/mst3k/* /WWW/Admin/httpd.setup cambot.mst
```

User `cambot` in group `mst` owns the directories.

<table>
<tr><td>

Protection *name*

</td><td>

Protection

</td></tr>
<tr><td colspan="2">

Beginning with version 3.0, the protection setup file information can be included in the server configuration file instead of in an outside file. You use the `Protection` directive for this, and syntax looks like:

```
Protection name {
     protection
     setup
     info
}
```

A `Protect` directive can then use the name of the `Protection` directive to specify its protection setup information.

You can save a step in the process by simply tacking the protection setup section onto the `Protect` directive where you would normally name the setup file. For example:

```
Protect /www/mst3k/* {
     UserId        cambot
     GroupId       mst
     AuthType      Basic
     ServerId      SatelliteOfLove
     PasswordFile  /WWW/Admin/passwd
     GroupFile     /WWW/Admin/group
     GetMask       all
}
```

Each `Protection` section uses the same directives used in a regular setup file. Two additional directives can be used here to specify the user and group ids of a protected directory when they differ from those of the server daemon: `UserId` and `GroupId`.

</td></tr>
</table>

UserId *user* Specifies the user name of the directory owner.	**UserId**

GroupId *group* Specifies the group name of the directory owner.	**GroupId**

CHAPTER 25

Netscape Server Configuration

Netscape provides a wide variety of high-end server products for the Internet. Their first generation of Web servers included the Commerce server and the Communications server. The second generation of server products is now available:

- The FastTrack server is geared toward Web hosting for individuals and small organizations.

- The Enterprise server is geared to larger organizations that run large, busy Web sites and have a need for advanced security features and enriched content.

Netscape servers are available on UNIX and Windows NT platforms. The FastTrack server is also available for Windows 95. This chapter discusses configuration features for the UNIX version only.

With the Netscape servers, you do not have to edit the configuration files manually. Netscape's servers come with a Web-based configuration system called the Server Manager. During installation, you provide an obscure port from which to run the Administration Server and a username and password for the administrator. You can then administer your server from any machine with a Net connection and the Netscape Navigator browser.

If you are familiar with any of the other UNIX servers, the Netscape servers' configuration may seem odd at first. Like the others, it uses configuration files that are composed of directives. Unlike the others, however, it has relatively few directives, with much broader purposes.

In this chapter we will discuss the basic configuration directives found in the main configuration files. We won't provide step-by-step instructions for making changes in the forms of the Server Manager.

For the 2.x servers, you should note that if you make manual changes to the configuration files and later work with the Server Manager, you will need to reload the files. Press Apply in the top frame of the Server Manager page and then select Load Configuration Files. The changes that you make manually are in effect the next time you restart the server (if you haven't made changes elsewhere). The Server Manager keeps its own copies of configuration files to make sure that changes will be in sync.

Most of the directives and options listed in this chapter are used in all of the Netscape Web servers. Some options do vary, however. This information is most specific to the Enterprise 2.0 server.

The Netscape server uses three files for configuration:

- *magnus.conf*—the server configuration file, which contains the basic server information (like *httpd.conf* for the NCSA and Apache servers)

- *obj.conf*—the object configuration file, which tells the server how to locate and serve resources (like *srm.conf* for the NCSA and Apache servers)

- *mime.types*—the MIME types file, which specifies what MIME or media types should be associated with what files

The *magnus.conf* file and its directives are very similar to their counterparts in other servers and simple to understand. The *obj.conf* file, however, is quite different. The directives have a more complex structure because of the way the Netscape server handles resources.

Basic Server Configuration — magnus.conf

The following directives are used in the *magnus.conf* file. The directives in this file follow a simple syntax of the directive name followed by its value. Directives should not be broken across lines.

ServerName	ServerName *name* This is the DNS hostname of the server machine. The name you use here must be a legitimate DNS name for the machine. Also, note that other legitimate names for the machine will also work if they correspond to the same IP address.
Port	Port *port* Specifies your server's port.
User	User *username* Specifies the user you want the server process to run as. The default setting is: User nobody

MaxProcs *n* Sets the maximum number of processes that can run at one time. The threads of a process then take turns handling requests.	**MaxProcs**
MinThreads *n* Specifies the minimum number of threads that can run under a process. The default is 4.	**MinThreads**
MaxThreads *n* Specifies the maximum number of threads that may run under a process. The default is 32. **NOTE** The 1.x servers used a different process handling method and different directives: **MaxProcs**, **MinProcs**, and **ProcessLife**. Performance tuning and optimization are different with the multi-threaded 2.x servers.	**MaxThreads**
ErrorLog *pathname* Specifies the name of the error log file. The name should be a full path to the file. The default value is `/logs/error` under the server root directory (`https-`*server/*).	**ErrorLog**
PidLog *pathname* Specifies the location of the file into which the server should place its process id when running. The default setting is *server-root/*`logs/pid`.	**PidLog**
LoadObjects *files...* The Netscape server treats every document as being an instance of an object. These are the objects described in the object configuration file. The **LoadObjects** directive specifies the names of the object configuration files. The files may be given as either absolute paths, paths relative to the server root directory, or filenames in the same directory as *magnus.conf*. If you create new objects and place them in another file, add another **LoadObjects** directive with its location. The default is *obj.conf* in the *config* directory.	**LoadObjects**

Server Configuration

RootObject	RootObject *name* When a request comes in, it needs to have an initial object assigned to it. This root object is the starting point for all request handling and is the arbitrator of what more specific object (if any) should handle the request. The RootObject directive specifies the name of this starting point object. By default, it is: RootObject default
DNS	DNS on|off Controls whether the server will attempt reverse DNS lookup of the client host during requests. The default setting is: DNS on
Chroot	Chroot *path* Limits the portion of the file system available to your server for security purposes.
Security	Security on|off Indicates whether security features are on or off. Having Security on means that the server will run using encrypted transactions via secure socket layer (SSL). Security features should be configured through the Server Manager. With security features enabled, other security-related directives will appear in *magnus.conf*.
ListenQ	ListenQ *n* Sets the listen-queue size of the server. This is the maximum number of connections that the system will accept at the socket level. The system will hold this number of connections until the server can process them. This directive should not be set to a larger size than the system can handle.
ACLFile	ACLFile *file* Specifies the name of the access control file. It should be a full path name.

The obj.conf File

The *obj.conf* file contains the configuration directives that tell the server exactly how to handle client requests. This file has two main functions, corresponding to the two main sections of the file. The first section initializes subsystems, a diverse set of tasks that includes opening and naming log files, loading the MIME types file, loading Java classes and LiveWire applications, and describing logging and directory index formats. The second section contains the object definitions, which tell the server how to handle resource requests.

Resource Handling

The Netscape servers are modeled on the idea that all resources to be served are instances of objects. To tell the server how to treat a set of documents, you assign them to an object. You give an object all of the properties you want the resources to have, including URL mapping, access and authorization, assigning MIME types, logging format, and directory listings. For example, there is no need for a special CGI program directory, since you can assign any document you want to a common cgi object.

Subsystem Initialization

The `Init` directive is used to initialize subsystems of the server. The `Init` directives for the subsystems being used by the server are grouped at the top of the *obj.conf* file. They take the following form:

```
Init fn=function argument1=value1 [argument2=value2 ...]
```

where *function* is the function name, and the arguments and values depend on the function.

Which subsystem is being initialized depends on the value of the `fn` function. The subsystems and available functions depend on which server you have and the functionality it supports. You may also have your own functions if you have written plug-in applications with the server API.

This section lists the `Init` functions corresponding to basic subsystems used by the server. Functions for Java and LiveWire subsystems commonly appear in this section as well, but they will not be discussed here.

cindex-init
The `cindex-init` function configures fancy directory indexing. These settings apply globally, and cannot be custom configured for specific directories. This function does not turn on fancy indexing for any directory; that is done in the object definitions, if desired. There are four arguments available for this function:

`icon-uri=`*path*
> This argument specifies the server path to the icon directory. Which icons are used with any given MIME type is determined by the *mime.types* file. The default server path for icons is `/mc-icons/`.

ignore=*expr*
> This argument specifies which files should be omitted from directory indices. The value should be a regular expression for filenames to ignore. For example, to exclude log files from listings, you could use the setting:
>
> ```
> Init fn=cindex-init ignore="*.log"
> ```
>
> Files whose names begin with a period are automatically omitted, with no option to un-omit them.

opts=s|i
> This argument specifies whether the icons are hyperlinked to the documents and whether the server should attempt to locate the titles of HTML documents to use as descriptions. If the value includes i, then icons are hyperlinked. If the value includes s, then the server will scan for HTML titles. The value should be one or both of these, e.g., opts=is.

widths=*a,b,c,d*
> This argument specifies the widths of the different columns in the directory index. Setting a column's width to 0 omits that column. The columns are the filename, the last-modified time, the size, and the description. For example, the value 16,0,8,30 would make a name column 16 characters wide, a size column 8 characters wide, and a description column 30 characters wide.

Note that this function does not turn on fancy directory indexing for any directories, but merely configures what a fancy directory would look like if it were turned on. To turn on fancy directory indexing, use the index-common function of the Service directive.

init-clf

The init-clf function is used to initialize logging in the common log format. This function tells the server to create one or more common log files and open them to record transactions.

Each log file needs to be assigned a name for internal use by the server. The default name for logging (but not for this directive) is global, but you can use whatever name or names you wish. The argument names should be the names you want to use with their values being the absolute paths to the log files. For example, you might want to call your three logs member, newsletter, and global (for everything else). You would do this like so:

```
Init fn=init-clf member=/https-server/logs/members.log
newsletter=/https-server/logs/newsletter.log
global=/https-server/logs/access.log
```

(Remember to not break Init directives across lines, despite how this example is formatted.) A more common use would be to create a single general file:

```
Init fn=init-clf global=/usr/local/etc/httpd/logs/access.log
```

Note that this directive merely initializes the logging system. It does not tell the server to write anything to the log files. That is done by including an AddLog directive in the relevant object, which specifies a logfile name that is defined here.

init-uhome

The `init-uhome` function tells the server to initialize user directory handling. User directory handling will work perfectly well without this directive, but when used, the user directory locations are pre-cached in a directory table file (by default */etc/passwd*) to improve performance.

The `init-uhome` function allows an optional second argument, `pwfile`, which specifies the name of the user directory table file other than */etc/passwd*. A basic initialization would be:

```
Init fn=init-uhome
```

while one using */usr/local/etc/httpd/users.db* as the user table would be:

```
Init fn=init-uhome pwfile=/usr/local/etc/httpd/users.db
```

load-types

The `load-types` function initializes the general MIME-type assignment subsystem. This function loads a types table, the *mime.types* file. The format of this file is simple, with one record per line:

type/subtype extension1 [extention2 ...] [icon=iconfile]

where *type/subtype* is a MIME type and subtype like `text/html`, *extension* is a filename extension such as `html`, and *iconfile* is the name of the icon to be shown if a file of that type is listed in a directory index. The icon names should be filenames in the index icon directory (specified by the `icon-uri` parameter of the `cindex-init` function).

This function can load two different types files, with one flagged as global and the other as local. The global file is given as the value of the `mime-types` argument, while the local file is defined by the `local-types` argument. The files may be specified as either absolute paths or file names inside the configuration directory. For example:

```
Init fn=load-types mime-types=mime.types local-types=clown.types
```

flex-init

This function is used to initialize the more enhanced logging system (called "flexible logging"). The first parameter gives the name of the logfile with the full path to its location. The second parameter is the format parameter, which takes a list of values for the various types of transaction information to log. The filename parameter looks like *logname=fullpathname*. Then the format parameter will be `format.`*logname=format options*. For example, the following line opens and specifies the format of a log named `access`:

```
Init fn="flex-init" access="/https-server/logs/access" for
mat.access="%Ses->client.ip% - %Req->vars.auth-
user% [%SYSDATE%] \"%Req->reqpb.clf-request%\" %Req->srvhdrs.clf-sta
tus% %Req->srvhdrs.content-length%"
```

The lines of the example are broken so poorly to remind you that the directive must be one long line and that all spaces in the format value count. Within the format value, everything between percent signs (%) is a transaction value parameter. Parameters surrounded by \" and "\ are "escaped" because their values may contain spaces. Any characters that are not escaped characters or between percents are literally printed to the logfile, giving your log lines spaces, separators, and readability. Here is the list of log parameter values:

`%Ses->client.ip%`
Client's hostname or IP address

`%Req->vars.auth-user%`
User authentication required

`%SYSDATE%`
System date

`%Req->reqpb.clf-request%`
Full client request (escapes required)

`%Req->srvhdrs.clf-status%`
Server response status

`%Req->srvhdrs.content-length%`
Content length

`%Req->headers.referer%`
Refering URL (escapes required)

`%Req->headers.user-agent%`
Client's browser identity (escapes required)

`%Req->reqpb.method%`
Client request method

`%Req->reqpb.uri%`
Requesting URL

`%Req->reqpb.query%`
URL query string

`%Req->reqpb.protocol%`
HTTP version (escapes required)

`%Req->headers.accept%`
Accept header(s)

`%Req->headers.date%`
Date header (escapes required)

`%Req->headers.if-modified-since%`
If-Modified-Since header

`%Req->headers.authorization%`
Authorization header

Object Configuration

The rest of the object file (beyond the `Init` directives) consists of a set of objects. Each object comes in a block surrounded by `<Object>` and `</Object>` tags. The `<Object>` tag uses one of two attributes: `name`, which gives a name to an object, or `ppath`, which gives a URL path or regular expression for resources belonging to the object.

An object consists of a series of directives that specify the behavior of documents within that object. The directives may specify that directory indexing is not allowed, that authentication is required, that the document should be treated as an imagemap, that requests for documents should be logged into a special log file, and so on.

An object named `research` looks like this:

```
<object name="research">
directive1
directive2
</object>
```

Alternatively, you could specify the object by the server path:

```
<object ppath="/secret/research/*">
directive1
directive2
</object>
```

There are two objects included by default: `default` and `cgi`. All resources are at first handled by one of these two objects. Directives in the object block may then redirect a specific resource to another named object for handling. In addition, directives within an object may be designated as applying only to (or only not to) specific client hosts (within `<client>` . . . `</client>` tags).

Client-specific directives are the same as other directives, but are wrapped within `<client>` . . . `</client>` labels. These labels can be qualified using either the `dns` argument, which matches against the DNS-resolved name for the remote client, or the `ip` argument, which matches against the IP address itself. Either can be a regular expression. For example, to enable specific directives only within the *ora.com* domain, you could write:

```
<client dns=*ora.com>
special-directive1
special-directive2
</client>
```

As with the `Init` lines, the object directives take the following form:

directive fn=*function argument1=value1* [*argument2=value2* ...]

where *directive* is the directive name, *function* is the function name, and the arguments and values depend on the directive and function.

There are only seven directives, and they correspond closely to the request processing pipeline. When a request comes in, it is assigned to an object by matching either a regular expression or the root object. Then:

1. Authentication is performed, as specified by any AuthTrans directives.

2. The path is translated to a specific resource by any NameTrans directives. At this point, the document may also be assigned to a different object, in which case the process starts over in that object.

3. The translated path is checked by any PathCheck directives.

4. The resource is assigned a type by any applicable ObjectType directives.

5. The request is serviced in some appropriate way by a Service directive.

6. The request is logged by an AddLog directives.

7. If any of these steps fail, a special message may be sent, depending on the status case, where these messages are specified by any Error directives.

Within each stage, the directives are processed in the order they appear in the object file. This can lead to occasional problems if you are not careful to put special cases before defaults.

AuthTrans

The AuthTrans directive is responsible for requesting and interpreting authentication whenever necessary. This directive can use one of two functions, either basic-auth or basic-ncsa. Both of these functions mean the same thing. basic-auth is used in 1.x servers. auth-ncsa supersedes it in 2.x servers.

The following parameters are used in the AuthTrans directive:

auth-type=basic
  Specifies the authorization type to be used. It is always basic.

dbm=*file*
  Indicates the name of a user database file. It should contain the full pathname of the file. If you use this parameter, you can't also list a userfile parameter.

userfile=*file*
  Specifies a userfile in the NCSA format. These are files with user:password listings created by the *htpasswd* program. You must supply a full pathname.

grpfile=*file*
  An optional parameter for specifying an NCSA-style group file. The group file contains lists of groups and their users in the format group:user1 user2 . . . . You must supply a full pathname.

The AuthTrans directive is usually used with the require-auth function of PathCheck.

NameTrans

The NameTrans directive is responsible for taking the requested server path and determining what actual resource corresponds to it. This includes resolving user directories, URL mapping, and redirections.

In addition, the NameTrans directive can assign documents to other objects for further processing. Any of the NameTrans functions, except for redirect, can take an extra argument name that specifies the name of the object to which the document should be transferred.

document-root
This function specifies the root directory of your server's document tree. If no other directive remaps the server path to an absolute path, it will be interpreted as being relative to this directory. The root directory is given as the value of the root argument. For example, to use *usr/local/etc/web/docs/* as the root directory, you would use this setting:

```
NameTrans fn=document-root root=/usr/local/etc/web/docs/
```

This function should be used in the default object.

home-page
The Netscape server allows you to assign a special document to the server home page request (i.e., a request for /) using this function. The home page documents path, absolute or relative to the document root, should be given as the value of the argument path. For example, to use *usr/local/etc/web/home.html* as the server's home page, you would use this setting:

```
NameTrans fn=home-page path=/usr/local/etc/web/home.html
```

pfx2dir
This function allows you to remap a server path to a new absolute path by assigning a prefix directory. That is, you can say that a whole server path tree actually resides at the end of a branch of another tree. This function takes two arguments:

from=*urlpath*
The server path tree being remapped.

dir=*path*
The absolute path that is being mapped to.

For example, if you want *children/kenny/* to map to the files in */monsters/gamera/kenny/*, you would use:

```
NameTrans fn=pfx2dir from=/children/kenny/ dir=/monsters/gamera/kenny/
```

The optional name parameter supplies the name of another object to which the mapped path should derive its configuration.

redirect

This function allows the server to redirect the user to a resource's location if it has moved. It uses the following arguments:

from=*path*
> The local server path that is being redirected.

url-prefix=*urlpath*
> If the new location is simply a new URL prefix for the server path (i.e., on the same server), the url-prefix argument should be used.

url=*url*
> If the new location is a full URL, then the url argument should be used.

For example, if you wanted to tell clients that everything in the */turtle/* directory had moved to *http://www.gamera.com/*, you would use this setting:

```
NameTrans fn=redirect from=/turtle/ url-prefix=http://www.gamera.com/
```

unix-home

This function sets up user directories with the following arguments:

from=*prefix*
> Specifies the prefix indicating a user directory, such as a tilde (~) or a path like /staff/.

subdir=*subdir*
> Specifies the subdirectory of each user's home directory to which the path should resolve.

pwfile=*file*
> This optional argument specifies the user database (in */etc/passwd* format) to use to locate user directories. If omitted, */etc/passwd* will be used, or NIS if it is running.

For example, to map a request of the form /~user/ to the user subdirectory *public_html*, using the standard user table, you would use this directive:

```
NameTrans fn=unix-home from="/~" subdir="public_html"
```

You can also supply a name parameter to refer the path's objects to another object's configuration settings.

PathCheck

The PathCheck directive tells the server to check various things about the translated path. This may be a security check to identify any suspicious directories, a scan for CGI path info spackled onto the end of an otherwise perfectly good path, or an instruction to require authentication. PathCheck's functions are less clearly unified than those of the other directives, but they have the common need to be applied after the path has been translated but before the processing of the request's content begins.

---

deny-existence

This function is used to hide the existence of a file from the user. It can take two arguments:

path=*path*
> Specifies which files should have their existences denied. If this argument is omitted, the server takes the severe stance of denying the existence of everything handled by the current object.

bong-msg=*file*
> Sends a special file instead of the standard error message.

For example, to deny the existence of everything in the */secrets/* directory and send back the file */docs/nosy.html*, you could use this setting:

```
PathCheck fn=deny-existence path=/secrets/ bong-msg=/docs/nosy.html
```

Alternatively, you could specify an entire object for that directory tree and only lock out outsiders:

```
<object ppath=/secrets/*>
<client dns=*~*.ora.com>
PathCheck fn=deny-existence bong-msg=/docs/nothing-to-see.html
</client>
</object>
```

find-index

When a user requests a directory, instead of a plain file, the server can either send a specified index file or create a directory listing (if enabled and authorized). The find-index function enables this ability. There is only one argument to this function:

index-names=*file1,file2, . . .*
> Supplies a comma-separated list (no spaces) of names to look for in a directory to be used as the default file.

For example, to look first for *index.html* and then *index.shtml* and then *index.cgi*, you would use this setting:

```
PathCheck fn=find-index index-names=index.html,index.shtml,index.cgi
```

find-links

This function allows you to specify when hard or soft links will be followed as part of path resolution. There are potential security problems with allowing links to be followable. If a request comes in for the path you have listed, the server will check for symbolic links that you don't want to be accessed, and if it finds any in the directory, it returns an error. Two parameters are used with this function:

disable=h|s|o
> Specifies which types of links you don't like. There are three choices that can be used in combination if you wish. h is used for hard symbolic links; s is used for soft links; and o means that you will allow symbolic links if the user owns the target link.

`dir=`*path*
>   Specifies the URL path that will be checked for symbolic links. All subdirectories of the path will be checked as well, if they are requested.

This example disables all symbolic links in user directories:

```
PathCheck fn=find-links dir=public_html disable=hs
```

find-pathinfo

When a user requests a document, he can put extra information (which may or may not get used) onto the end of the document's server path in the form of additional directory levels. In a CGI environment, this is what makes up the PATH_INFO variable. The Netscape server does not identify and strip out this information by default, which means if you want it to do so, you have to tell it to. The `find-pathinfo` function does just that. There are no arguments. To handle path info correctly, just include this directive:

```
PathCheck fn-find-pathinfo
```

require-auth

This function tells the server that it must be able to authenticate the user before any further processing can take place. If the authentication information has already been sent, this function causes it to be used. If it has not been sent, the user will be prompted for a user name and password which will be returned to your server. The following arguments are used:

`auth-type=`*type*
>   Gives the type of authorization used, usually `auth-type=basic`. Required.

`realm=`*name*
>   Provides a realm name (enclosed in quotes) to the server, so it will have a better idea of which username and password to send. Required.

`auth-user=`*users*
>   Used to specify a user or list of users who are authorized. The list is enclosed in parentheses and usernames are separated by | symbols.

`auth-group=`*groups*
>   Specifies a group or list of authorized groups.

For example:

```
PathCheck fn=require-auth auth-type=realm realm="web"
    auth-user=(linda|val|stephen)
```

unix-uri-clean

Users may try to break out of your server's document space by inserting extraneous path elements into their server paths. The `unix-uri-clean` function looks for `/../`, `/./`, and `//`, and denies access if any of them are present. There are no parameters.

```
PathCheck fn=unix-uri-clean
```

Remember that all PathCheck functions will be applied in order, so if your path info may contain these, you should make sure the find-pathinfo function is listed before the unix-uri-clean function.

load-config

This function tells the server to look for local configuration files in document directories. Local configuration files use *obj.conf* configuration directives to apply localized configuration options to specific directories. The following parameters are used:

file=*name*
: Identifies the name of the file to look for in the directory.

disable-types=*types*
: Allows you to disable local configuration for specific file types.

basdir=*directory*
: Gives the directory in which to look for configuration files. Without this parameter, the server looks in the root directory given by the name translation.

descend=1
: Tells the server to look in subdirectories of the base directories.

check-acl

This function tells the server to check a specific access control list for authorization requirements on the requested object. Access control lists (ACLs) are contained in sections of the ACLFile, which is set in *magnus.conf*. The function is executed before any require-auth settings in PathCheck. The following parameters can be used:

acl=*name*
: Gives the name of the ACL to use.

shexp=*expr*
: Gives a shell expression for the path that the ACL apply to.

bong-file=*file*
: Gives the name of the file to return if access is denied.

ObjectType

The ObjectType directive is used to tell the server how to assign a MIME type, encoding, and/or language to an object. This may be by looking up the extension in the *mime.types* file or by forcing it directly. Unlike some other directives, multiple ObjectType directives do not override each other, but fortify each other. If one sets the MIME type and another sets the encoding, fine. If, however, one sets the type and another tries to set it again, the second loses rather than the first.

In addition, like many servers, the Netscape servers use several "magic" MIME types to cause special treatment to occur. They are called internal server types, but they are the same as magic types.

force-type

This function sets the MIME type by fiat. It may optionally also set the encoding and/or language.

type=*type*
: Sets the MIME or media type.

enc=*encoding*
: Sets the encoding type.

lang=*language*
: Sets the language to be used.

For example, to make the type *text/plain* the default for a given object, you would add the following directive after all the other ObjectType directives:

```
ObjectType fn=force-type type=text/plain
```

type-by-exp

This function tells the server to assign a given type if the translated path matches a given regular expression. As with the force-type function, the server may also set the encoding and/or language.

exp=*expr*
: Gives the regular expression to be matched for files to be assigned the specified type.

type=*type*
: Sets the MIME or media type.

enc=*encoding*
: Sets the encoding type.

lang=*language*
: Sets the language to be used.

For example, to tell the server that everything in the directory */scratch-n-sniff/* should be assigned the type *odor/oif*, regardless of extensions, you could use this directive:

```
ObjectType fn=type-by-exp type=odor/oif exp=/scratch-n-sniff/*
```

type-by-extension

Rather than having to use a special ObjectType directive for every file type, you can set up most of them in a *mime.types* file in advance and use the type-by-extension function to have the server look the file type up. This lookup is done based on the document's extension, which explains the name of this directive. There are no arguments; you simply use:

```
ObjectType fn=type-by-extension
```

image-switch

This function allows you to send the client an image of a different type, if it exists in the directory, when the client can't accept a certain image type. For example, if a user requests *image.gif*, and there is also *image.jpg* in the same directory, the server will send the JPEG instead. There are no parameters for this function.

Service

The Service directive is where the server finally gets down to business and does something material to respond to a request. Up until now, the server has checked paths, remapped them, checked them again, and picked some MIME types. With the Service directive, it will finally decide what to do with the file it has found. Since an applicable Service directive tells the server how to handle a request, further Service directives are ignored, unless the first uses the append-trailer function.

Any Service function can take either (or none) of two constraint arguments. The type argument can take a regular expression to match against the MIME type. If this argument is present and it doesn't match, that Service directive is deemed inapplicable and the next one is tried. Similarly, the method argument, if present, must match the request method for the directive to apply. The value is GET, HEAD, or POST, or any combination delimited by vertical bars (|) within parentheses. For example, (GET|HEAD) will match GET requests and HEAD requests, but not POST requests.

append-trailer

append-trailer is the only Service function that does not actually send data to the client. Instead, it merely tells the server that when it does send data, it should append a fragment of HTML to any HTML file it does send.

trailer=*html-string*
> Gives the HTML formatted string to append. It should be in quotes if you use spaces. If you want to include the last-modified time for the file, include the :LASTMOD: variable in the string and it will be replaced appropriately.

timefmt=*format*
> Specifies the format of the time string; required when you use :LASTMOD:. Takes a *strftime* format string.

For example, to append the string "Copyright ©1996" to the end of every file, you would use this directive:

```
Service fn=append-trailer type=text/html trailer="Copyright &copy;1996"
```

imagemap

This function tells the server to process a request as an imagemap with type=magnus-internal/imagemap:

```
Service type=magnus-internal/imagemap fn=imagemap
```

index-common

This function generates a fancy directory index. Much of the format is controlled not here, but by the `cindex-init` function of the `Init` directive. What is controlled here is whether to build one (that is, whether this function is used) and what header and footer files to use, if any. The type given in this directive is `type=magnus-internal/directory`. You may also use these parameters:

header=*file*
    Specifies the filename to be looked for in the requested directory containing information to be placed at the top of the directory listing.

readme=*file*
    Specifies the filename to be looked for in the requested directory containing information to be placed at the bottom of the directory listing.

index-simple

This function tells the server to produce a simple directory index. This does not include icons, sizes, etc., but only a bulleted list of linked file names. As with `index-common`, this function uses `type=magnus_internal/directory`.

parse-html

This function is used to serve server-side include files.

query-handler

Specifies a CGI program to act as a handler for non-CGI GET requests that include a query string. As such, it is only seen as applicable if the request matches those criteria. The program should be given as an absolute path in the `path` argument. For example, to use */10/cgi-bin/doc_searcher*, you would use this setting:

```
Service fn=query-handler path=/10/cgi-bin/doc_searcher
```

This program is executed with the original document path stored in the PATH_INFO CGI variable.

send-cgi

This function tells the server to execute a requested object as a CGI program. For example, an object that runs everything in the server path */cgi-bin/* would be:

```
<object ppath=/cgi-bin/>
Service fn=send-cgi
</object>
```

send-error

This function sends a specified file when an error occurs. The absolute path to the file should be given in the `path` argument.

send-file

This function tells the server to send the file. It is often useful to provide this as a default behavior by adding this directive after all other Service directives:

```
Service method(GET|HEAD) fn=send-file
```

Error

The `Error` directive is where the server confesses to being unable to complete a request. It can use the same functions as the `Service` directive, but it is only used when an error has occurred, and it has different constraint arguments, `reason` and `code`, which correspond to the textual description of the error and the status code, respectively. You cannot place both `code` and `reason` in the same `Error` directive. There are four sets of values:

401, Unauthorized

Authorization was required and the user failed to deliver proper information.

403, Forbidden

The server was unable to read a file.

404, Not Found

The document could not be found.

500, Server Error

This could mean anything from a hardware or OS problem to a CGI program that returned bad data.

send-error

This function sends a specified file to the user when an error occurs. The absolute path to the file should be given in the `path` argument.

query-handler

You may want to use a CGI program to customize a response resulting from an error. Use the `query-handler` function to specify a CGI file (with the `path` parameter) for a given error code.

AddLog

The `AddLog` directive is applied after the server has handled the request and is purely for local bookkeeping. Its functions let you write a normal transaction log and record what user-agent was responsible for the transaction. If you have more than one, all `AddLog` directives in an object will be used.

common-log

This function is used to record transaction data in the common NCSA log format. This is the format used by most log analysis tools. It uses these parameters:

name=*logname*

Specifies the name of a log file to use. This must be a logfile name that you initialized with `Init fn=init-clf name=...` at the top of the *obj.conf* file. Without this parameter, it logs to the global access log.

iponly=*n*

Tells the server not to perform host-name lookup for logging. Any value for `iponly` will do. The Server Manager creates `iponly="1"`.

flex-log

This function tells the server to log transaction data in the extended or flexible logging format. This format is specified in the `Init` directives with the `flex-init` function. It uses the same parameters as the `common-log` function:

name=*logname*
> Specifies the name of a log file to use. This must be a logfile name that you initialized with `Init fn=init-clf name=` . . . at the top of the *obj.conf* file. Without this parameter, it logs to the global access log.

iponly=*n*
> Tells the server not to perform host-name lookup for logging. Any value for `iponly` will do. The Server Manager creates `iponly="1"`.

record-useragent

This function tells the server to write the client IP address followed by the value of the User-Agent header into a log file. As with the `common-log` function, the argument `name` tells the server which log file to write to. If it is omitted, the information will be written to the global access log.

CHAPTER 26

WebSite Server Configuration

WebSite is a Web server on Windows NT and Windows 95. In addition to the server itself, WebSite includes many other tools to help you develop and maintain your own Web site: a graphical environment to help you develop documents (WebView), an HTML editor (HotDog), an image maps editor (MapThis!), and a tool for creating searchable indexes (WebIndex).

The WebSite server itself is configured using the Server Admin tool, which has an easy-to-use graphical interface.

There is also a secure version of the WebSite server, called WebSite Professional. WebSite Pro contains all the features and tools included with WebSite, adding cryptographic security with S-HTTP and SSL capability; the WebSite API, with an SDK (Software Developers Kit) and online documentation; support for Microsoft's ISAPI; ODBC/SQL database access with Cold Fusion 1.5; Perl 5 for Win32; server-side Java SDK; one-button publishing with Netscape Navigator Gold; support for Microsoft's FrontPage; and three books in its documentation set.

WebSite was developed as a team effort by Bob Denny, Jay Weber (and others from Enterprise Integration Technologies), and O'Reilly & Associates (publishers of this book). Although it is a commercial product, WebSite is available for free evaluation from *http://software.ora.com*. For additional information about WebSite, refer to *http://website.ora.com*.

This chapter describes the Server Admin items common to WebSite 1.1 and Web-Site Pro, but does not cover the secure-specific features. The material in this chapter comes from the book *Building Your Own WebSite* by Susan B. Peck and Stephen Arrants, which is included with the commercial WebSite distribution.

Server Configuration

Server Admin

Server Admin is the tool for administering the WebSite server. WebSite uses the Windows 95 or Windows NT Registry to maintain information about your server. This configuration information is used by many of the WebSite applications, including Server Admin.

You can launch Server Admin either by selecting Properties from the server's Control menu, or by launching the application from the WebSite program list or group. Figure 26-1 shows the Server Admin application displaying the General properties page.

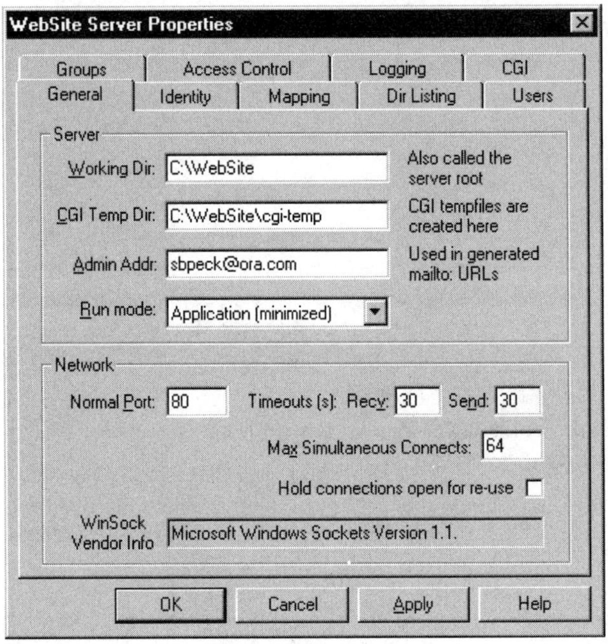

Figure 26-1: Server Admin General page

All of the configuration options for WebSite are available in Server Admin. The property sheet contains the following pages:

General

    Contains general server properties, such as the server root directory, port number, and administrator's address.

Mapping

    Sets the mappings from URLs to physical pathnames; CGI directory locations; mappings of content types to file extensions; and directory index icons.

Identity

    Contains the settings for "virtual servers" or multi-homed servers.

Dir Listing

    Contains the settings for the enabling and formatting of directory listings when no default file is available.

Users

> Used to manage users for your system, with their own usernames and passwords.

Groups

> Used to manage special groups of users who may access certain parts of your web.

Access Control

> Used to configure access control to URLs in your web, either by user/group authentication or class restriction (IP address or hostname), or both.

Logging

> Specifies the locations of your logging files, the type of access file format, and tracing options for the server log.

CGI

> The CGI page of Server Admin should be used by advanced users only. Many of the fields on this page are used to set command-line options for the various types of CGI programs that WebSite runs. This page will not be described here.

The settings available on each of these pages are described in the following sections. When you make a change to Server Admin and close it (or press Apply), a dialog pops up asking if it should update immediately (and terminate any active connections) or wait until the server is idle to update. Whichever you choose, you'll hear a beep when the update is made, indicating that the server's configuration has been updated. If the server is not running, you will not hear a beep, but the configuration is in effect the next time you start the server.

General Properties

The General page of Server Admin lists some of the basic settings for the WebSite server:

Working Directory

> Indicates where WebSite is installed. This directory is also called the server root. Do not change this entry unless you move WebSite to a new location.

CGI Temporary Directory

> Indicates the temporary location Common Gateway Interface (CGI) programs use. You can change this directory if necessary by typing in a new one.

Administrator Address

> Shows the complete email address of the WebSite server administrator. Notice that the address is the Internet address you entered during setup. You can change the address here by typing in a new one.

Run Mode

> Specifies how WebSite will run the next time it is started. Under Windows 95 there is only one run mode: desktop application. Under Windows NT, the pulldown list has three choices: desktop application, system service with icon, and system service without icon. If you want to run WebSite as a service, you must first select a new run mode here and then restart the server as a service.

Normal Port

> Tells the server what port number to use. The standard TCP/IP port is 80.

Timeouts (Receive and Send)
>Fairly standard settings. You may need to increase the timeouts if you are on a slow line, or if users complain that your server seems "slow" or "cuts off" documents. Increase the timeouts to 180 seconds for a PPP/SLIP connection.

Maximum Simultaneous Connects
>Limits the number of simultaneous connections. You may need to adjust this for your line speed, to guarantee a minimum level of service. For example, if you have a 28.8 line and 10 simultaneous connections, each user sees only a 2800 baud line, which is very slow for Web traffic. In this case, you would want to decrease the number of maximum connects. If you are on a high-speed line (ISDN, T1, or T3) or running on an internal network, the number can be higher.

Hold Connection Open for Reuse
>Specifies whether the server should use the Connection: Keep Alive feature, which allows browsers to reuse a connection for fetching inline graphics and other elements referenced in a document.

Winsock Vendor Information
>Lists the valid Winsock programs detected on your system. WebSite uses Microsoft's Winsock Version 1.1. You cannot change this field.

Mapping

When a browser requests a URL, the WebSite server first compares the URL to several Web server mapping tables to see how the URL should be translated on your web. For example, a URL may be mapped to a physical location on your computer or one halfway around the world, or it may be mapped to a CGI program that creates a virtual document.

The WebSite server supports three types of mapping:

- URL mapping, including:

    - Document mapping, which maps a logical URL to a physical location on your system

    - Redirection mapping, which maps one URL to another URL, often on another server and generally used only temporarily

    - Executable or CGI mapping, which maps URLs for CGI programs to the location of the specific type of CGI program (Standard, Windows, or DOS) and tells the server to execute rather than display the CGI program

- Content type mapping, which maps the type of document (as defined by the file extension) to a standard MIME (Multipurpose Internet Mail Extensions) protocol type, used by the Web browser to correctly display the document

- Directory icon mapping, which maps icon images used in automatic directory listing to specific content (or MIME) types

Each of these mappings is controlled by the Mapping page of Server Admin, shown in Figure 26-2. The List Selector box lists the different types of mappings available. By selecting one from the list, the current mappings are displayed in the top window. You can add, change, or delete mapping values using the two edit boxes and Delete, Replace, and Add buttons in the lower right corner of the page. When you select a value to change it, edit the value in the second box only. If you change the value in the first box, you are actually creating a *new* value to be mapped.

After you have made all the changes to the mapping type, press Apply. You may then select another mapping type to modify or update the WebSite server by pressing Close.

Document mapping

Document mapping lets you assign the logical pieces of your web (as defined by URLs) to physical locations on your computer or any other computer on your network. The WebSite default document mappings are shown in Figure 26-2.

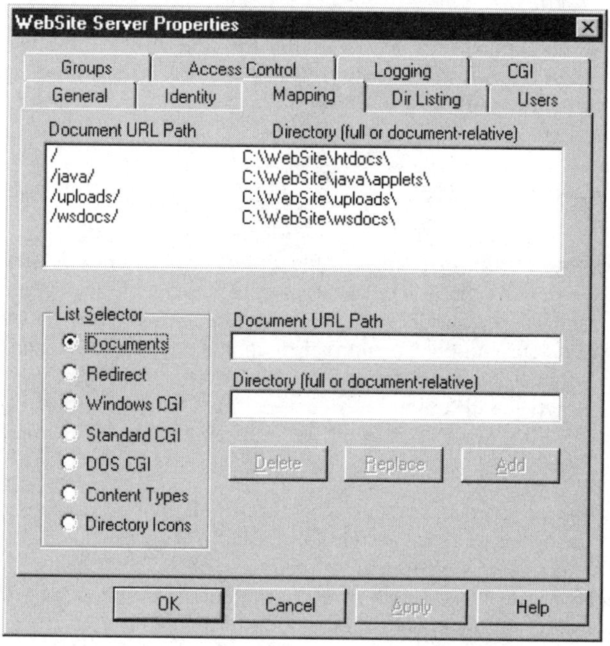

Figure 26-2: Default WebSite Document mappings

The document root (/) must be a full path name (including drive letter) or a path relative to the server root (displayed on the General page of Server Admin). Other mappings must be full path names or paths relative to the document root. It is suggested that you use full path names for all mappings to avoid confusion.

Redirect mapping

This mapping type maps a URL on your web to another URL, usually on another computer. When the server receives a request for a redirected URL, it automatically sends the browser to the new URL. The redirection is transparent to the user. The original URL must be a URL path for your server. The redirected URL must be a full URL (including protocol and/or hostname and path) if it is on another computer.

CGI mapping

There are three types of CGI mapping in WebSite, one for each of the types of CGI programs WebSite supports: Windows CGI, Standard CGI, and DOS CGI. CGI mapping identifies URLs that require the browser to execute a program instead of sending a document, and the type and location of the program. CGI mappings must use full path names or paths relative to the server root. Mappings must not fall within either a document-mapped directory tree or the tree mapped for another CGI type. See Chapter 9, *CGI Overview*, for more information on CGI. See Chapter 14, *Windows CGI*, for information particular to the Windows CGI.

Content Type mapping

This mapping selection displays the mappings of file extensions to content types or MIME types. The server returns the content type of a requested file as header information in its response to the browser. Since WebSite runs under Windows 95 and Windows NT, file extensions can be any number of characters. Multiple extensions often indicate the same file type, such as *.htm* and *.html* for *text/html* files. When adding new content types with multiple extensions, each extension must be mapped to the content type separately. You cannot map extensions more than one at a time.

WebSite includes about 50 predefined content types and their mappings. There are five standard types included: text, image, video, audio, and application. One type special to the WebSite server is also included: *wwwserver*. Six subtypes exist for *wwwserver*; three map to the three kinds of CGI programs, and the others to special files. The CGI subtypes allow you to include CGI programs in your document trees and let the server know that it should execute them when requested. The *wwwserver* subtypes are described as follows:

wwwserver/shellcgi
> Mapped to *.cgi* and *.scgi*. Used for Standard CGI files. See Chapter 9 for more information on CGI.

wwwserver/doscgi
> Mapped to *.dcgi*. Used for DOS CGI files.

wwwserver/wincgi
> Mapped to *.wcgi*. Used for Windows CGI files. See Chapter 14 for more information on WinCGI.

wwwserver/redirection

Mapped to *.url*. Used for files that contain only a URL, which the server reads and redirects the browser to. Works with Internet Shortcut files in Windows 95.

wwwserver/imagemap

Mapped to *.map*. Used to process NCSA-format clickable image maps.

wwwserver/html-ssi

Mapped to *.html-ssi*. Used for HTML files that contain Server Side Includes (see Chapter 13, *Server Side Includes*).

Directory Icon Mapping

This section of the mapping page is used to map icons to file types for use in directory indexing. The icons are placed to the left of filenames in enhanced directory indexes. Settings for how directory indexes are displayed are available from the Dir Index page of Server Admin. WebSite includes many default icon mappings. Icon files are GIF images that are stored in the directory */WebSite/icons*. New icon files that you create should be placed there.

Directory index icons can be mapped to files either by content type, i.e., *images/**, which covers all image subtypes, or by specific subtypes. A specific subtype mapping will be used over a more general content type mapping.

Virtual Servers

The Identity page of Server Admin (shown in Figure 26-3) is used for multi-homed or virtual servers' settings for WebSite. Setting up differently named and addressed sites on the same computer and server is a complex issue and is not discussed in detail in this book. However, the Windows platforms are quite capable of supporting multiple IP addresses on the same machine. Windows NT supports multiple IP addresses using a single or multiple adapters. Windows 95 supports multiple IP addresses only with multiple adapters—one IP address per adapter. The WebSite server can support an unlimited number of IP addresses, or as many as the operating system can.

WebSite handles multiple virtual servers in a rather elegant way by using unique "nicknames" for each address. When WebSite receives a request for a specific IP address, it prefixes the URL with that address's nickname. Document and CGI mapping are critically important under this scheme, and URLs for each virtual server must be mapped using the nickname. The use of the nickname is of no concern to your users. They simply request URLs using whatever IP address or hostname they require.

WebSite gives you an easy way and a hard way to set up virtual servers. Both paths begin on the Identity page of Server Admin. When you click the Multiple Identities box, an alert box pops up to tell you that IP addresses have been added to the server's configuration. Press OK and the page changes to show all the IP addresses on the system in the pulldown list box. The first address shown is always 127.0.0.1, *localhost*. You must configure this address just like any other virtual server you set up. To set up a new IP address, select it from the list and press

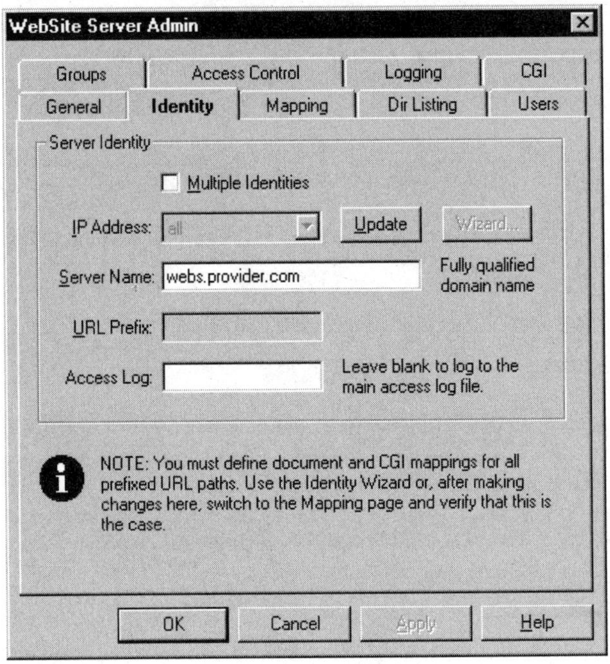

Figure 26-3: Identity page in Server Admin

the Wizard button. The Identity Wizard will appear and ask you to supply information about the new address. The Identity Wizard automates the setup of nicknames and documents and CGI mapping for you. It will also create new directories if you wish to use them for the new web. Using the Wizard is the easy way.

The hard way is the path you take if you do not press the Wizard button after selecting the new address to be configured. You must then provide the fully qualified domain name for the new address, the URL prefix you wish to use (it must begin with a slash /), and the name of an access log file, if you don't wish to use the main access file. You must supply *.log* with the access log filename; WebSite will not add it automatically.

Once you have filled in all of the fields, press the Update button. Follow the same steps to configure any other new addresses you may have. When all new addresses are set up, press Apply.

Filling in the Identity page is only part of manually setting up a new IP address. You now have to go to the Mapping page and create mappings for the new address by using its nickname. Make sure you use the address' nickname in front of every URL path you map. For example, a new virtual server has been set up on the Identity page with the server name *webs.provider.com* and the nickname */webs*. Figure 26-4 shows the Document URL mappings from the Mapping page with the document root directory set for */webs*.

All mapped URLs for that server must begin with */webs/*. CGI mappings also must be mapped using the nicknames. Keep in mind that URLs mapped by nicknames for different virtual servers can use the same physical directory. This will probably be the case for some of your CGI programs.

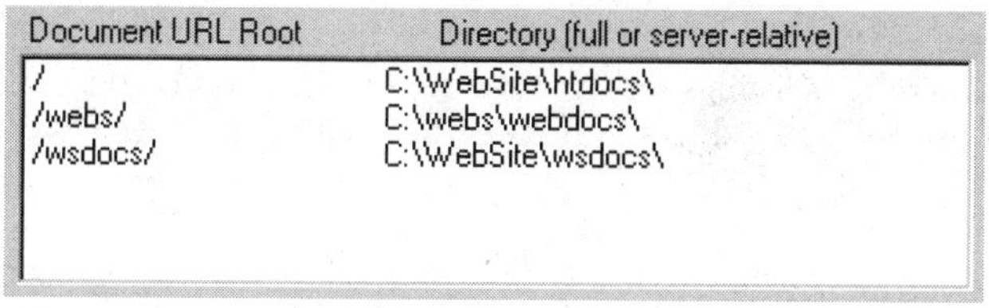

Document URL Root	Directory (full or server-relative)
/	C:\WebSite\htdocs\
/webs/	C:\webs\webdocs\
/wsdocs/	C:\WebSite\wsdocs\

Figure 26-4: Document Mapping for a virtual server

Directory Listings

Automatic directory index listings in WebSite are configured on the Dir Listing page of Server Admin. The Default settings for the page are shown in Figure 26-5.

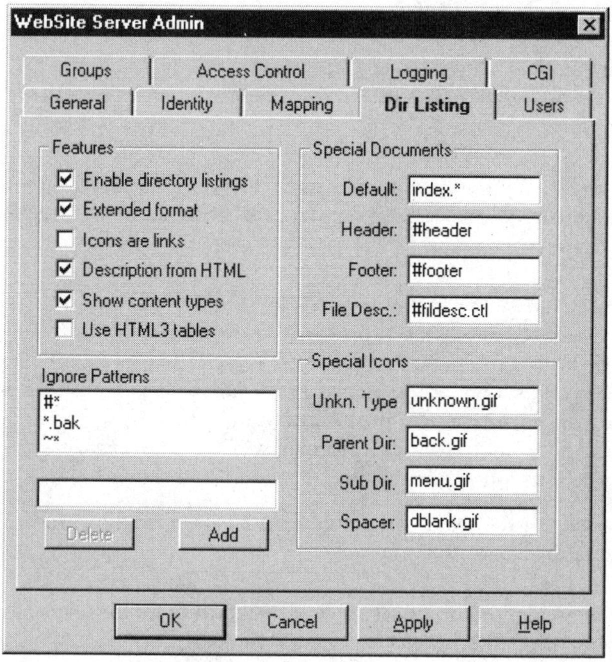

Figure 26-5: Default Dir Listing page

WebSite provides two types of directory indexing. Simple indexing will list all of the files in a directory as a bulleted list with filenames as links. Extended format is the default, and provides icons, file descriptions, modification times and dates, and header and footer files. These options are configurable as well.

If you wish, you can disable all directory indexes. If you want to restrict access to specific directory indexes, you use the Access Control page of Server Admin. The features of the Dir Listing page are described in the following sections.

The Features area of the page provides general setup options for directory listings.

Enable directory listings

This box controls directory listings for your server. It is checked by default. You can turn off listings on a URL basis on the Access Control page of Server Admin.

Extended format

This option controls which type of index format you desire. It is checked by default. If it is not checked, simple format indexes will be used, and all options on the page are unavailable except the Default document box and the Ignore Patterns listing.

Icons are links

Icons in directory listings are enabled as links to the files. The icons used for links are borderless.

Description from HTML

When this option is enabled, the contents of the `<title>` ... `</title>` tags for each file are used as the file description. The HTML title tags must occur in the first 250 bytes of the file, and the title tags must be uppercase. Annotations defined in a description file take precedence over HTML titles used as file descriptions.

Show content types

This option enables content types to be used for the file description. Description file annotations and HTML titles take precedence over content types for file descriptions.

Use HTML3 tables

With this option selected, WebSite serves extended format directory listings as HTML3 style tables (i.e., tables as supported by the Netscape browser). This option provides nicer formatting for the listing; for example, a long file description is displayed as a multi-line block of text rather than a single long line. Table listings can be selected or deselected via the URL. By appending */?table* to the end of the URL, the table format will be sent by WebSite. Appending */?plain* returns a non-table listing.

The Special Documents area of the Dir Listing page identifies special files used to enhance extended directory listings.

Default

This field indicates the name of the file that will be returned for any URL that does not contain an exact filename. The default value is `index.*`, which will make WebSite look for *index* with any extension. If a file using this name does not exist in the requested directory, a listing of the directory will be returned (or an error if indexing is disabled).

Header

This field specifies a filename that contains a partial HTML file (or plain text file) to include at the top of a directory listing. The default is *#header*, and the server will look for this name followed by either *.html*, *.htm*, or *.txt*. You do not have to supply an extension. An HTML header file should contain all appropriate tagging except closing `</body>` and `</html>` tags.

Footer

This field specifies a filename that contains a partial HTML file (or plain text file) to include at the bottom of a directory listing. You should not use any starting tags such as those used in the header file. Additionally, do not use the closing tags `</body>` or `</html>` as the server will supply them.

File Desc.

This field is used to specify the name of a file that contains annotations for files in the directory to be used in the file description field of a directory listing. These descriptions require a special format in the file:

[filename]| [comment or hypertext link]

Lines that begin with whitespace in the file are considered comments. You can list descriptions for some or all of the files in the directory. You can also specify an annotation for the parent directory (..). The server reads this file as HTML, so you should use the HTML coding for special characters such as ampersand (&).

The Ignore Patterns section of the Dir Listing page specifies full or partial filenames that you want to exclude from all directory listings. You can use the wildcard characters ? and * here for pattern matching. The default patterns are:

```
#*
*.bak
~*
*.ctr
```

Notice that the # pattern hides all files that begin with the hash character, such as the default filenames for the header and footer files. You should hide any file types that you don't want to provide a link to, such as *.exe* executables. Keep in mind that the patterns you set apply to all directory listings available from your site.

To add a new pattern, type it into the edit field and press Add. To remove a pattern, select it from the list and press Delete.

The Special Icons section of the Dir Listing page specifies icon images to be used with file listings that don't have an associated content type. The other directory icons are mapped from the Mapping page according to file type or subtype. The default filenames shown exist in the */icons/* URL directory of WebSite. If you add a new icon file, you must put it there.

Unkn. Type

This specifies the icon used for files whose type is undefined. The default is a blank page image.

Parent Dir.

This specifies the icon used for the parent directory (..) listing. The default is an up arrow.

Sub Dir.

This specifies the icon used for a listing of a subdirectory of the correct directory. The default is a folder image.

Spacer

This specifies the icon used as a blank placeholder in the header of a directory listing. This icon fills the space to the left of "Name" in the header row, aligning it with the filenames below.

Logging

WebSite has three main logs: the access log, the error log, and the server log. The access log records each request to the server and the server's response in one of three formats: Common (older NCSA/CERN), Combined NCSA/CERN, and Windows Log format. The error log records access errors, such as failed user authentication. The server log records each time the server is restarted or its configuration is updated. You can also set a variety of tracing options to have the server log collect more or less detailed information. The tracing information is used primarily for troubleshooting and debugging.

WebSite log configuration occurs on the Logging page of Server Admin. Figure 26-6 shows the default Logging page.

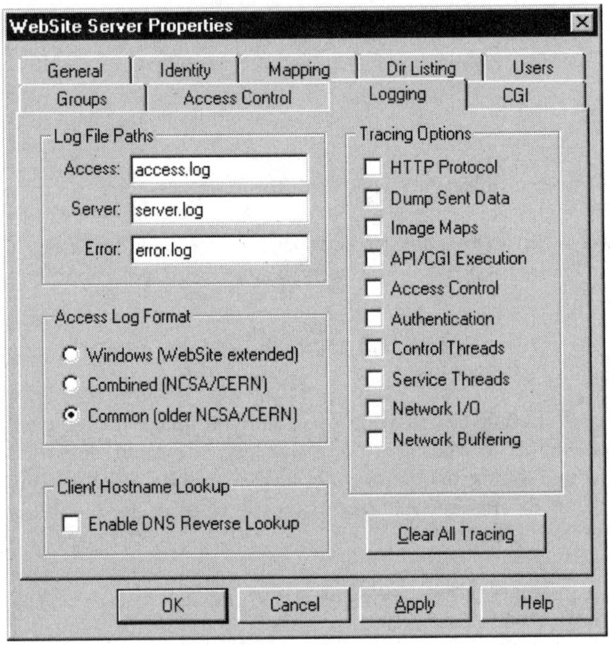

Figure 26-6: Default Logging page

The Log File Paths section allows you to choose the path and filenames of the log files. The default files are in the directory */WebSite/logs*. You can place a full pathname to put the logs in another location. The server will shut down if it cannot maintain log files. Therefore, if you locate the logging directories on a remote computer, make sure that it will always be available when the server is running.

The Access Log Format section of the page allows you to select the format of the access log file. The three formats are described as follows:

Windows (WebSite Extended)
This format collects server access data in a format that can be easily imported into most Microsoft Windows Office productivity packages. The entries are tab delimited and require no additional parsing using Visual Basic or Perl. This format creates larger files than the other logging formats.

Combined (NCSA/CERN)

This format collects server access data in a more standard Web log format with fields delimited by quotation marks. Two extra fields are included to identify the URL from which the browser made the current request (Referer), and to identify the browser type (User_Agent).

Common (older NCSA/CERN)

This is the default format for WebSite and is the standard Web log format used by most Web servers.

Instead of the IP address, you can have WebSite find and put the requesting client's hostname in the log files. To do this, select the Enable DNS Reverse Lookup box in the Client Hostname Lookup section of the Logging page. For every logged access, the server will contact its DNS server with the browser's IP address and ask for its corresponding DNS hostname. It is not suggested that you use this feature without a compelling reason as it will slow transaction time noticeably.

WebSite has 10 different tracing options that provide detailed data about the server's activity in the server log. You can select one or more of these options by clicking on the appropriate checkboxes in the Tracing Options sections of the Logging page. The first six options listed are useful to the server administrator, while the last five are used mainly by technical support. The last five will not be described here. You can remove any tracing option by clicking on a checked box, or press Clear All Tracing to remove them all. The first six tracing options are as follows:

HTTP Protocol

This tracing option records the incoming header data for each request from a browser and the action the server takes responding to the request. See Chapters 17 through 20 for more information on HTTP.

Dump Sent Data

This tracing option records all of the outgoing data to the browser in the server's response (header and file data). This option generates huge server logs.

Image Maps

This tracing option records the information about a client requesting a location on a clickable image map, and shows the server's response.

API/CGI Execution

This option records the server's activity when a browser requests a URL containing a CGI or WSAPI execution. It is useful for debugging CGI programs. When this tracing option is enabled, the server notifies the various types of CGI or API programs to enable their own debugging features, such as displaying standard output and saving temporary files. See Chapter 9 for more information on CGI.

Access Control

This tracing option records the server's actions in checking access control restrictions and then denying or allowing access to a specific URL path by requestor. Access Control tracing shows both the class restrictions (IP address or hostname) and user authentication requirements. User and group names are not included with this tracing option.

Authentication

This tracing option records all user authentication attempts, whether successful or unsuccessful, and why they weren't. Passwords are shown only in encrypted form. The URL path for the authentication attempt is not included with this tracing. Enabling both Access Control and Authentication tracing provides a complete picture of how your server is handling access control restrictions.

Access Control

Your options for controlling access to your web with WebSite are similar to the access schemes used by other servers. You can restrict access by user with a user/password system, by the requesting IP address or hostname (class restrictions), or both. Three pages of Server Admin are used for access control.

The Users and Groups pages are where you create users and give them passwords and create groups of users. WebSite also uses the concept of "realms," which are large collections of groups and users. When you want to control access to a URL path on your web, you pick a realm first, and then groups and users in that realm who are permitted access.

The Users page of Server Admin (shown in Figure 26-7) is for managing users and their passwords; it has three sections:

Authentication Realm

You can select an existing realm to use (such as Web Server), create a new realm (by pressing the New button), or delete an existing realm. Your web can have one or multiple realms. You may want to have a separate realm for each virtual server you have. When you create a realm, it has no users.

User

You can select an existing user in the realm, change a user's password (by pressing the Password button), or delete a user. The default Web Server realm has an Admin user.

Group Membership

You can view and change the group membership status for the selected user. Every realm automatically has an Administrators group and a Users group. All groups you have created within a realm on the Groups page are available here for selection. Every user in a realm is a member of Users, and cannot be removed unless they are deleted altogether.

The Groups page of Server Admin (shown in Figure 26-8) is used for managing groups and groups membership. It has three sections:

Authentication Realm

This area works exactly the same as it does on the Users page. Here you select which realm will be affected by the changes you make on the rest of the page. Note that on both the Users and Groups pages, you can create or delete realms.

Group

You can select an existing group in a realm, add a new group, or delete a group. Every realm automatically has an Administrators and a Users group. All users in a realm are members of Users and cannot be removed.

Group Membership

You can view and change the selected group's membership list. All available users in the selected realm will appear in the non-members box (if they aren't already members). To add a user to the group, select her name and

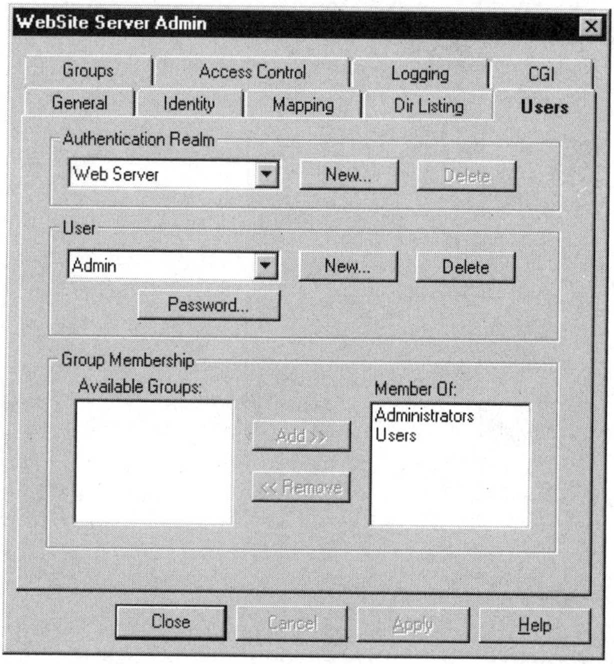

Figure 26-7: Server Admin Users page

press the Add button. It is easier to add users to groups on the Users page when you create them and set their passwords. If the group(s) you want to add them to are already created, you can add them there and save a possible extra step.

Once you have your users, groups, and realms set up, you can assign access based on them on the Access Control page. Access can also be assigned based on IP address or hostname of the requesting browser. You also use this page to disable automatic directory listings and determine how the server will control access restrictions per URL.

The Access Control page is shown in Figure 26-9. It has several sections:

URL Path or Special Function

You can select, add, or delete a URL path or special function. The URL path cannot specify a file, so all files and subdirectories under that directory have the restrictions applied to them. You can protect any document or CGI directory. To add a new URL path, press the New button. In the popup dialog, type in the new URL path and select a realm to which it will be restricted.

Since restrictions are applied by path, many "control points" may exist along a path. The deepest access control point determines the access restrictions at a particular level. In other words, when the server receives a request from a browser, it starts at the level of the request and works up levels until it finds a control point. The server applies the restrictions at that point and stops; it does not look at restrictions above that point.

The special functions are URLs that start with a tilde (˜) character and are handled in a special way by the server. Some special function URLs only

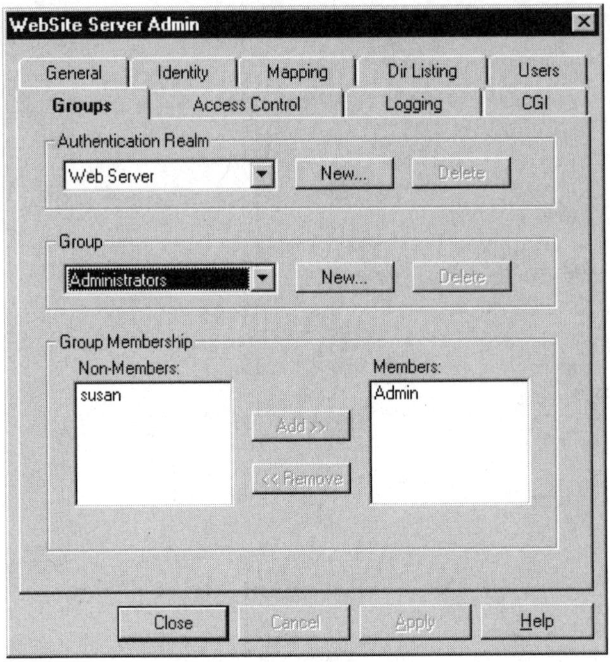

Figure 26-8: Server Admin Groups page

retrieve data, such a ˜*stats* or ˜*imagemap*. Other special function URLs cause the server to perform an administrative task, such as ˜*cycle-acc* or ˜*cycle-err* to cycle the access and error logs. All of the special function URLs in WebSite are on the Access Control list, although only those that cause the server to do something are protected. You cannot delete special functions from the access control list.

Disable Directory Listings

This checkbox disables automatic directory listings for the selected URL. Users will be able to view or download documents in that URL directory hierarchy only with the specific filename. You can also add user authentication and class restrictions to a URL with disabled directory listings (i.e., authorized users can receive a directory listing).

Logical OR Users and Class

This checkbox tells the server how to evaluate access control. When the box is not checked, the server uses the default method, first looking for class restrictions and then for user authentication (if the class restrictions are met). If the box is checked, the server evaluates both class restrictions and user authentication. If either condition is met, the server returns the requested URL.

Authorized Users & Groups

You can view or change the users and/or groups authorized for the selected URL path or special function. The realm for this URL is displayed above the list. If no users or groups are shown in this box, then the URL has no user authentication restrictions.

Class Restrictions

In this section of the Access Control page, you specify which connections to the Web are allowed and which are denied. First decide the logic the server should follow in testing connections. Should it first deny and then allow, or first allow and then deny? Which you should choose depends on the scope of restriction. To delete an entry, select the entry from the appropriate box and press Delete. To add a new entry, place the cursor in the appropriate box and press New. A popup dialog will open where you type in the address.

Class restrictions accept three kinds of entries: all, a full or partial IP address, or a full or partial domain name. You can use metacharacters (* and ?) to match all or part of either IP addresses or domain names. If you use domain names, you must turn on DNS reverse lookup on the Logging page. The server then looks up the name for the IP address of each requesting node. It is recommended that you don't use domain names or DNS reverse lookup because the extra DNS traffic and waiting time may adversely affect server performance.

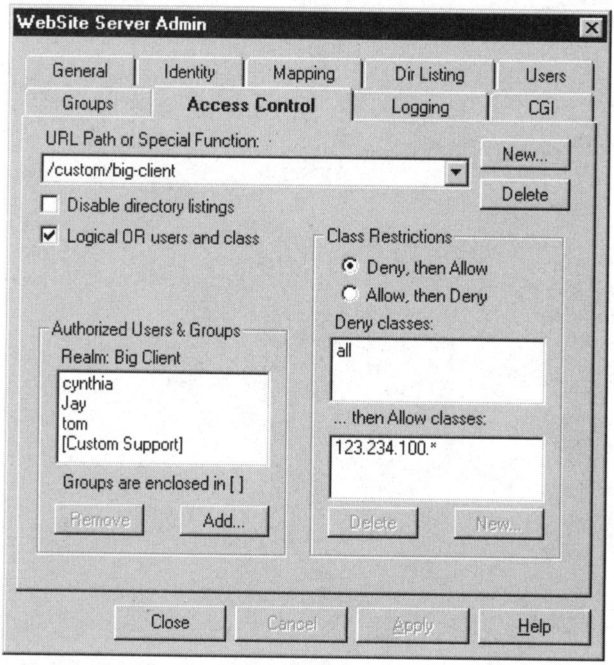

Figure 26-9: Access Control page

Index

flex-log function, 322
floating frame, 47
floor( ), 218
focus( ), 199, 227, 239, 241, 246
font, 14, 18, 234
<font> tag, 18, 234
fontcolor( ), 234
fontsize( ), 234
footers, table, 36
Forbidden (403) HTTP error, 155, 289, 321
ForceType directive, 269
force-type function, 318
foreground color (see color)
Form External section, CGI data file, 107
Form File section, CGI data file, 108
Form Huge section, CGI data file, 108
Form Literal section, CGI data file, 107
Form object, 199
<form> tag, 18, 79, 199
format
    Perl functions for, 127
    SSI (see config directive)
    (see also layout)
forms, HTML, 79-86, 199
    decoding, 108
    transferring data, 74
    (see also CGI)
forms[] property, 194
forward( ), 206
frame attribute, <table>, 35, 54, 66
Frame object, 201
<frame> tag, 18, 45-47
frameborder attribute
    <frame> tag, 19, 47
    <frameset> tag, 19, 67
    <iframe> tag, 21
frames, HTML, 18, 21, 41-47, 201, 243-249
frames[] property, 244
<frameset> tag, 19, 42-44, 67
framespacing attribute, <frameset>, 20, 47, 66
From header, 163
fsize directive (SSI), 97
full URLs (see absolute URLs)
Function( ), 202
Function object, 202

functions
    CGI, 104
    Perl, 117-123, 127

GATEWAY_INTERFACE variable, 87
general HTTP headers, 159
GET method, 74, 149
getClass( ), 203
getDate( ), 190
getDay( ), 190
getHours( ), 190
GetMask directive, 299
getMinutes( ), 190
getMonth( ), 190
getSeconds( ), 190
getTime( ), 190
getTimezoneOffset( ), 190
getYear( ), 190
global, Perl variables, 134
go( ), 206
group authentication, 274
Group directive, 260
group file, 298
GroupFile directive, 299
GroupId directive, 284
gutter attribute, <multicol>, 29

<h#> (heading) tags, 20
hash mark (#) in server configuration files, 258, 283
hash property, 213, 215
HEAD method, 150
<head> tag, 8, 20
HeaderName directive, 269
headers
    extra, 107
    HTTP, 75, 148, 159-171, 254
    table, 37, 52
headings, 20
height (see size)
height attribute
    <applet> tag, 13
    <embed> tag, 17
    <iframe> tag, 21
    <img> tag, 22
    <marquee> tag, 28
    <object> tag, 30
    <spacer> tag, 33
height property, 207
help (see documentation)

LOG2E (constant), 217
logarithms, 218
LogDirGroupWriteOk directive, 260
LogDirPublicWriteOk directive, 260
LogFileDateExt directive, 290
LogFormat directive, 291
LogOptions directive, 260
LogTime directive, 291
loop attribute
    <bgsound> tag, 14
    <img> tag, 22, 66
    <marquee> tag, 28
lowsrc attribute, <img>, 22, 67
lowsrc property, 207

magnus.conf file, 304-306
Main() routine, 101
Map directive, 289
<map> tag, 27
mapping WebSite, 326-329
marginheight attribute
    <frame> tag, 19, 45
    <iframe> tag, 21
margins
    frame, 19, 21, 45, 47
    HTML document, 14
    table, 51
marginwidth attribute
    <frame> tag, 19, 45
    <iframe> tag, 21
markers (see tags)
<marquee> tag, 27, 66
Math object, 216-219
Math property, 245
max(), 218
MaxClients directive, 261
MaxContentLengthBuffer directive, 287
Max-Forwards header, 164
MaxKeepAliveRequests directive, 261
maxlength attribute, <input>, 23-25, 80
MaxProcs directive, 305
Max-Proxy-Authorization header, 164
MaxRequestsPerChild directive, 261
MaxServers directive, 261
MaxSpareServers directive, 261
MaxThreads directive, 305
MAX_value constant, 221
MD5 message digest, 258
media types, 80, 254, 309
    forcing, 318
    HTTP, 171-174

mapping (WebSite), 328
    specifying icons for, 267
menu lists, 28
<menu> tag, 28
<meta> tag, 28
MetaDir directive, 287
MetaSuffix directive, 288
method attribute, <form>, 18, 74
method property, 200
methods, 149-152
methods attribute
    <a> tag, 11
    <link> tag, 27
MIME (Multipurpose Internet Mail
    Extensions), 171, 266
MIME types (see media types)
MimeType object, 219
mimeTypes[] property, 220, 228
MIME-Version header, 161
min(), 218
MinSpareServers directive, 262
MinThreads directive, 305
minute (see date and time)
MIN_value constant, 221
modification time, 97, 99
modules, Perl, 116
month (see date and time)
mouse events, 213
<multicol> tag, 29, 67
multihoming, 259, 329-330
multiline text input area, 25, 36, 82,
    240-242
multipart/form-data media type, 80
multiple attribute, <select>, 33, 83,
    107, 231

name attribute
    <a> tag, 12
    <applet> tag, 13
    <embed> tag, 17
    <frame> tag, 19, 42, 45
    <iframe> tag, 21
    <input> tag, 23-26, 80
    <map> tag, 27
    <meta> tag, 29
    <object> tag, 30
    <param> tag, 31
    <select> tag, 33, 83
names
    color, 56-57
    entities (see entities)

About the Author

Stephen Spainhour is a writer for O'Reilly & Associates who focuses on Internet-related topics (when he's wearing his glasses). He has worked at O'Reilly since 1993, originally as a production editor. He studied physics and writing at the Massachusetts Institute of Technology, but really only remembers singing a lot in the all-male *a capella* group, the MIT Logarhythms. He enjoys cooking and watching low-rated television, and fantasizes about having his own cooking show/situation comedy one day.

Valerie Quercia is a writer for O'Reilly & Associates. Val and Tim O'Reilly have coauthored several editions of the *X Window System User's Guide*. She is also coauthor of *X User Tools*, with Linda Mui, who happens to be the editor of *WebMaster in a Nutshell*. Once unfairly labeled Madame X, Ms. Quercia is now writing about the World Wide Web, and, occasionally, about baseball. Val has been a Red Sox fan since her grandmother taught her what a grand slam was in 1967. Despite a suspiciously yellowing high school diploma, Val insists she was an embryo at the time.

Colophon

Our look is the result of reader comments, our own experimentation, and feedback from distribution channels. Distinctive covers complement our distinctive approach to technical topics, breathing personality and life into potentially dry subjects.

A crab spider is featured on the cover of *WebMaster in a Nutshell*. Like the crustaceans after which they are named, crab spiders walk sideways or backwards. They feed on bees and other pollenizing insects, often laying in wait for them by hiding on flowers. Some species of crab spider can, over a period of several days, change color from white to yellow and back again to blend into the flower on which they are sitting. The spider can grab its prey quickly with its forward-facing front legs. It then injects its victims with a fast-acting, highly poisonous venom, in this way protecting itself from the bee's sting.

Spiders are similar to, but not the same as, insects. They belong to the class *Arachnida*, named after Arachne, a maiden in Greek mythology. She defeated the goddess Athena in a weaving contest. In a fury of anger, Athena destroyed Arachne's weaving and beat her about the head. In utter disgrace, Arachne hanged herself. A regretful Athena changed Arachne into a spider so that she could weave forever.

While they are certainly not going to win any popularity contests, spiders' insect-eating habits are extremely helpful to humans. Every year, billions of spiders do away with a large number of disease-carrying and crop-destroying insects. If every spider ate just one a day for a year, those insects, piled in one spot, would weigh as much as 50 million people. Spiders are, by far, the most important predator of insects in the world.

Edie Freedman designed the cover of this book, using a 19th-century engraving from the Dover Pictorial Archive. The cover layout was produced with Quark XPress 3.3 using the ITC Garamond font.

The inside layout was designed by Edie Freedman and Nancy Priest and implemented in gtroff by Lenny Muellner. The text and heading fonts are ITC Garamond Light and Garamond Book. Figures were created by Chris Reilley in Macromedia Freehand 5.0 and Adobe Photoshop. This colophon was written by Clairemarie Fisher O'Leary, with help from Elaine and Michael Kalantarian.

More Titles from O'REILLY™

Developing Web content

Building Your Own WebSite

By Susan B. Peck & Stephen Arrants
1st Edition July 1996
514 pages, ISBN 1-56592-232-8

This is a hands-on reference for Windows® 95 and Windows NT™ users who want to host a site on the Web or on a corporate intranet. This step-by-step guide will have you creating live Web pages in minutes. You'll also learn how to connect your web to information in other Windows applications, such as word processing documents and databases.
The book is packed with examples and tutorials on every aspect of Web management, and it includes the highly acclaimed WebSite™ server software 1.1 on CD-ROM.

Web Client Programming with Perl

By Clinton Wong
1st Edition Fall 1996
250 pages (est.), ISBN 1-56592-214-X

Web Client Programming with Perl teaches you how to extend scripting skills to the Web. This book teaches you the basics of how browsers communicate with servers and how to write your own customized Web clients to automate common tasks. It is intended for those who are motivated to develop software that offers a more flexible and dynamic response than a standard Web browser.

JavaScript: The Definitive Guide, Beta version

By David Flanagan
1st Edition August 1996
472 pages, ISBN 1-56592-193-3

Includes coverage of the frustrating bugs encountered in the beta version of JavaScript, the HTML extension that gives Web pages programming-language capabilities. With JavaScript you can control Web browser behavior, add dynamically created text to Web pages, interact with users through HTML forms, and even control and interact with Java applets and Navigator plugins. Available online (http://www.ora.com) and at your bookstore.

HTML: The Definitive Guide

By Chuck Musciano & Bill Kennedy
1st Edition April 1996
410 pages, ISBN 1-56592-175-5

A complete guide to creating documents on the World Wide Web. This book describes basic syntax and semantics and goes on to show you how to create beautiful, informative Web documents you'll be proud to display. The HTML 2.0 standard and Netscape extensions are fully explained.

Designing for the Web: Getting Started in a New Medium

By Jennifer Niederst with Edie Freedman
1st Edition April 1996
180 pages, ISBN 1-56592-165-8

Designing for the Web gives you the basics you need to hit the ground running. Although geared toward designers, it covers information and techniques useful to anyone who wants to put graphics online.
It explains how to work with HTML documents from a designer's point of view, outlines special problems with presenting information online, and walks through incorporating images into Web pages, with emphasis on resolution and improving efficiency.

WebMaster in a Nutshell

By Stephen Spainhour & Valerie Quercia
1st Edition October 1996
374 pages, ISBN 1-56592-229-8

Web content providers and administrators have many sources of information, both in print and online. *WebMaster in a Nutshell* pulls it all together into one slim volume— for easy desktop access. This quick-reference covers HTML, CGI, Perl, HTTP, server configuration, and tools for Web administration.

For information: **800-998-9938**, 707-829-0515; **info@ora.com; http://www.ora.com/**
To order: **800-889-8969** (credit card orders only); **order@ora.com**

Stay in touch with O'REILLY™

Visit Our Award-Winning World Wide Web Site

http://www.ora.com/

VOTED

"Top 100 Sites on the Web" —*PC Magazine*
"Top 5% Websites" —*Point Communications*
"3-Star site" —*The McKinley Group*

Our Web site contains a library of comprehensive product information (including book excerpts and tables of contents), downloadable software, background articles, interviews with technology leaders, links to relevant sites, book cover art, and more. File us in your Bookmarks or Hotlist!

Join Our Two Email Mailing Lists

LIST #1   NEW PRODUCT RELEASES: To receive automatic email with brief descriptions of all new O'Reilly products as they are released, send email to:
listproc@online.ora.com and put the following information in the first line of your message (NOT in the Subject: field, which is ignored): **subscribe ora-news "Your Name" of "Your Organization"**
(for example: **subscribe ora-news Kris Webber of Fine Enterprises**)

List #2   O'REILLY EVENTS: If you'd also like us to send information about trade show events, special promotions, and other O'Reilly events, send email to:
listproc@online.ora.com and put the following information in the first line of your message (NOT in the Subject: field, which is ignored): **subscribe ora-events "Your Name" of "Your Organization"**

Visit Our Gopher Site

• Connect your Gopher to **gopher.ora.com**, or
• Point your Web browser to **gopher://gopher.ora.com/**, or
• telnet to **gopher.ora.com** (login: **gopher**)

Get Example Files from Our Books Via FTP

There are two ways to access an archive of example files from our books:

REGULAR FTP — ftp to: **ftp.ora.com**
(login: **anonymous**—use your email address as the password) or point your Web browser to:
ftp://ftp.ora.com/

FTPMAIL — Send an email message to:
ftpmail@online.ora.com (write "help" in the message body)

Contact Us Via Email

order@ora.com — To place a book or software order online. Good for North American and international customers.

subscriptions@ora.com — To place an order for any of our newsletters or periodicals.

software@ora.com — For general questions and product information about our software.
• Check out O'Reilly Software Online at **http://software.ora.com/** for software and technical support information.
• Registered O'Reilly software users send your questions to **website-support@ora.com**

books@ora.com — General questions about any of our books.

cs@ora.com — For answers to problems regarding your order or our products.

booktech@ora.com — For book content technical questions or corrections.

proposals@ora.com — To submit new book or software proposals to our editors and product managers.

international@ora.com — For information about our international distributors or translation queries.
• For a list of our distributors outside of North America check out:
http://www.ora.com/www/order/country.html

O'REILLY™

101 Morris Street, Sebastopol, CA 95472 USA
TEL 707-829-0515 or 800-998-9938 (6 A.M. to 5 P.M. PST)
FAX 707-829-0104

TO ORDER: **800-889-8969** (CREDIT CARD ORDERS ONLY); **order@ora.com**; **http://www.ora.com**
OUR PRODUCTS ARE AVAILABLE AT A BOOKSTORE OR SOFTWARE STORE NEAR YOU.

Titles from O'REILLY™

INTERNET PROGRAMMING

CGI Programming on the
World Wide Web
Designing for the Web
Exploring Java
HTML: The Definitive Guide
Web Client Programming with Perl
Learning Perl
Programming Perl, 2nd Edition
(Fall '96)
JavaScript: The Definitive Guide,
Beta Edition
WebMaster in a Nutshell
The World Wide Web Journal

USING THE INTERNET

Smileys
The Whole Internet User's Guide
and Catalog
The Whole Internet for Windows 95
What You Need to Know:
Using Email Effectively
Marketing on the Internet (Fall '96)
What You Need to Know: Bandits on
the Information Superhighway

JAVA SERIES

Exploring Java
Java in a Nutshell
Java Language Reference
(Fall '96 est.)
Java Virtual Machine

WINDOWS

Inside the Windows 95 Registry

SOFTWARE

WebSite™ 1.1
WebSite Professional™
WebBoard™
PolyForm™
Statisphere™

SONGLINE GUIDES

NetLearning
NetSuccess for Realtors
NetActivism
Gif Animation
Shockwave Studio (Winter '97 est.)

SYSTEM ADMINISTRATION

Building Internet Firewalls
Computer Crime:
A Crimefighter's Handbook
Computer Security Basics
DNS and BIND
Essential System Administration,
2nd Edition
Getting Connected:
The Internet at 56K and Up
Linux Network Administrator's
Guide
Managing Internet Information
Services
Managing Usenet (Fall '96)
Managing NFS and NIS
Networking Personal Computers
with TCP/IP
Practical UNIX & Internet Security
PGP: Pretty Good Privacy
sendmail
System Performance Tuning
TCP/IP Network Administration
termcap & terminfo
Using & Managing UUCP
Volume 8: X Window System
Administrator's Guide

UNIX

Exploring Expect
Learning GNU Emacs, 2nd Edition
Learning the bash Shell
Learning the Korn Shell
Learning the UNIX Operating
System
Learning the vi Editor
Linux in a Nutshell (Fall '96)
Making TeX Work
Linux Multimedia Guide (Fall '96)
Running Linux, 2nd Edition
Running Linux Companion
CD-ROM, 2nd Edition
SCO UNIX in a Nutshell
sed & awk
Unix in a Nutshell: System V Edition
UNIX Power Tools
UNIX Systems Programming
Using csh and tsch
What You Need to Know:
When You Can't Find Your
UNIX System Administrator

PROGRAMMING

Applying RCS and SCCS
C++: The Core Language
Checking C Programs with lint
DCE Security Programming
Distributing Applications Across
DCE and Windows NT
Encyclopedia of Graphics File
Formats, 2nd Edition
Guide to Writing DCE Applications
lex & yacc
Managing Projects with make
ORACLE Performance Tuning
ORACLE PL/SQL Programming
Porting UNIX Software
POSIX Programmer's Guide
POSIX.4: Programming for
the Real World
Power Programming with RPC
Practical C Programming
Practical C++ Programming
Programming Python (Fall '96)
Programming with curses
Programming with GNU Software
(Fall '96 est.)
Programming with Pthreads
Software Portability with imake
Understanding DCE
Understanding Japanese
Information Processing
UNIX Systems Programming
for SVR4

BERKELEY 4.4 SOFTWARE DISTRIBUTION

4.4BSD System Manager's Manual
4.4BSD User's Reference Manual
4.4BSD User's Supplementary
Documents
4.4BSD Programmer's Reference
Manual
4.4BSD Programmer's
Supplementary Documents

X PROGRAMMING
THE X WINDOW SYSTEM

Volume 0: X Protocol Reference
Manual
Volume 1: Xlib Programming
Manual
Volume 2: Xlib Reference Manual
Volume. 3M: X Window System
User's Guide, Motif Edition
Volume. 4: X Toolkit Intrinsics
Programming Manual
Volume 4M: X Toolkit Intrinsics
Programming Manual,
Motif Ediotion
Volume 5: X Toolkit Intrinsics
Reference Manual
Volume 6A: Motif Programming
Manual
Volume 6B: Motif Reference Manual
Volume 6C: Motif Tools
Volume 8 : X Window System
Administrator's Guide
Programmer's Supplement
for Release 6
X User Tools (with CD-ROM)
The X Window System in a Nutshell

HEALTH, CAREER, & BUSINESS

Building a Successful Software
Business
The Computer User's Survival Guide
Dictionary of Computer Terms
The Future Does Not Compute
Love Your Job!
Publishing with CD-ROM

TRAVEL

Travelers' Tales: Brazil (Fall '96)
Travelers' Tales: Food (Fall '96)
Travelers' Tales: France
Travelers' Tales: Hong Kong
Travelers' Tales: India
Travelers' Tales: Mexico
Travelers' Tales: San Francisco
Travelers' Tales: Spain
Travelers' Tales: Thailand
Travelers' Tales: A Woman's World

International Distributors

Customers outside North America can now order O'Reilly & Associates books through the following distributors. They offer our international customers faster order processing, more bookstores, increased representation at tradeshows worldwide, and the high-quality, responsive service our customers have come to expect.

EUROPE, MIDDLE EAST AND NORTHERN AFRICA (except Germany, Switzerland, and Austria)

INQUIRIES
International Thomson Publishing Europe
Berkshire House
168-173 High Holborn
London WC1V 7AA, United Kingdom
Telephone: 44-171-497-1422
Fax: 44-171-497-1426
Email: **itpint@itps.co.uk**

ORDERS
International Thomson Publishing Services, Ltd.
Cheriton House, North Way
Andover, Hampshire SP10 5BE,
United Kingdom
Telephone: 44-264-342-832 (UK orders)
Telephone: 44-264-342-806 (outside UK)
Fax: 44-264-364418 (UK orders)
Fax: 44-264-342761 (outside UK)
UK & Eire orders: **itpuk@itps.co.uk**
International orders: **itpint@itps.co.uk**

GERMANY, SWITZERLAND, AND AUSTRIA

International Thomson Publishing GmbH
O'Reilly International Thomson Verlag
Königswinterer Straße 418
53227 Bonn, Germany
Telephone: 49-228-97024 0
Fax: 49-228-441342
Email: **anfragen@arade.ora.de**

AUSTRALIA

WoodsLane Pty. Ltd.
7/5 Vuko Place, Warriewood NSW 2102
P.O. Box 935, Mona Vale NSW 2103
Australia
Telephone: 61-2-9970-5111
Fax: 61-2-9970-5002
Email: **info@woodslane.com.au**

NEW ZEALAND

WoodsLane New Zealand Ltd.
21 Cooks Street (P.O. Box 575)
Wanganui, New Zealand
Telephone: 64-6-347-6543
Fax: 64-6-345-4840
Email: **info@woodslane.com.au**

ASIA (except Japan & India)

INQUIRIES
International Thomson Publishing Asia
60 Albert Street #15-01
Albert Complex
Singapore 189969
Telephone: 65-336-6411
Fax: 65-336-7411

ORDERS
Telephone: 65-336-6411
Fax: 65-334-1617

JAPAN

O'Reilly Japan, Inc.
Kiyoshige Building 2F
12-Banchi, Sanei-cho
Shinjuku-ku
Tokyo 160 Japan
Telephone: 81-3-3356-5227
Fax: 81-3-3356-5261
Email: **kenji@ora.com**

INDIA

Computer Bookshop (India) PVT. LTD.
190 Dr. D.N. Road, Fort
Bombay 400 001
India
Telephone: 91-22-207-0989
Fax: 91-22-262-3551
Email: **cbsbom@giasbm01.vsnl.net.in**

THE AMERICAS

O'Reilly & Associates, Inc.
101 Morris Street
Sebastopol, CA 95472 U.S.A.
Telephone: 707-829-0515
Telephone: 800-998-9938 (U.S. & Canada)
Fax: 707-829-0104
Email: **order@ora.com**

SOUTHERN AFRICA

International Thomson Publishing Southern Africa
Building 18, Constantia Park
240 Old Pretoria Road
P.O. Box 2459
Halfway House, 1685 South Africa
Telephone: 27-11-805-4819
Fax: 27-11-805-3648

O'REILLY™

Here's a page we encourage readers to tear out...

O'REILLY WOULD LIKE TO HEAR FROM YOU

Nineteenth century wood engraving
of the rhesas monkey from the O'Reilly
& Associates Nutshell Handbook®
Exploring Expect.

POST CARD

O'Reilly & Associates, Inc., 103A Morris Street, Sebastopol, CA 95472-9902

BUSINESS REPLY MAIL
FIRST CLASS MAIL   PERMIT NO. 80   SEBASTOPOL, CA

Postage will be paid by addressee

O'Reilly & Associates, Inc.
103A Morris Street
Sebastopol, CA 95472-9902